Interpretation
and
Instruction Path Coprocessing

Computer Systems
Herb Schwetman, editor

Metamodeling: A Study of Approximations in Queueing Models, Subhash Chandra Agrawal, 1985

Logic Testing and Design for Testability, Hideo Fujiwara, 1985

Performance and Evaluation of LISP Systems, Richard P. Gabriel, 1985

The LOCUS Distributed System Architecture, edited by Gerald Popek and Bruce J. Walker, 1985

Performance Models of Multiprocessor Systems, M. Ajmone Marsan, G. Balbo, and G. Conte, 1986

Analysis of Polling Systems, Hideaki Takagi, 1986

Performance Analysis of Multiple Access Protocols, Shuji Tasaka, 1986

A Commonsense Approach to Theory of Error-Correcting Codes, Benjamin Arazi, 1987

Microprogrammable Parallel Computer: MUNAP and Its Applications, Takanobu Baba, 1987

Simulating Computer Systems: Techniques and Tools, M. H. MacDougall, 1987

Research Directions in Object-Oriented Programming, edited by Bruce Shriver and Peter Wegner, 1987

Object-Oriented Concurrent Programming, edited by Akinori Yonezawa and Mario Tokoro, 1987

Networks and Distributed Computation: Concepts, Tools, and Algorithms, Michel Raynal, 1988

Fault Tolerance Through Reconfiguration of VLSI and WSI Arrays, R. Negrini, M. G. Sami, and R. Stefanelli, 1989

Queueing Networks - Exact Computational Algorithms: A Unified Theory Based on Decomposition and Aggregation, by Adrian Conway and Nicolas Georganas, 1989

ABCL: An Object-Oriented Concurrent System, edited by Akinori Yonezawa, 1989

Interpretation and Instruction Path Coprocessing, by Eddy H. Debaere and Jan M. Van Campenhout, 1990

Interpretation
and
Instruction Path Coprocessing

Eddy H. Debaere
Jan M. Van Campenhout

The MIT Press
Cambridge, Massachusetts
London, England

© 1990 Massachusetts Institute of Technology

All rights reserved. No part of this book may be reproduced in any form by any electronic or mechanical means (including photocopying, recording, or information storage and retrieval) without permission in writing from the publisher.

This book was printed and bound in the United States of America

Library of Congress Cataloging-in-Publication Data

Debaere, Eddy, H.
    Interpretation and instruction path coprocessing / Eddy H. Debaere, Jan M. Van Campenhout.
       p.   cm. — (Computer systems)
    Includes bibliographical references.
    ISBN 0-262-04107-3
    1. Programming languages (Electronic computers)
2. Microprocessors. 3. Computer architecture. I. Campenhout, Jan M. van. II. Title. III. Series: Computer systems (Cambridge, Mass.)
QA76.7D4   1989   89-12864
005.13—dc20   CIP

Contents

List of Figures		viii
List of Tables		x
Series Foreword		xi
Preface		xiii

1	ARCHITECTURES AND LANGUAGES	1
1.1	The Evolution of Computer Architecture	1
	1.1.1 Early calculating machines	2
	1.1.2 The first stored program computers	3
	1.1.3 Architectural refinements of the von Neumann computer	4
	1.1.4 Technology and Packaging	12
1.2	Microprocessor Architecture	15
	1.2.1 A classification of microprocessor architectures	15
	1.2.2 Microprocessors and the von Neumann bottleneck	18
1.3	Programming Languages	21
	1.3.1 A brief history	21
	1.3.2 A classification of high level languages	24
1.4	Bridging the Semantic Gap	30
	1.4.1 Language implementation techniques	31
	1.4.2 Aspects of microprocessor instruction sets	36
	1.4.3 Architectural techniques to bridge the semantic gap	41
1.5	Conclusion	45

2	A CLOSER LOOK AT INTERPRETATION	47
2.1	Intermediate Language Representations	48
	2.1.1 The interpretive loop	48
	2.1.2 The intermediate instruction encoding level	50
	2.1.3 The intermediate representation of program structures	53
	2.1.4 On the space/time trade-off of intermediate representations	58
2.2	Examples of Intermediate Languages	64
	2.2.1 MODULA-2 and M-code	64
	2.2.2 FORTH and threaded code	72

	2.2.3	Lispkit LISP and SECD-code	84
2.3	Bibliographical Notes on Interpretation		90
2.4	Conclusion		97

3	OPTIMIZING INTERPRETIVE EXECUTION	99
3.1	Why are Interpreters Slow?	99
	3.1.1 The effect of the intermediate representation	99
	3.1.2 The interpretive overhead	100
	3.1.3 The architectural gap	106
3.2	Interpreter Optimization Techniques	108
	3.2.1 Improvements at the intermediate language level	108
	3.2.2 Reducing the interpretive overhead	110
	3.2.3 Bridging the architectural gap	111
3.3	Conclusion	123

4	INTERPRETIVE COPROCESSORS	125
4.1	Data Path Coprocessors	125
	4.1.1 A classification of coprocessor interfaces	126
4.2	Instruction Path Coprocessors: the Concept	129
	4.2.1 The prefetch engine	131
	4.2.2 A true instruction path coprocessor	134
4.3	Two Concrete Instruction Path Coprocessors	136
	4.3.1 An instruction path coprocessor for M-code	136
	4.3.2 An instruction path coprocessor for threaded code	146
4.4	An Analysis of ICP Performance	152
	4.4.1 Instruction path coprocessor speedup	152
	4.4.2 Weak points of instruction path coprocessors	156
4.5	Conclusion	165

5	CONCLUDING REMARKS	167
5.1	An Overview of Related Work	167
	5.1.1 The instruction fetch unit of the Dorado	167

	5.1.2	The instruction fetch unit of the G-machine	168
	5.1.3	The Prolog Preprocessor	168
5.2	On the Applicability of Instruction Path Coprocessors		169
	5.2.1	RISCs and the ICP concept	169
	5.2.2	ICPs and other interpretive applications	172
5.3	Conclusion		173
	Bibliography		175
	Index		187

List of Figures

1.1	The connection of ALU and registers	5
1.2	The memory hierarchy	6
1.3	The evolution of the integrating density of some popular microprocessor families	14
1.4	A typical microcontroller chip	16
1.5	Internal parallelism in modern microprocessors (after Intel's 80286)	16
1.6	A typical microprogrammed architecture using bit-slice components	17
1.7	A decoupled access/execute architecture	20
1.8	A pedigree of computer languages (after Schindler, 1988)	25
1.9	Implementation techniques of high level languages	32
1.10	Language oriented computer architectures	42
2.1	Subroutine encoding of intermediate instructions	51
2.2	Pointer encoding of intermediate instructions	52
2.3	Tokenized encoding of intermediate instructions	53
2.4	Sequential intermediate program representations	56
2.5	Threaded intermediate program representations	57
2.6	Linked intermediate program representations	58
2.7	The architecture of the M-machine	66
2.8	The architecture of a threaded code machine	75
2.9	The data structure of the SECD intermediate LISP engine	85
2.10	Intermediate representation of the APPEND function on the SECD machine	87
3.1	The interpretive overhead of M-code on various processors	102
3.2	The Sieve Benchmark in FORTH	103
3.3	The Sieve Benchmark in MODULA-2	104
3.4	The effect of in-line mapping instructions and pointer alignment in i8086 threaded code FORTH implementations	112
3.5	Statistics of the depth variations of the M-machine expression stack	114
3.6	Improvements achieved by top of stack optimization	118
3.7	Parallel operation of CPU and NDP during interpretation	119

List of Figures

3.8	Speedup obtained by intertwining the semantic and fetch/decode operations for some M-codes on the Am29000 processor	122
3.9	The effectiveness of a small M-code cache	124
4.1	Instruction flow to data path coprocessors: (a) peripheral coprocessor; (b) spying coprocessor; (c) independent coprocessor	127
4.2	The instruction flow and data flow in a prefetch engine type interpretive coprocessor	133
4.3	The instruction flow in a true instruction path coprocessor	134
4.4	The architecture of an M-code instruction path coprocessor	138
4.5	A timing trace of the DMA activity of an i8086 interpretive coprocessor: (1) the coprocessor requests the bus; (2) bus is granted; (3) DMA address is output; (4) data is read and bus released; (5) and(6) bytes are clocked internally	139
4.6	A timing trace of an instruction stream without transfers of control	143
4.7	A timing trace of the execution of an intermediate unconditional transfer of control	144
4.8	A timing trace of conditional code generation	147
4.9	The architecture of an instruction path coprocessor for indirect threaded code	148
4.10	A typical deadlock situation in the ICP/CPU relation	157

List of Tables

1.1	Some addressing modes implemented in the MC68020. Symbols: M[Addr] = memory contents at address Addr; [R] = contents of register; R = general register; A = address register; X = index register	9
1.2	A comparison of RISC-style and CISC-style properties	40
2.1	A classification of intermediate representations	50
2.2	An overview of research papers dealing with interpretation	91
3.1	The interpretive slowdown of the Sieve benchmark on the i8086	105
3.2	The effect of raising the semantic level of intermediate instructions	109
4.1	The M-code ICP viewed as a memory device. Note : a0000H is base address where coprocessor segment is located	137
4.2	The microcode control bits in the M-code coprocessor	140
4.3	The microcode control operations in the threaded code coprocessor	149
4.4	The encoding of operands of microcode control operations in the threaded code coprocessor	150
4.5	Relative speedups of the ten most frequent M-machine instructions. Figures in parentheses do not count intermediate fetch DMA cycles	153

Series Foreword

This series is devoted to all aspects of computer systems. This means that subjects ranging from circuit components and microprocessors to architecture to supercomputers and systems programming will be appropriate. Analysis of systems will be important as well. System theories are developing, theories that permit deeper understanding of complex interrelationships and their effects on performance, reliability, and usefulness.

We expect to offer books that not only develop new material but also describe projects and systems. In addition to understanding concepts, we need to benefit from the decision making that goes into actual development projects; selection from various alternatives can be crucial to success. We are soliciting contributions in which several aspects of systems are classified and compared. A better understanding of both the similarities and the differences found in systems is needed.

It is an exciting time in the area of computer systems. New technologies mean that architectures that were at one time interesting but not feasible are now feasible. Better software engineering means that we can consider several software alternatives, instead of "more of the same old thing," in terms of operating systems and system software. Faster and cheaper communications mean that intercomponent distances are less important. We hope that this series contributes to this excitement in the area of computer systems by chronicling past achievements and publicizing new concepts. The format allows publication of lengthy presentations that are of interest to a select readership.

Herb Schwetman

Preface

This monograph is about interpretive implementations of high level programming languages on contemporary microprocessor systems. Interpretation is nearly as old as the von Neumann architecture itself; it has found its way to various parts of computer systems. The significance of interpretive techniques has constantly changed as the result of the fast evolution of hardware and software technology. A discussion and analysis of the delicate relationship between programming languages and the ways in which computer hardware can support them is not very meaningful without explicit reference to this evolution. We therefore start our presentation with a brief historic overview of the development of key concepts of computer systems and programming languages, ending with a review of its current status. Due to space limitations, our overview will be very short and incomplete. Yet, we shall identify some specific aspects and trends that allow to ponder the relevance of the concepts presented in the following chapters.

In the second chapter, we zoom in on interpretive techniques. Interpretive techniques have been used to serve many purposes and goals, among which portability, interactivity, and code compaction play an important role. Interpretation assumes the presence of a program representation that is not directly executable by the processor. We start the chapter with an overview of intermediate program representation techniques. Three concrete examples are given, each illustrating a particular aspect of intermediate program representations. We end the chapter with an overview of the contexts in which interpretation has been used.

In the third chapter we focus on the chief drawback of interpretive techniques: their relative slowness. For some applications, this slowness is bothersome; for others, it is not. We identify the main reasons why interpretation on general purpose microprocessors is much slower than the comparable execution of compiled, native code programs. We proceed with the analysis of interpreter optimization techniques. Despite the fact that several improvements can be identified, the global improvement of interpreter speed using these techniques is limited. As an example, a commercially available M-code interpreter was improved by a factor of 2, which, unfortunately, is only a fraction of the total interpretive slowdown.

The main contributions of this monograph lie in Chapter 4. There we investigate how, and to what extent, interpretive execution can be accelerated using dedicated coprocessors. To set the scene, we first review traditional coprocessor architectures. These coprocessors all provide support in the *datapath*, that is, they help in executing instructions. While useful to accelerate interpreters that heavily use floating-point or graphics operations, datapath coprocessors are of little use in accelerating the interpretive mechanism. To that end, we present *instruction path* coprocessors as a possible solution. Instruction path coprocessors aid the interpretive processor in locating the instructions it must actually execute. We present two coprocessors for the Intel i8086, together with an analysis of their strengths and weaknesses. For *existing* intermediate representations, an overall additional acceleration by factors of more than 2 can be achieved over well-optimized software interpreters. Much of the remaining slowdown is intrinsically connected to the properties of the intermediate language. A careful redefinition of the intermediate program representation would allow even higher gains, thus increasing interpretive execution speed to almost that of the code generated by an average native code compiler.

In the last chapter we relate our work to other published developments. The recent upsurge in artificial intelligence techniques has spurred the research on interpretive support in a broader sense. Coprocessors supporting interpretation seem to be a natural solution, also for many other interpretive language implementations or applications on modern RISC architectures.

This monograph was neither intended to be a tutorial, nor a textbook on interpretation with worked-out examples. Rather, it groups and presents concepts that are seldom found together, and it elaborates on ideas that are not in the main thrust of recent hardware developments. Yet, interpretive techniques are frequently used and important, and are bound to stay that way in the foreseeable future. Then who should read our monograph? We feel that anyone, whether student or practitioner, with an interest in interpretive techniques on modern microprocessor architectures may benefit from reading this book.

This monograph would not have been possible without the contributions of a great many people. Several students at the State University of Ghent have been involved in theses gathering valuable data. We are also indebted to researchers and collegues for their useful suggestions and contributions, among which: R. Blomme, D. Brokken, K. De Bosschere, R. Deloor, C. Manhaeghe, P. Notredame, P. Veelaert, and many others whose names would make this list too long. In particular, we thank Prof. M. Vanwormhoudt, director of the Electronics Laboratory of the State University of Ghent, for his encouragement, and allowing us to conduct this research.

Partial financial support was obtained through funding from the Belgian Institute for the Encouragement of Scientific Research in Industry and Agriculture (IWONL), and the Science Policy Programming Services of the Belgian Prime Minister's Office.

Gent, Belgium *Eddy H. Debaere*
June 1989 *Jan M. Van Campenhout*

Interpretation
and
Instruction Path Coprocessing

1 ARCHITECTURES AND LANGUAGES

The least one can say about computer hardware and software is that, since their first successful realizations after the second world war, their development and evolution has been no less than stormy. Despite the demonstrated existence of fundamental limits in physics and formal deductive systems, ultimately limiting the attainable performance, computer systems are becoming faster and more powerful every day.

Several factors have influenced the development of computer hardware and programming languages. Hardware and software have influenced each other's development thoroughly. Nevertheless we shall treat hardware and software separately. We shall take three major viewpoints:

- Computer architecture: the technological evolution and the structure of the basic building blocks of computer systems;

- High level programming languages;

- Instruction set processing, providing the bridge between architecture and programming language.

Because of the wide scope of this chapter, our treatment is bound to be shallow; however, many excellent publications on this matter are available [Myer82,Kuck78], and can be consulted for more detail.

1.1 The Evolution of Computer Architecture

Since the earliest written records of mathematics around 4000 B.C., people have experienced the need to apply mathematical knowledge to such fields as trade, land surveying, navigation, astronomy, ballistics, and the like. Obtaining reliable and precise results was possible through the punctual application of stepwise computation procedures. Such procedures are called *algorithms*, after the mathematician Al-Chwarizmi († Bagdad, 850). Algorithms consist of some form of memory, a *state*, which can record and hold information; and of a sequence of elementary *operations*, which modify the state in an unambiguous and well-defined way. The sequence of operations can be *conditional*, i.e., it may depend on the present or previous values of the state.

Simple algorithms, such as for the addition of two-digit numbers, can be executed solely by the human mind. For the execution of more complex algorithms, the human mind alone is insufficient; external support is needed. Computation support devices have known a long evolution, of which contemporary von Neumann computers are the current stage. Although non-von Neumann architectures are gradually gaining importance, the basic properties of algorithmic calculation are rooted so deeply that the von Neumann architecture is bound to keep playing an extremely important role in the foreseeable future. But before looking into the future, let us first look at past stages and review some important steps in the evolution of the von Neumann architecture.

1.1.1 Early calculating machines

For humans performing computation algorithms, external support is needed most in the state memory function, i.e., to remember the computation state. Some of the oldest forms of algorithmic memory support devices were paper (or any substrate used for writing), pebble stones, and the abacus. With such memory devices the human user remains responsible for the transformations of the state, and for the sequencing of the operations. A major consequence of this early step in the evolution is the separation of data storage from data transformation and operation sequencing. This separation has since been omnipresent in the evolution of digital computer hardware[1].

Gradually, devices were designed and built which, besides storing information, could also perform some *elementary transformations* on the stored data. Pascal's (1642) and Leibnitz' (1671) calculating machines were early examples of this evolution. Still, the sequencing of elementary operations needed to obtain a desired result remained the responsibility of the user. A step forward in the mechanical support of operation sequencing came from the weaving industry. Several inventions led to the development of the *Jacquard loom* (1801), in which the elementary weaving steps (warp-control) for pattern weaving were stored in some binary form on perforated paper cards.

Data storage, data transformation, and operation sequencing were all present in Babbage's *Analytical Engine* (1833). In many ways, this never-completed mechanical computer was a blue-print of today's computers. It contained several registers for data storage (the 'store'), a special register with arithmetic capabilities (the 'mill'), and a sequence of punched instruction cards. The instructions would control the interconnections between registers, and supply input data for the computation. Even an elementary form of conditional execution was present, by means of skipping cards based on the outcome of the previous operation.

Several technological inventions allowed a gradual implementation of Babbage's ideas. The use of electromechanical relays, the invention of the flipflop memory cell [Eccl19], and the use of vacuum tubes led to the development of various computing machines. Aiken's MARK I, developed at Harvard University [Aike46], was a

---

[1]Note, however, that there exist alternative means of computation in which this separation is *not* present. Take for instance the analog slide-rule. When using a slide-rule to compute the product $c = a \times b$, the position of the mobile part w.r.t. the fixed part represents the first factor a, and *simultaneously* defines the entire function $f_a(x) = a \times x$. The result $a \times b$ is immediately obtained by reading the scale on the fixed part at the location indicated by the operand b on the mobile part. Thus the memory function and the transformation function are combined, and the calculation involves no incremental transformations on the state. Graphical computation techniques have similar properties.

general-purpose calculator. The MARK I contained 60 24-digit registers, was electromechanical, and was controlled by paper tape. A major step forward was the construction of the ENIAC (Univ. of Pennsylvania, 1946), by a group of researchers headed by Eckert and Mauchly. The ENIAC is accepted as the first general-purpose computer. The system contained some 18,000 vacuum tubes, and was programmed by interconnecting (wiring) different units using a patchboard. Later on, cards containing sequences of operations were used. There were about 20 accumulator registers which could operate simultaneously. The use of vacuum tube technology resulted in a dramatic increase of the computation speed: the addition time was 200 μs; a multiplication took 2.8 ms. This was approximately 1,000 times faster than the MARK I.

1.1.2 The first stored program computers

Operation sequencing in computers of the ENIAC era was done either by punched cards, or by using patchboards. Programming was done manually, and in binary machine-readable form. The support of sequencing control structures like (conditional) program loops was very awkward and slow with paper tape programming. On the Harvard MARK I, for instance, a program control loop was realized by cutting and pasting the program tape into a loop! Patchboard programs could be executed faster, but these programs could not be generated by the machine.

In von Neumann's report on the EDVAC [vonN45], the concept of *stored program computer* was introduced. The *same memory medium* was to be used to store both data and program steps. Consequently, programs could be accessed as quickly as data items, and programs could be manipulated as if they were data items. *Programs were numbers*, as observed earlier by Turing in his theoretical work on computability [Turi36].

A great technological barrier hampering the breakthrough of the von Neumann concept was the absence of large, low-cost random access memories. The first usable form of storage was serial, but was used in a random access type fashion: magnetic drums, and ultrasonic mercury delay lines used in radar systems. With this technology, the construction of the EDVAC was started in 1945; it became operational in 1952. The EDVAC was the first true realization of Babbage's ideas: it consisted of a memory, an arithmetic/logic unit (ALU), and a control unit. In turn, the EDVAC architecture has thoroughly influenced the large number of stored program computers we know today. In England, Wilkes completed the EDSAC in 1949, although its construction was started later than that of the EDVAC. The EDSAC was similar to the EDVAC.

The first true random access memory, i.e., memory in which the access time does not depend on the address, was the electrostatic Williams tube, developed at Manchester in 1948. At Princeton University, von Neumann's team constructed the IAS machine, using some 40 Williams tubes (1952). At MIT, Forrester's team studied magnetic core memory, and used it in the Whirlwind I aircraft simulation computer (1953). Almost simultaneously, the first commercial stored program computers became available: Eckert and Mauchly's first UNIVAC (1951), and the IBM-700 series (1952). The modern computer era had begun.

1.1.3 Architectural refinements of the von Neumann computer

As a result of the above evolution, all stored program computers contain the following basic building blocks: (1) a memory, storing data and instructions; (2) an arithmetic/logic unit, capable of computing a small set of elementary unary (one-operand) or binary (two-operand) functions; (3) a control unit, capable of obtaining instructions from memory and issuing control signals to the ALU and the memory in order to execute the instructions; and (4) provisions to transfer data and programs to and from the memory.

Modern von Neumann machines exhibit a great variety of ways in which these building blocks can be combined into efficient computing systems. Some relevant aspects of modern architectures are the following:

1. The exploitation of the memory hierarchy;

2. The use of complex addressing modes;

3. Instruction sets, and the implementation of control units;

4. The implementation of input/output systems;

5. The use of parallelism.

We shall now briefly review these aspects.

The exploitation of the memory hierarchy. Initially, memory was only available in small quantities, in the form of discrete registers tightly connected to the ALU transformation logic. During the execution of an elementary binary instruction, at least two, and sometimes three registers must be simultaneously connected to the ALU (fig.1.1): the two source operands S_1 and S_2, and the destination operand D.

The interconnection and communication channels between basic system building blocks are called *data paths*. Thus, the nature of the calculations involved requires a certain degree of parallelism in the data paths. Early registers and ALUs operated in a digit or bit serial fashion, and the required data path parallelism was not a matter of great concern. However, as soon as technology permitted, ALUs were constructed to operate in a digit or bit parallel fashion. Long data words were required to guarantee sufficient precision in arithmetic operations. Consequently, data path parallelism resulted in large numbers of conductors operating

1.1. The Evolution of Computer Architecture

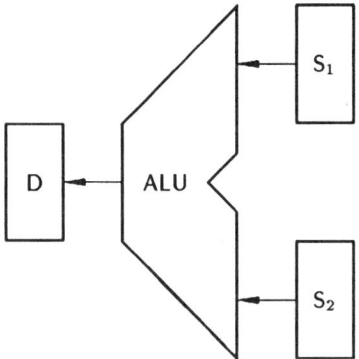

Figure 1.1
The connection of ALU and registers

at high switching speeds. In addition, programs involving large data arrays, or even the mere storing of programs in memory resulted in a vast increase in memory requirements.

However, no single memory technology was (and still is) capable of combining the size, parallelism in operation, speed and random accessibility asked for, in an economically feasible way. Big memories with parallel accessibility could not be realized economically with register technology; random access memories with limited parallelism emerged. Random access memories can only be accessed one word at a time. They exhibit only digit or bit parallelism, and hence, are not suited to *directly* provide the data for the ALU.

The quest for even bigger memories to store programs or large data sets could only be satisfied using serial magnetic drums, discs or tapes. Consequently, every stored program computer soon contained several forms of memory, interconnected in a hierarchical way: the *memory hierarchy* (fig. 1.2).

Because of the data path cost the parallelism in the memory interconnections was limited to the absolute minimum, i.e., to the parallel interconnection of registers to the ALU and the control unit. During the execution of a program, data and instructions alike must migrate to the top of the memory hierarchy, the registers. Thus the rate at which a program can be executed is limited by the available transfer bandwidth between successive stages of the memory hierarchy, and by the speed of memory at each layer. When the attainable processing rate of the ALU is increased by architectural or technological means, for example by using parallelism, the bandwidth of the memory system becomes a true limit for further

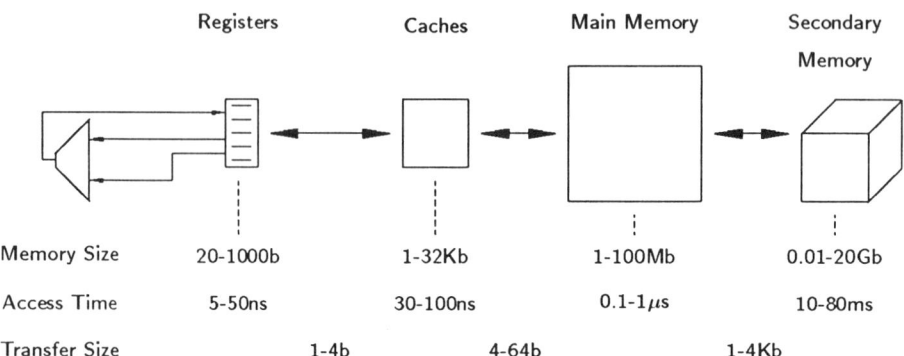

Figure 1.2
The memory hierarchy

speed increase. This limit is known as the *von Neumann Bottleneck*.

The von Neumann Bottleneck is fundamentally caused by the separation of state memory and transformation logic, and by the fact that programs are stored in memory. Several ways have been devised by means of which the limitations of the von Neumann bottleneck can be relaxed:

1. Reducing the rate at which data items or instructions have to cross memory hierarchy stage boundaries;

2. Accelerating transfers between memory layers;

3. Increasing the amount of information transferred in a given number of bits.

The computations performed by stored program computers are intrinsically sequential. With respect to memory, a computation can be modeled as a sequence of memory references

$$r_1, r_2, r_3, \ldots$$

where each reference r_i is a tuple $< a_i, d_i, c_i >$ consisting of the address a_i, the data involved d_i, and the control information c_i (read, write, etc.). Soon it was realized that a high correlation exists between successive addresses in a reference stream: instruction word addresses occur predominantly in cyclic patterns of sequential runs; often accesses, to individual data locations are grouped in bursts instead of being spread evenly in space and time. In a given time span, 'reasonable' programs address only a small fraction of their total address space, and this working set of 'active' addresses changes slowly with respect to its frequency of use.

This basic property of the memory behavior of programs has been called the *principle of locality*. It has been exploited at various places in the memory hierarchy. Well-known examples are register optimization, programmed overlays, hardware stack support, caches [Smit82], and virtual memory [Denn70]. Register optimization is a *static* optimization technique, i.e., it is applied when the program is written. The goal is to use the registers in such a way that their contents can be used as many times as possible without having to reload them from memory. Program overlays are also static, in that the program is decomposed in a tree-like structure. At any time, only the entire path from the root to the active leaf node must be in memory, which can be significantly smaller than the entire program. Caches optimize the transfers between registers and main memory, whereas virtual memory optimizes the transfers to and from secondary memory (disks or drums). Both the caching and the virtual memory techniques are *dynamic*: the true contents of the faster memory level is determined at run time, and is based on the actual program behavior. Of course, dynamic optimization techniques are more expensive than static ones, but no *a priori* static program analysis is required, and the optimization adapts itself to the true program behavior, which might be difficult to predict.

In all the above examples, the efficient exploitation of the memory hierarchy rests on a few simple principles:

1. **Decoupling logical from physical addresses.** Each object (memory word) in the address space of a program has a unique logical address. However, the *physical* address of this object at a certain level of the memory hierarchy is not necessarily equal to the logical address; it may even vary in time. At each level L_i there exists an address translation mechanism allowing to find out whether the object, identified by its logical address, is present, and if so, where it is in physical space. The address translation techniques strongly depend on the memory level. For example, in register optimization, physical addresses are determined beforehand by the programmer or by an optimizing compiler; no dynamic translation is needed. In caches, the address translation is done by means of a mixture of indexing and associative table lookup. Virtual memory address translations use memory-based tables (paging tables), but accelerate the translation process using caching techniques: TLBs, or translation look aside buffers.

2. **Maintaining a working set.** One tries to keep objects that are likely to be accessed in the near future at the highest level possible. Objects that have been referenced recently are likely to be referenced again, and should preferably not migrate to lower levels (the least recently used or LRU policy). Objects in the immediate neighborhood of referenced objects are also likely to be referenced (spatial correlation). Good replacement algorithms maximize

the chance that a referenced memory word is present in the highest possible layer of the memory hierarchy.

3. **Performing block transfers.** Transfers from level L_{i+1} to level L_i are typically not done on an individual word basis, but rather by blocks of *consecutive* memory locations. This sequentiality enables one to fully exploit the physical communication bandwidth, independent of the memory access or cycle times, using techniques like memory interleaving or burst mode memories. Furthermore, block transfers exploit the spatial correlation of memory accesses.

Besides controlling the migration of bit patterns through the memory hierarchy, one can also try to increase the *information content* of the bit patterns that are transferred. Multiple data formats (bytes, short integers, words, long words, etc.) provide a more dense data encoding. Significant gains can be obtained using a denser encoding of the instruction stream. Instruction compactness will form a major point of interest in this monograph; we shall discuss it at a greater length later on.

The use of complex addressing modes. Originally, memory locations were addressed directly by instructions. Any instruction referencing a memory cell contains the physical address of the cell. For example, the Whirlwind I had provisions for 2048 memory cells; memory reference instructions were composed of a 5-bit opcode part, and an 11-bit direct address field.

With the increase of memory sizes and the associated growth in algorithm complexity, the need for more flexible memory addressing methods became imminent. Several significant improvements were introduced between 1950 and 1970. Direct effective addresses were complemented with *address expressions*, specifying how to compute the effective address of an instruction or data item at run time. Note that there is no avail in using address expressions when the address stream generated by a computation would be totally random and unpredictable. The fact that address expressions are indeed very useful is yet another manifestation of locality in program behavior, which in fact results in a compaction of the instruction stream. Major steps in the development of contemporary addressing modes are:

- **index registers** (University of Manchester, 1949). Effective addresses can be formed by adding the contents of an index register to an offset field in the instruction. Offsets no longer must span the entire address range, and generating consecutive address streams, e.g. to index arrays, is simple.

- **indirect addressing** (IBM 704, 1954). A memory cell contains the *address* of another memory cell. This concept embodies the notion of a *pointer*.

- **segmented memory.** Memory is no longer viewed as one linear array of cells, but rather as a collection of logically separate segments. An ad-

1.1. The Evolution of Computer Architecture

Expression	Operand	Addressing Mode Name
#Data	Data	literal
R	[R]	register direct
(Addr)	M[Addr]	absolute
(A)	M[[A]]	register indirect
(A)+	M[[A]] ; A:=A+i	reg. indir. with postincrement
-(A)	A:=A-i ; M[[A]]	reg. indir. with predecrement
(Addr,A)	M[Addr+[A]]	reg. indir. with displacement
(Addr,A,X)	M[Addr+[A]+[X]]	reg. indir. with index and displacement
([Addr,A],X,Offs)	M[M[Addr+[A]]+[X]+Offs]	mem. indir. with post index
([Addr,A,X],Offs)	M[M[Addr+[A]+[X]]+Offs]	mem. indir. with preindex

Table 1.1
Some addressing modes implemented in the MC68020. Symbols: M[Addr] = memory contents at address Addr; [R] = contents of register; R = general register; A = address register; X = index register

dress is formed by means of the pair `segment name, cell offset`. Among other things, memory segments support structured memory views imposed by the application, and provide segment-bound protection against unauthorized memory accesses, an essential requirement for multi-user operation.

Some contemporary computers possess very complex addressing modes. Table 1.1 represents some of the most commonly used ones.

Instruction sets, and the implementation of control units. Even in the earliest calculating machines, operations like multiplication or the computation of the square root were executed through the use of sequences of primitive hardware operations such as register to register transfers, additions, and shifts. In von Neumann architectures this situation remained largely the same. The control unit of a von Neumann computer is responsible for obtaining the instructions from memory, and generating the corresponding sequences of hardware operations for its execution.

Designing a control unit for a complex instruction set was not an easy matter. A control unit is a complex automaton that must execute its operations very quickly, since it is located at the heart of the computer system. Control units of early computers were realized using asynchronous finite state machine techniques; to say the least, designing such automata was a true challenge. Soon it was realized that systematic design techniques for control units were badly needed. As early as 1951, one of the early computer architects, M.V. Wilkes, proposed the use of *microprogramming* as a systematic, synchronous way to design control units [Wilk51]. The idea is the following: since the execution of a machine instruction consists of a sequence of elementary hardware operations, it is in fact a *microprogram*, written in a language that consists of combinations of the primitive hardware operations. Each statement, a *microinstruction*, can be directly executed by the hardware, in one single clock period. The underlying hardware needed to sequence the microinstruction execution is much simpler than the original control unit.

This technique worked, even in the early days, when memory was scarce and slow. The reason why it worked was that the microcoded engine, although executing microinstruction stored in a memory, the *control store*, was *not* a von Neumann machine. Indeed, there was a strict separation between data, residing in registers and main memory, and microinstructions, residing in control store. The contents of the control store was fixed; control store could thus be realized using *read only storage* (ROS). Early ROS technologies (1960-1970) were capacitive, inductive, or used diode arrays [Huss70]. These technologies allowed the realization of control stores that operated much faster than the random access memories of that era. Later, with the introduction of semiconductor memory, control store became writable (WCS, or Writable Control Store), permitting the dynamic modification of its contents. In fact, WCS can be seen as the top level in the instruction memory hierarchy, and has been exploited as such [Raus78,Raus80].

As long as there was a clear distinction between the speed of control store and main memory, the usefulness of microprogramming instruction sets was not questioned. Even now, nearly all complex instruction sets are implemented using microprogramming. Minicomputers and mainframes typically use writable control store, while most microprocessors use read-only control stores. The recent technological evolution has strongly reduced the speed discrepancy between control stores and main memories, as a result of which computer architects have reconsidered the complexity and implementation technique of microprocessor instruction sets. Memory parameters have become such that the execution of *microinstructions* directly from main memory has become feasible. Such computer are called RISCs (Reduced Instruction Set Computers), while the traditional computers with complex, microprogrammed instruction sets are called CISCs (Complex Instruction Set Computers). We shall encounter this distinction at various occasions later in this monograph.

The implementation of I/O systems. Input/Output operations are concerned with getting data (and programs) into the computer system, and with obtaining results from it. The transfers should take place between the memory of the computer system and the external world. Often, I/O operations are much slower than the computation proper, either due to the presence of a human operator, or due to the mechanical nature of I/O devices. A certain degree of overlap between internal computation and I/O transfers, with as little intervention of the central processing unit as possible, are desirable features of an efficient I/O system. I/O systems have

1.1. The Evolution of Computer Architecture

indeed evolved according to these goals. Several stages characterize the evolution of I/O systems:

1. **Direct processor control.** The central processor directly issues control signals to the peripheral device. Very little overlap between computation and I/O operations is possible. Processor involvement is high.

2. **Simple I/O controllers.** These controllers take over the generation of control pulses. The central processor activates the controller, and polls its status to await the completion of the I/O operation. Some concurrency is allowed between the operation of the I/O device and the processor.

3. **Interrupts** are added to signal the completion of the I/O operation to the processor. This removes the need for explicit polling, allowing more parallelism. The actual data transfers to and from memory are still performed by the central processor.

4. **Direct memory access** is added to offload the processor also from executing block data transfers. The central processor is only responsible for initializing the DMA controller; interrupts are used to signal the termination of the block transfer.

5. **I/O coprocessors** are no longer given detailed commands by the central processor. The intelligent I/O coprocessor obtains its own instructions from private or main memory, and can also perform transformations on the data being transferred.

The global evolution of I/O systems exhibits a cyclic nature: at stage 5, one can re-enter stage 1 at the level of the coprocessor ('the wheel of reincarnation' [Siew85]).

The use of parallelism. Various forms of concurrency and parallel operation have found their way to von Neumann computers, both microscopically and macroscopically. Microscopic forms of parallelism concern the parallelization of the stages in the execution of a single instruction. Possible forms are the pipelining of instruction fetching, decoding, and execution, possibly in parallel with the calculation of effective addresses. Sometimes one separates and parallelizes the data transformations performed by the ALU from the transfer of data and instructions to and from memory. Such architectures are called *decoupled access/execute architectures* [Smit84,Smit82]. Various forms of pipelining of arithmetic operations have been realized, e.g. pipelined Wallace-tree multipliers and vector processors.

A useful characterization of macroscopic parallelism is due to Flynn [Flyn72]. It is based on the number of simultaneous instruction and data streams. Some classes considered by Flynn are the following:

- Single Instruction stream - Single Data stream systems (SISD);

- Single Instruction stream - Multiple Data stream systems (SIMD);

- Multiple Instruction stream - Multiple Data stream systems (MIMD).

The first class, SISD machines, contains most familiar systems (e.g. personal computers, mono-microprocessor systems, etc.): only one instruction stream and only one data stream can be processed at a time. Note that we take a macroscopic point of view and are not concerned with the detailed implementation of instruction execution, possibly containing additional forms of microscopic parallelism.

SIMD machines include array processors (one control unit and several independently working processors), pipelined processors (one control unit controls dedicated servers in a production line fashion) and associative processors (the servers only execute when a match occurs between the input instruction and the capabilities of the server).

MIMD machines conform to multiprocessors: these are systems consisting of machines which are loosely or tightly coupled, and work in a largely independent way. Shared memory multiprocessors and distributed multiprocessors are typical examples. Whether processors connected by means of a network are to be considered as communicating computers or as true multiprocessors is not always clear.

1.1.4 Technology and Packaging

After the breakthrough of the first generation of general purpose digital computers, technological developments have kept influencing the further development of von Neumann computers. Key innovative concepts were the use of solid state technology, and later, the use of planar lithographical techniques allowing integration and miniaturization.

- **The invention of the transistor** (Bardeen, Brattain, Shockley, 1948). The vacuum tube was very power consuming, bulky, and fragile. The transistor, offering the same functionality, eliminated most of these disadvantages. This was the first step towards integrated technology.

- **The use of integrated circuits** (1965). The capability to integrate transistors and other circuit elements onto one piece of silicon opened a totally new perspective w.r.t. the size and speed of digital systems. Gradually, technology allowed the integration of ever larger numbers of components: Small Scale Integration (SSI) around 1965 (1 to 10 transistors), Medium Scale Integration (MSI) by the 1970's (10 to 1,000 transistors), Large Scale Integration (LSI) by the 1980's (1,000 to 100,000 transistors), and Very Large Scale Integration (VLSI) from 1980 on (more than 100,000 transistors).

1.1. The Evolution of Computer Architecture

The use of integrated semiconductor technology has become one of the great success stories of this century. Several aspects account for this success, among which there are

- **Reduction of costs.** Complex digital systems are integrated into one package. As a consequence, the required board space, power dissipation, handling costs and assembly operations are reduced [Tred88].

- **Higher reliability.** A tested integrated circuit causes less reliability problems than an assembled board with equal functionality. The integrated circuit is largely free of defects such as bad contacts (soldering, sockets), interconnections suffering from mechanical stress and electromagnetic interference.

- **Advantages of mass production and standardization.** Well designed standard integrated circuits attain high production volumes because of their high universality. Mass production leads to low unit costs and highly reliable products that are well understood. Mass products provide a *de facto* standard in the environments where they are used.

- **Increased performance possibilities.** The technological limits for integrated circuits are less restrictive than those for interconnected devices (assembled by the system integrator). Indeed, the dimensions of the wires that transmit switching signals among primitive devices determine the minimal time and energy to transmit one bit of information. As the dimensions in integrated devices are about four magnitudes lower than those in assembled boards, the achievable performance is correspondingly higher.

The evolution of computer architectural concepts, together with the simultaneous advances in integrating technology eventually resulted in the realization of the first microprocessor: the Intel i4004 (1971).

There is no conceptual difference between general purpose mini or mainframe computers, and microprocessors. In fact, microprocessors are general purpose computers integrated on one or a few chips. Compared to the minicomputers and mainframes of their era, early microprocessors were very primitive. However, since their introduction in 1971, microprocessors have undergone a complete metamorphosis. This development is highly parallel to earlier developments in the traditional computer forms. Siewiorek *et al.* suggest that similar development waves in mainframe computers, minicomputers, and integrated microcomputers are separated by some 10 to 15 years [Siew85]. Microprocessors like the Intel i8080 (1974) were as powerful as the mini's from the mid sixties and, more recently, a RISC like the AMD29000 outperforms 12 VAX11/780s in raw CPU speed.

The extremely fast evolution of the microprocessor complexity can be illustrated by the number of transistors needed to build them. The Intel i4004 consisted of

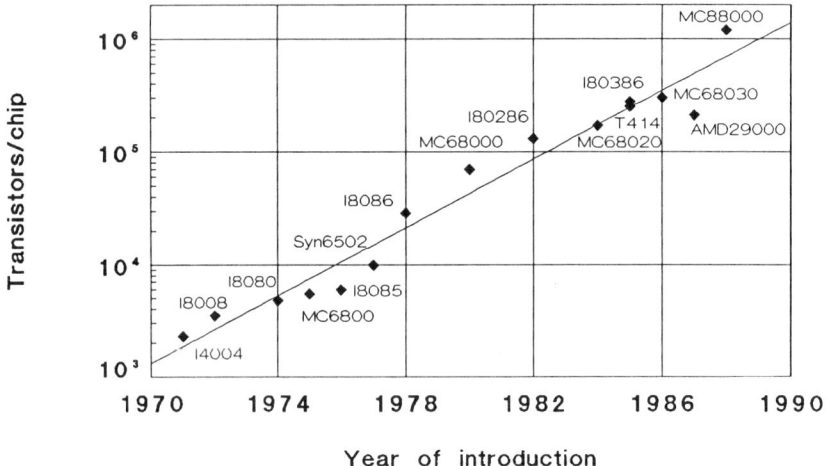

Figure 1.3
The evolution of the integrating density of some popular microprocessor families

approximately 2300 transistors [Myer86]. Its latest descendant, the i80386 (1985), has 275000 transistors, while the i80486 and i80860 are being announced (1989) as having over one million transistors. This shows that the integrating capabilities improved by a factor of 100 during 15 years! Figure 1.3 shows the evolution of the transistor count for a sample of popular microprocessors.

The gap between microprocessors, minicomputers and mainframes is very temporary. It is getting more and more difficult for mini's to be ahead of contemporary microprocessors and it appears that microprocessors will take the leadership role in the near future [Alli86].

What are the limits of this evolution ? To answer this question, we must investigate the restrictive technological aspects. Scaling down the dimensions of interconnections improves circuit performance. Both the transmission delays and switching energies are reduced. However, the reduction of circuit dimensions is fundamentally limited [Keye81], on the basis of quantum mechanical considerations. Also practical limits exist, which are even more limitative than the theoretical ones. A practical limit for CMOS technology seems to be a 0.25 μm transistor channel length, a dissipation of 1 W per chip, a cycle time of 100 Mhz, 50 mm × 50 mm die size and gate delays of some tens of picoseconds [Myer86,Park83,Flag78,DeMa89]. Extrapolations indicate that this will be achieved before the end of this century! By that time, the resulting microprocessors would contain about 5 million transistors and achieve a performance equivalent to 50 VAX-MIPS.

Since only microprocessors will be considered in this monograph, it worthwhile to briefly look into the different microprocessor varieties that have come into existence. That is what we do in the next section.

1.2 Microprocessor Architecture

A computer system based on a microprocessor is called a *microcomputer*. Typically, such systems consist of a microprocessor, an amount of primary and/or secondary storage and peripheral devices. The peripheral units are the gateways to the outside world: keyboard interfaces, serial/parallel data communication, screen management, and network interfaces. As a result of the current technological limitations on the complexity of integrated circuits, contemporary integrated microprocessors are available in a large variety of forms and shapes.

1.2.1 A classification of microprocessor architectures

A useful classification criterion is the way in which the basic system building blocks are partitioned into integrated circuits. We distinguish among three classes: microcontrollers, general purpose microprocessors, and bit-slice components.

Microcontrollers. This variety requires the fewest number of chips to construct a system. A microcontroller chip [Crag80] consists of a CPU, some data memory in the form of registers, some program storage, and some peripheral devices (serial/parallel controllers). Figure 1.4 shows the internal structure of a microcontroller chip. The microcontroller is aimed at high volume and low cost applications requiring only a small amount of computing power. Some microcontrollers have been extremely successful: for example, of the TMS1000 4-bit controller, several tens of millions have been built [Gupt83].

General Purpose Microprocessors. This microprocessor form is the most commonly used. It is the form which is gradually replacing larger, traditional computer systems. Consequently, the performance requirements are much more stringent than in microcontrollers, and on-chip resources are dedicated to obtaining as high a performance as possible. Therefore, general purpose microprocessors do not contain on-chip program memory. Several chips are needed to construct a microcomputer.

16   Chapter 1. ARCHITECTURES AND LANGUAGES

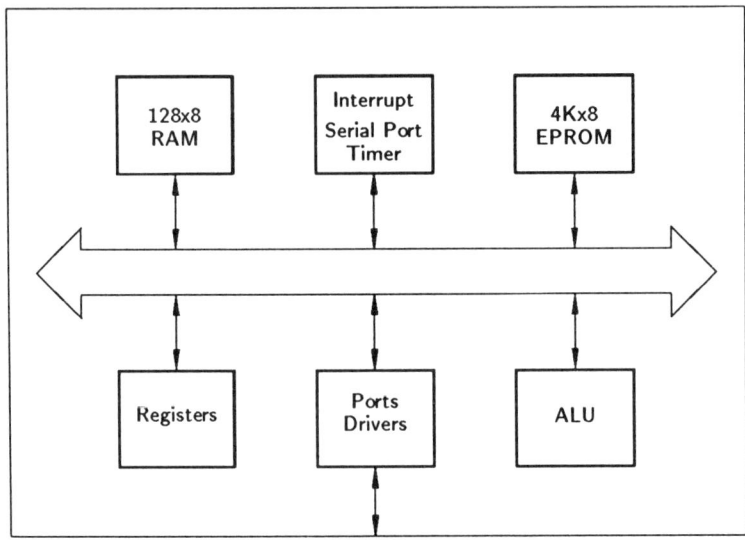

Figure 1.4
A typical microcontroller chip

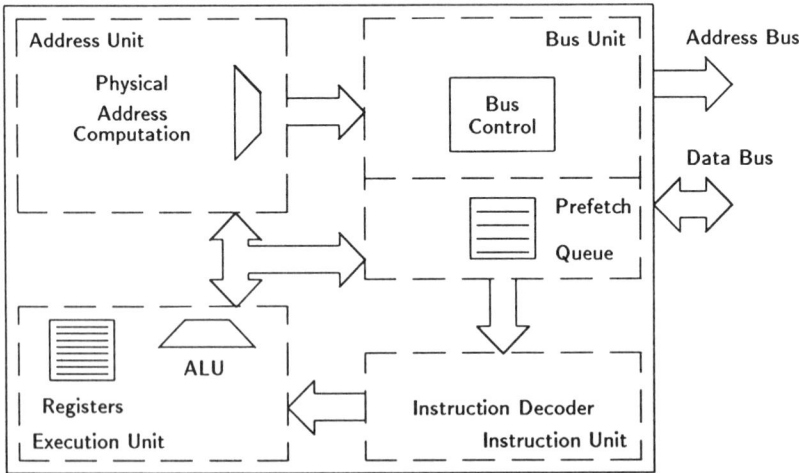

Figure 1.5
Internal parallelism in modern microprocessors (after Intel's 80286)

1.2. Microprocessor Architecture

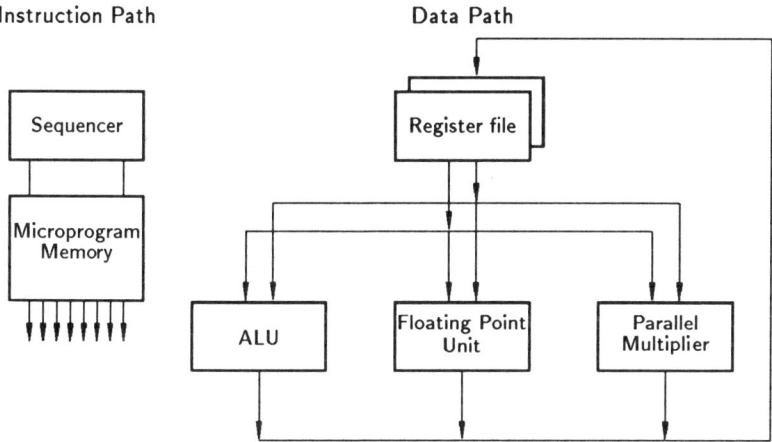

Figure 1.6
A typical microprogrammed architecture using bit-slice components

So as to fulfill the performance requirements, various forms of microscopic parallelism are exploited on general purpose microprocessor chips (fig. 1.5). Commonplace are instruction prefetch; pipelining of instruction decoding and execution; simultaneous internal operations and external transfers. The instruction sets of general purpose processors are not directed towards any particular application. As a result, for many applications requiring a performance unattainable by the general purpose von Neumann processor, dedicated coprocessors are available. Typical coprocessor application fields include numeric (floating point) calculations, graphics, I/O-transfer to and from peripheral equipment, communications, and networking. In Chapter 4 of this monograph, we look deeper into coprocessors for general purpose microprocessors. We present an additional field of interest for coprocessor support: the interpretive execution of programs written in high level programming languages.

Bit-slice components. While microcontrollers go one step further in integrating functionality than microprocessors do, bit-slice components go one step backward [Bane82]. Bit-slice components may be viewed as functional blocks which are not integrated on one chip, and only when connected into a system, give rise to computers (fig. 1.6). The data path components (operators and data registers) are cleanly separated from the instruction path (instruction sequencing and program manipulations). Both subfunctions can be *sliced* into fixed bit length building blocks (4,

8, 32 bits wide) that can be concatenated into units of almost arbitrary width. The advantage of bit-slice systems is that the control signals of the components are available to the system designer. The hardware operations invoked by these signals are rather primitive, and are intended to microprogram more complex operations. This allows an application oriented definition of the architecture and the instruction set. Parallelism and pipelining can be used at will.

Bit-slice components have been used as building blocks for microprogrammed general purpose minicomputers, but also in specific applications such as graphics engines, signal processing, and language oriented work stations. In these applications, much higher performance levels have been obtained than would have been possible with traditional microprocessors. However, due to the large number of chips needed to realize a system, the low level at which the design must take place, and the limited production volumes of application oriented designs, systems based on bit-slice technology tend to be expensive. Bit-slice components are also available as library functions for custom chip design. The recent technological evolution has made bit-slice technology somewhat obsolete: modern RISC processors offer typical bit-slice functionality (visible parallelism at the instruction level, very low level instruction encoding) with 32-bit wide data paths *on one chip*, with low cycle times, at a fraction of the cost.

1.2.2 Microprocessors and the von Neumann bottleneck

In modern microprocessor systems, the von Neumann bottleneck remains as relevant as ever. Since the arrival of the Intel i4004, processor clock rates have been increased by a factor of 35; the bandwidth of dynamic random access memories has been increased by a factor of 4; storage capacities have increased by a factor of 1,000. The internal data transfer rates at the top of the memory hierarchy in modern microprocessors reaches extreme values: rates of several hundred megabytes per second are no exception. The internal data paths of the Intel i80860 RISC are rated at 1 Gigabytes per second! Unfortunately, microprocessor system data paths (buses) have not been able to keep up with this evolution[2]. Bus timing depends also on other factors than those governing on-chip integration: bus interfacing circuits, signal travel time, arbitration overhead, etc. Furthermore, bus protocols have greater longevity than processors or memory chips, so they are bound to lag behind in speed. As a result, besides registers, some top line microprocessors also contain on-chip caches. Other processors are specifically designed to keep the external data rates low (National 32000). Even so there will be a need for additional bandwidth. Increasing the bandwidth of the external microprocessor data paths can only be done by increasing the parallelism, i.e., the width of the data path. Early microprocessors had narrow, time-multiplexed buses, that were often narrower than the

---

[2] Well-known standardized buses are the Multibus (IEEE 796) and the VME bus (IEEE 1014).

internal data path (see Intel's i8088 and Motorola's MC68000). Modern 32-bit microprocessors have separate data and address buses, and some architectures may even have separate data and instruction buses (e.g. the TMS320 DSP chip, and the Motorola MC88000 RISC). This is a deviation from the basic von Neumann architecture; such architectures conform to the so-called *Harvard Architecture*.

Meyers [Myer86] conjectures that, eventually, 64-bit wide buses will emerge. Providing such wide and fast data paths is an expensive matter, also on-chip: in the Stanford 32-bit MIPS, no less than 38% of the operating power is dissipated to drive the external connection pads of the chip [Chow88].

Another way to look at the von Neumann bottleneck is due to Flynn [Flyn78]. The set of instructions representing a program can be divided in three classes:

1. **F-type instructions,** functional instructions, specifying the operations actually transforming the state of the algorithm into a new state;

2. **M-type instructions,** movement instructions, which move data to the locations where it is needed to compute or to save;

3. **P-type instructions,** procedural instructions, controlling the sequencing through the program.

Flynn observed that there are 2.6 to 5.5 times more non-functional instructions (M-type or P-type) than functional instructions. This illustrates how many instructions are required to support the computation, and how few are actually performing useful transformations on the state.

Even if the bandwidth of the memory system in a von Neumann microprocessor system were not limited, the execution speed would be limited. Indeed, the execution process in von Neumann computer consists of repeatedly fetching an instruction, decoding it and performing the corresponding semantic operations. In SISD-systems, as microprocessors are, the next instruction cannot be decoded before the current instruction is, as the length of each instruction is encoded in the instruction itself. This length is needed to find the beginning of the next instruction. Therefore, the SISD-type microprocessors (however complex they may be) cannot execute instructions in less time than the time required to decode the instructions. In other words, in microprocessors there is a limitation of the execution speed of 1 instruction per instruction decoding time. This is called *the Flynn Bottleneck* [Flyn66]. In more complex systems, such as Very Long Instruction Word architectures [Nowa87,Nico84] several independent operations are simultaneously decoded and executed from a single, wide instruction. This is not possible with contemporary microprocessors, as these are of the SISD-type. Instructions in VLIW-architectures may be compared to horizontal microcode instructions, as these also specify different independent operations which are performed simultaneously.

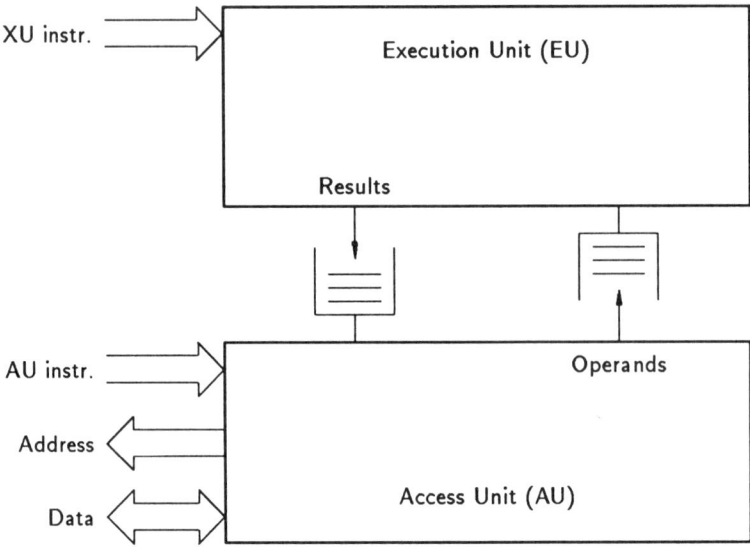

Figure 1.7
A decoupled access/execute architecture

Another attempt to fight both the von Neumann and the Flynn bottlenecks is known as the concept of *decoupled access/execute architectures* [Smit84,Smit82]. Here (fig. 1.7), the CPU is decomposed into two execution units: one for the F-type instructions (the execution unit, producing the result) and one for the M-type instructions (the access unit, fetching operands and storing results). Both units have their own instruction stream and decode and execute simultaneously. The P-type instructions are handled by both units. The operands produced by the access unit are passed to the execution unit by means of a queue. Similarly, the results of the execution unit are passed to the access unit. This architecture reduces the von Neumann bottleneck, since multiple memory-CPU channels are used; it relaxes the Flynn bottleneck, since fetching, decoding and executing occur concurrently. It is clear that this configuration is no longer a von Neumann architecture.

1.3 Programming Languages

1.3.1 A brief history

Until the arrival of the first practically usable computers, mathematics had been applied by mathematicians and engineers in a very informal way. They needed no formal notational system in which algorithms could be expressed unambiguously, and which could be 'understood' by a machine. The problem with computers was that they could not be driven with the same informal method humans used. They needed an unambiguous and correct representation of the algorithms they had to execute. This representation had to be in binary, and could only use operations and sequencing steps that could directly be executed by the computer hardware. Such representations were unavailable.

True, in the 19-th century, Boole and Frege had established formal logic as a model of mathematical reasoning. In 1936, Turing, Kleene and Church obtained deep results in computability, which started research on formal language and automata theory. In 1962, Church, Rosser, Curry, and Kleene established λ-calculus as a formal model of mathematical functions and their manipulation. But these developments did not reach the practitioner of the early fifties (and we feel it hasn't reached most of them now, either). Consequently, the only appropriate formal representation system for algorithms was the *binary machine language* of the computer, hardly readable for humans. Programs were hand *coded*, not expressed, in binary, machine readable form.

Soon, coding was done *symbolically*, using human-readable mnemonic representation of numbers and basic binary control patterns, but this only had a cosmetic meaning. Assembly language was born; it is still as alive as ever. So as to increase its expressive power, *macro-expansion* was used: routines were coded in a readable form and were expanded at compile time. These translation programs were among the more sophisticated tasks for computers of that time. Even if high level languages were available at that time, the computers wouldn't have been able to process them.

With the increasing number of computer applications, the need for more appropriate and less machine dependent algorithm representations grew quickly. As early as 1954, Backus presented the first high level language, Fortran, intended to specify, code and communicate numerical algorithms [Husk76]. Its constructs were such that *computers* could execute them easily: memory variables, conditional jumps, iteration, sequences of instructions, etc. were all 'higher level' versions of the basic machine ingredients [Back78]. During the early fifties, the main goal of high level languages was to provide the ability to *program the computer* in a rather natural language (e.g. Fortran). Later, in the early sixties, emphasis was put on *representing the algorithm*. Algorithmic language expressiveness became important, and led to the development of languages like Algol60 and PLI/1; languages such as Cobol and Lisp were used to increase expressive capabilities in specific application domains, such as business administration and artificial intelligence. Languages became 'fat'. As it became clear that the programmer did not fully exploit the complex syntax provided in rich languages such as Algol68, a reaction towards simple yet powerful languages led to the development of Pascal and comparable languages, around 1970.

While the evolution of computer hardware progressed as a separate discipline throughout the 1950's, in the period 1960 - 1970 a truly intertwined evolution of both hardware and software technology began. In the software domain, from 1960 on, efforts were made to describe and analyze programming languages, leading to mathematical models, formal languages and automata theory [Wegn76]. The results of this research were used to build parsers, compiler compilers and tools for building correctness proofs and program verification.

After 1970 one became concerned with the problems associated with building and maintaining large and complex software applications. This movement was mainly initiated by the increasing impact of software cost on the price of computer applications, and the fact that writing complex software applications requires a form of teamwork. The software cost takes up to 80% of that of the total system development and the future tends to increase this ratio even more [Wall83]. The production of software had to become an engineering discipline: *software engineering*. The associated problems clearly transcend the language level, although many language characteristics are relevant. Aspects like reusability of software, software validation, life-cycle support, etc. became important. In this context, structured programming, documentation, software libraries, software production tools, modularity, verifiability and reliability deserved special attention. In the mid-seventies, languages like Modula-2, Ada, and Smalltalk were developed, stressing aspects like modularity and information hiding. At the other end of the spectrum, simplicity, hardware accessibility, and the generation of efficient code led to the development of C.

But languages only serve as media through which the programmer can dictate his solution of a given problem; they do not provide support in the early stages of system design. Problem analysis, specification and formalization have become the most difficult, and at the same time very critical steps in the development of a software product. This situation naturally leads to efforts for the creation of tools which automate one or more steps of the system design process [Wass82]. Several difficult problems must be solved:

- In the initial conceptual stage, the ordering party often does not always exactly know what he or she wants; there is a need to quickly provide insight in what the implications are of early decisions concerning the functionality

1.3. Programming Languages

or implementation of the product. We need *requirement capturing and rapid prototyping tools*.

- Another difficult step is to formalize the given specifications, and to validate the formalization w.r.t. to the original requirements. We need *formal specification tools* that do not enforce early implementation decisions.

- Once a machine-readable and unambiguous specification has been made, we need support for the further implementation of the specification. *Verification tools* should allow to match the actual implementation with the original specification.

At this moment and in the near future, considerable effort is, and will be spent on the development of tools for these kinds of operations [Wass82]. Good programming environments equipped with high level languages are essential for the productivity of the programmers and for the quality of their products.

Besides the actual generation of software, also the iterative process of coding and testing is responsible for the software development cost [Somm85]. Hence, the programming environments emphasize both production and debugging facilities, and integrate these in one environment in order to reduce the needs for environment switching and to increase the accessibility of design information. For several years to come, the supported high level languages will be those currently available. The inertia in language utilization is due to the extremely large investment in trained programmers and programs in existing languages [Wass82].

Later on, as the developments in the areas above mature, we may expect a general movement towards environments in which a *declarative* specification of the problems is input, rather than a specification of the proposed solution. Such specifications allow programmers to input the problem specification in a more natural way. The absence of an explicitly sequential algorithmic solution will allow the software environment to determine the appropriate realization method, possibly with large-scale parallelism. Declarative languages and rule based systems are one step in this direction. However, the understanding of the problem and finding an unambiguous specification will still remain weak points of the design process.

It is known that declarative and logic programming systems require enormous computing power to attain a reasonable performance and interactivity. Therefore, the progress in hardware performance is essential and, luckily, the prospects in this area are favorable. Myers [Myer82] forecasts a doubling of the performance in microcomputer systems every 2.25 years for at least the next years. But, as history taught us, we will never have enough sequential computing power to solve all the problems we want. Therefore, other techniques such as parallelism (multiprocessing, coprocessing) must be applied and improved to fulfill this necessity.

1.3.2 A classification of high level languages

Since the development of Fortran 0 by J. Backus in 1954, several hundreds of high level languages have been presented. A Tower of Babel has been erected, which is still growing [Marc86]! Of course, most of the languages are based on their predecessors and only a few are really revolutionary. Some of the 'basic' languages are Fortran, Cobol, Algol 58, and Lisp [Horo84].

As the tie of kinship becomes less close, the resemblance with the ancestors fades away. In this sense, Smalltalk, based on Simula, in turn influenced by Algol 60, which was inspired by Fortran, has little correspondence left with Fortran, and can be considered a completely new language: Fig. 1.8 (after [Schi88]).

In view of these complex inheritance relationships, it is difficult to classify the existing high level languages in strictly separate groups. One may distinguish between the following classes:

- imperative languages;
- applicative languages;
- object-oriented languages;
- logic languages;
- dedicated languages;
- interactive applications.

The applicative and logic languages are often grouped into the superclass of *declarative languages*. To some extent, object-oriented languages could also be considered declarative, although many would consider them non-declarative. Many other classifications are possible; there is no unanimity concerning the terminology used.

Imperative languages. In an imperative language, the programmer specifies a sequence of imperative, state-transforming operations that must be executed in a particular order. Fortran is the oldest and most widely known example and has many successors: Cobol, Algol, Basic, PL/1, Pascal, C, Modula-2, Ada, etc. Most of the existing languages belong to this class and, therefore, they are called *conventional languages*.

The order of the statements in imperative languages is important and must be obeyed during execution. Hence, it is difficult to detect and exploit parallelism: to execute a statement, often the results of the previous statements are required [Nico84,Flyn66]. The maximal execution speed of programs written in imperative languages is limited by a rather low number of statements executable in parallel during each cycle.

1.3. Programming Languages

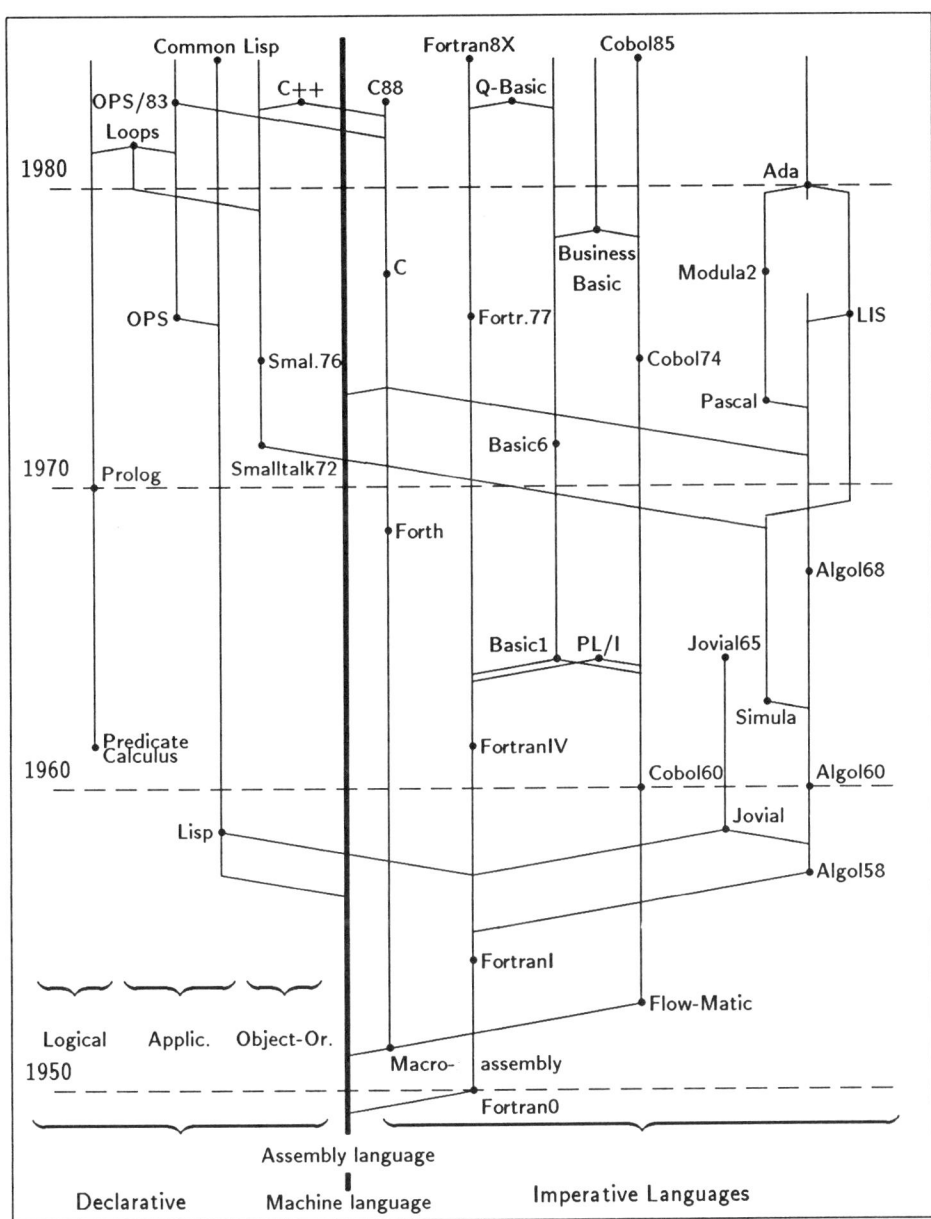

Figure 1.8
A pedigree of computer languages (after Schindler, 1988)

A second disadvantage concerns the productivity of a programmer using imperative languages. The primitive elements of execution are incremental modifications of values held in variables (memory locations). So, the progress of the computation is defined by the global state represented in the computer's memory. In order to code and debug a program, the programmer has to be aware of the values of *all* variables. He must think in terms of incremental manipulation of data and not directly in terms of the problem. This tends to reduce productivity [Hend80].

Although imperative languages do not seem to be particularly favorable with respect to either programmer productivity, the reliability of programs, or maximum potential execution speed, for a number of reasons they are the most frequently used languages at this moment.

A first reason is, of course, their long-time presence in the programmer's world. A lot of knowledge, equipment and experienced people are available.

Second, imperative languages map very well on current von Neumann machines. Backus has pointed out that the design of the first imperative languages was inspired by the existing von Neumann machines [Back78]. Hence, imperative languages are said to be the high level versions of von Neumann computers. Indeed, program variables, control structures and assignments correspond to memory cells, jump instructions and read/write statements of the machines, respectively. This high level of correspondence results in a relatively high execution speed of imperative language programs on today's computers.

Third, it must be admitted that certain applications are inherently sequential in nature (I/O routines, protocols). For these applications, attempts to parallelize do not seem useful, as the data dependency is implied by the problem itself and not by the implementation. In such cases, of course, the sequential nature of imperative languages is not a disadvantage.

Imperative languages are expected to remain common for at least some decades.

Applicative languages. Applicative, or functional, languages are based on the application of functions to arguments [Alle78]. As in mathematics, each function has arguments (inputs) and returns a result (output). There is no notion of time or evolution; a purely functional program is a static representation of the result of the computation. The computation itself is a mere transformation of the program into a directly usable but equivalent form. There is also no notion of a computation state kept in memory.

The key concept of applicative languages is known as *referential transparency* [Horo84]. This means that the result of a function application depends only on the arguments, and is in no way influenced by computational history of the system. In other words, replacing a function with its arguments by its result will not change anything to the result of the program (this is the *equational logic* underlying functional computation: substituting equals for equals). Obviously, referential transparency requires that, during the evaluation of a function, neither its arguments nor any other program element is modified. Hence, in contrast to imperative languages, side effects, time dependencies and state of a program are not present in pure functional languages. The programmer does not have to reason in terms of modifying values of state variables: he is able to concentrate more on the solution proper of the problem. For that reason, advocates of applicative languages claim that functional programming increases programmer productivity, and makes verification easier [Hend80].

Another advantage of functional languages is their relationship to purely mathematical concepts. This provides more solid ground for tools to verify and to prove correctness.

But what about the execution of functional languages on today's computers ? There is no direct relationship between functional languages and the currently available von Neumann systems. As a result, several architectures dedicated to the execution of functional programs and increasing the architectural correspondence have been presented [Vegd88,Gabr85]. However, most of them have remained in prototype stage. In [Vegd88] some reasons for the inefficient execution of functional languages on von Neumann computers were identified:

- the use of linked lists [McCa60] does not correspond to the linear structure of conventional memory;

- the extremely high frequency of function calls results in significant overhead;

- garbage collection is not directly supported on von Neumann machines;

- as no existing data is modified, the computation of a result requires the generation of an entirely new data structure (modifying takes less time).

Applicative languages clearly have certain advantages over conventional languages. However, when considering their use, one should take into account both the low execution speed on von Neumann machines, and their suitability for the formalization of the particular problems. Artificial intelligence and symbolic list processing are two typical areas for applicative languages.

Object oriented languages. In object-oriented languages, the basic programming element is the *object*. An object is a modular concept which groups all definitions of state variables and the procedures to change them, and hides this information from the outside world. Only the names of the local procedures (*methods*) are made available. Objects can be created dynamically, during the execution of the program. Creation of objects is made easy through the use of *classes* and *inheritance*. A class is a template from which new objects can be instantiated. By default, newly created objects or classes inherit the properties laid down in the class definition. Properties may be overridden locally.

The breakthrough of object-oriented programming languages came with Smalltalk by the end of the 1970s [Gold83]. Smalltalk achieves a high level of abstraction. Computation occurs by sending messages to objects. The class to which the receiving object belongs determines the method (routine) which corresponds to the received message. This method is executed by sequentially evaluating its expressions.

This way of computing is akin to procedure calling in imperative languages; one these grounds one may regard object-oriented languages as being imperative. The difference is in the binding of procedure call and procedure body: in imperative languages this is done at compile time, while in Smalltalk the receiver performs a runtime search for the body corresponding to the message. This is called *polymorphism*: the execution of the message can take on many forms, depending on the receiver. In a way, one could say that the programmer need not be concerned with precisely how a task is carried out, but only with what this task accomplishes. This provides a more declarative view on the language. Although the expressiveness provided by this dynamic binding is very powerful, this mechanism also causes a lot of overhead during execution on conventional architectures. Indeed, the corresponding method has to be identified from a list of available methods for that class, with only the name of the message as input.

One of the beautiful features of Smalltalk, also found in Lisp and Forth, is the extreme uniformity. Message passing is the *only* way to activate, *everything* is an object (also the classes), the debugger and the interpreter are Smalltalk programs, etc. This uniformity has also disadvantages: simple operations such as incrementing an integer must be done conforming to the Smalltalk style. A message (increment) must be sent to an integer whose class determines the corresponding method.

As a consequence, a reasonably fast Smalltalk system requires an optimized implementation of the Smalltalk kernel and fast, possibly Smalltalk-oriented computer hardware. Typical application areas of Smalltalk include robotics (for world models), AI (for frame-based knowledge representation), small-scale simulation, and rapid prototyping.

Logic languages. In imperative languages the programmer specifies *how* the computer has to compute (i.e., the sequence of operations) a result. In contrast, using logic languages, a program consists of a declaration of the logic properties the solution should have, i.e., *what* the computer should compute. A very popular member of this class of languages is Prolog.

A Prolog program consists of a list of Horn clauses, a representation of a subset of first order predicate logic. Horn clauses either represent *facts* or *rules*. A goals is formulated, which may be proved or disproved by the system. Using these declarations, the system tries to prove or refute the goal, by means of its built-in inference mechanism. In this way the computer actively searches a solution only guided by

1.3. Programming Languages

general rules. This relieves the programmer from detailed implementation analysis and setting up algorithms for the problem. Since the programming is a declaration of the essential properties of the solution, the programmer does not have to be concerned with the sequencing of the actions needed to find it.

However, things are not as easy as presented. One difficulty lies in the understanding of how to find a complete and consistent declaration of the properties of the problem. This requires a very deep understanding of the problem, somewhat akin to the specification problem of software engineering. Furthermore, in the current implementations, the programmer has to be aware of the underlying inference mechanism. In fact, this underlying algorithm replaces the algorithm in imperative languages and the declarations are the data upon which it operates. In the case of Prolog for example, the ordering of declarations not only influences the execution speed of the evaluation but, in some cases, is essential to find any solution at all. Therefore, programming in Prolog still requires a profound experience and knowledge.

Another class of logic-type languages is formed by rule-based systems (e.g., OPS-5). In such environments the programmer specifies what must happen depending on the evaluation of a boolean expression. These IF-THEN-ELSE rules allow the user to program the system in a way that does not require a full *a priori* comprehension of the problem. The computer evaluates the IF expressions, and 'fires' the corresponding bodies. As can be noted, rule-based systems are also influenced by imperative languages and are not strictly declarative.

The operations performed during the execution of logic languages are very specific: unification, binding, matching, searching, etc. This is the reason why today's von Neumann machines are not well suited for logic languages. Once again, in this field much effort is spent to the design of special purpose architectures. These perform the particular operations by means of special hardware, at a high rate. Logic languages cover application domains such as artificial intelligence and logic programming.

Dedicated languages. In several applications, languages have been developed to support the application-specific semantics. Fortran 0, being a language designed for scientific computation, was the first dedicated language. Although tuned to a particular application, dedicated languages can be general. This means that they can perform any calculation that can be expressed in another language. Several languages, including Fortran, started off as dedicated and evolved to a more general purpose one. Others started merely as a possibility to enter data and, in order to increase their expressiveness, grew out to true (application specific) languages. Dedicated languages are often a mixture of programming styles. This is not surprising, since many problem classes can be best described using such a mixture. Consequently, it may be very difficult to categorize dedicated languages, or even to distinguish a language from e.g. an unstructured set of interactive commands.

Several areas exist which benefit from the existence of a dedicated (high level) language: business administration (COBOL, SQL, BUSINESS BASIC), numeric array manipulations (APL, spreadsheet languages), systems programming (BLISS), command level languages (DCL), real-time control (Forth), document formatting (LaTeX, GML, NROFF, PostScript, Desktop Publishers), symbolic calculation (Reduce, MacSyma), etc. The merits of these dedicated languages are the enhanced capabilities of expressiveness in their particular application fields.

Interactive applications. Many contemporary computer applications can only be used in a productive way when they are used interactively. One may define interactive applications as application specific on-line languages of keystrokes. Indeed, keystroke sequences must meet certain syntactic and semantic restrictions. The fact that these are tested and executed immediately after entry is more or less immaterial. Well known examples are databases, spreadsheets, graphics (CAD) packages, and desktop publishing languages.

Interactivity is an important feature: it allows the user to approach the solution of his problem in a stepwize and quick way. It gives the user the feeling that he is fully controlling the system, and that he can specify in a natural way what he wants the computer to do [Koko88]. From the user's point of view the problem and the programming environment are integrated. This differs from a system with separate editor, compiler, linker and debugger. The step between programming and debugging is not as large as in non-interactive programming environments.

Interactive applications are user-oriented, and in most cases, programming experience is not required for their use. Generally, an on-line help facility is included in the environment. Moreover, to provide a kind of programming facilities, often a script recording capability is incorporated which stores the keystrokes during a certain sequence of steps. In this way, even an unexperienced programmer can easily program and automate his application by replaying command files.

In [Wass82], interactive environments are said to quickly gain importance. They reduce the cost of programming: the user — who is supposed to know the problem well — specifies and implements the solution in a natural way. Of course, not every problem can be solved in this way and, therefore, other language environments will still maintain an important position in the programmer's world.

1.4 Bridging the Semantic Gap

In the previous section, we have sketched the evolution of high level programming languages. We have seen that initially, language designers were concerned with the ease of execution of the language constructs on von Neumann architectures. Later on, language design was (rightfully) directed towards the programmer and

1.4. Bridging the Semantic Gap

the application. At the same time, we see a reduction of the semantic level of the basic machine instructions. Very early computers had complex calculator-like instructions like multiply or square root. As soon as program translators became available, there was no need to maintain this high semantic instruction level. Thus a gap has developed between the semantics of the basic machine instructions and the primitive operations provided by programming languages: the *semantic gap*.

1.4.1 Language implementation techniques

The execution of a program written in a high level language requires that each statement of the program be replaced by a semantically equivalent sequence of machine instructions. Clearly, a transformation of the source program is called for. This transformation can be realized in a number of ways. A useful criterion to distinguish among them is the *instant* at which the translation takes place. We have the following possibilities (fig. 1.9):

- the high level language program is translated to a form only using machine instructions (native code) *before* the execution;

- the high level language program is translated to an intermediate from, which does not consist of machine instructions. During the execution, each statement of the intermediate program representation is *dynamically* translated into immediately executed machine instructions by another program.

A few definitions. The first execution method is called *direct execution of compiled native code*. The program representation is directly executable by the microprocessor and is built of instructions native to the microprocessor. The execution machine is called a *host machine* executing host instructions. The second execution method, in which the high level language program representation is not directly executable, is called *interpretation of intermediate instructions*. The program representation can be that of the high level language, or of an intermediate level between the native code and the high level language (HLL). The program representation is interpreted by a program consisting of directly executable instructions. The latter program is called an *interpreter program* or *interpreter* for short. The interpreted program consists of *intermediate instructions*. The intermediate instructions define an instruction set architecture called the *image machine*. This process of interpretation of image instructions is also called *emulation*. The host machine, also called *base machine*, is the *emulating machine*; the intermediate architecture is the *emulated architecture*. One often uses the verb *simulate* instead of emulate. The slight difference between these synonyms deals with the purpose and context in which they are used. Emulation emphasizes that the instruction set architecture of the image machine has also been implemented as a host machine. Emulation

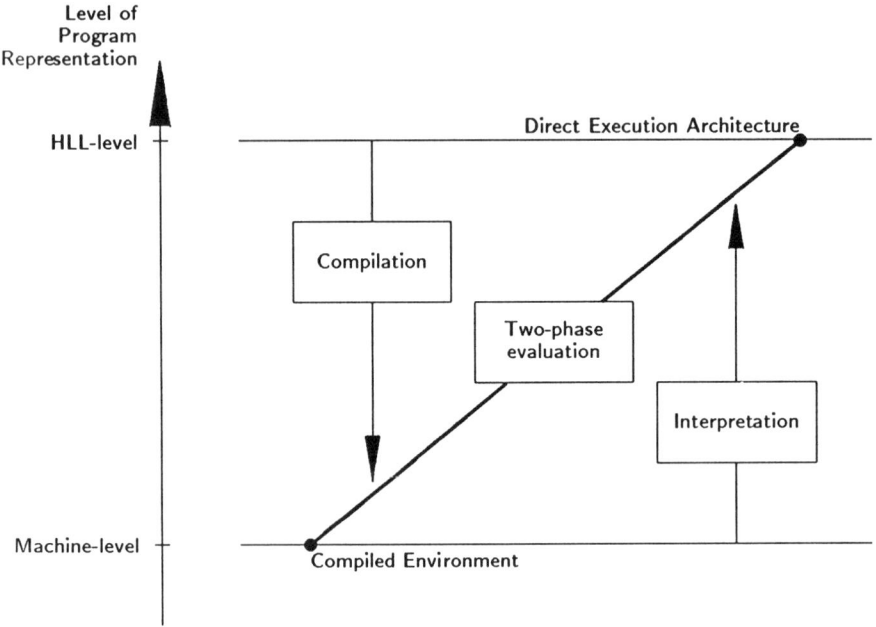

Figure 1.9
Implementation techniques of high level languages

is a technique to support portability of code. Simulation suggests that the image machine has not been realized. Simulation is a technique to investigate an as yet unrealized instruction set. The term interpretation is more general and can be used in the case of an image instruction set as well as to perform operations depending on data of any other kind.

The image machine can also act as a host machine to emulate yet another instruction set. In this case, we have a two-level interpreter. In [Hoff83], Hoffmann categorizes interpretive systems based on the number of levels involved: one level, two levels, or interpreters with three or more levels. According to his formalism, $P \xrightarrow{i} I \xmapsto{h} H$ denotes a one-level interpreter where the intermediate instructions i of program P are interpreted by an interpreter program I consisting of machine instructions h, directly executed by a host machine H. Similarly, $P \xrightarrow{l} L \xrightarrow{i} I \xmapsto{h} H$ refers to a two-level interpreter.

Here, we only consider execution techniques observable *outside* the processor and ignore internal instruction execution mechanisms of the machine such as microcoding. Since the internal interpretive mechanism is fixed, it is out of reach for

1.4. Bridging the Semantic Gap

the language implementor. Except for bit-sliced or otherwise microprogrammable systems with writable control store, instruction sets must be considered as fixed boundary conditions.

Direct execution of native code. In the direct execution technique the high level language program source is compiled into a sequence of native machine instructions. These are directly executed by the processor. The compilation technique has the following main properties:

- **Execution speed.** The program representation is directly executed and no extra instructions are required to process it. The execution speed can only be improved by a more optimal program representation. Hence, the quality of the compiler is essential.

- **Portability.** The native code representation can be executed by another machine as far as the instruction sets are compatible. Unless processors belong to the same family, this is in general not the case.

- **Debugging.** The debugging of programs is done at the level of the executing machine, and additional software is required to link HLL statements with corresponding machine instructions. Even then, compiler optimization can make generated machine code difficult to correlate with the source program. Without symbolic HLL debuggers, the gap between the HLL source and that of the representation is too large to allow easy debugging.

- **Representation size.** The compactness of the generated program representation obviously depends on the processor instruction set; program sizes can vary by factors of more than 2 among contemporary microprocessors (see below). Obviously, the compiler plays an important role in obtaining compact code.

- **Extensibility.** A modification of the high level language requires a modification of the compiler. This is also true if the target instruction set changes.

- **Interactivity.** The programming process consists of repeatedly editing the source, compiling the program and running/debugging the program. Viewing the results immediately after the modification of a program source is impossible. An incremental compilation capability is rare. This is caused by the fact that the binding of the program source to the machine is realized very early [Myer82]. For example, the offsets of jump instructions are computed at compile time, which fixes the distance (in bytes) between instructions.

Compilers can optimize two aspects of their generated code: execution speed and compactness. Often, chief interest goes to the reduction of execution time. Some compilers use an intermediate form during the compiling process and optimization can be done at the level of that intermediate form and/or at the target instruction level. Some traditional optimization techniques are the following [AhoS86]:

- **Peephole optimization.** The generated code is scanned in order to detect short sequences of instructions which can be replaced by a single instruction. This is more space-time efficient.

- **Elimination of common subexpressions.** The instruction sequences are scanned to discover common instruction sequences. If these exist, the result of a previously executed sequence can be directly used instead of recomputating it by the current, identical sequence. This is especially valuable in addressing of complex data structures. In some languages the programmer can use a WITH statement to enforce the compiler to use this optimization technique.

- **Code motion.** Instructions that compute loop-invariant results may be moved outside the loop and executed only once.

Interpretation of intermediate instruction sets. The interpretation of intermediate instruction sets refers to the execution by means of another program which is independent of the HLL program. Here, we exclude program representations equal to the HLL program source, because they are spatially inefficient. We limit ourselves to truly intermediate program representations. The interpretive technique has the following properties:

- **Execution speed.** The execution mechanism is indirect. A native code interpreter consults the program representation and, based on the intermediate instruction found, executes the corresponding machine instructions. Hence, the execution speed is inherently lower than the direct execution of native code.

- **Portability.** The program representation is not dependent on the machine instruction set and can be ported to other machines. The interpretation of a ported program only requires that an interpreter be written in the instruction set of the new host. Hence, to support m languages on n machines the interpretive technique requires m compilers and n interpreters (if the same image architecture is used), while $m \times n$ compilers are needed with the compilation technique.

- **Debugging.** The debugging of intermediate instruction sequences is less cumbersome compared to that of native instruction sequences as the program representation corresponds more to the HLL source. Easy modifications in the interpreter may provide mechanisms for tracing (see Chapter 2) [Klin81].

1.4. Bridging the Semantic Gap

- **Representation size.** The intermediate form of the program, being independent of the host machine, allows optimization w.r.t. one or more criteria (space, time). Generally, the image instructions are oriented towards a particular HLL and allow a compact program representation. Of course, the size of the interpreter must be added to the program size, but this is only an additive constant. The compactness relative to native code depends on the semantic level of the intermediate instruction set. Intermediate languages with complex dynamic semantics (dynamic type checking, exception checking, etc.) allow a very compact representation.

- **Extensibility.** In order to extend a HLL, the compiler has only to be changed if the modification cannot be expressed by a change in the semantics of intermediate instructions. A modification of the semantics of intermediate instruction requires just a modification of the interpreter program which is of considerably lower complexity and size than the compiler.

- **Interactivity.** Compared to the native execution, interactivity is better supported in interpretive systems. There are two reasons for this: (1) the compilation required is less time-consuming, as there is a closer correspondence between the intermediate instructions and the HLL; (2) the intermediate representation can be chosen in such a way that interactive source editing and incremental compilation of the changes become feasible. The reason for this is that the binding of the program to the machine is done at run-time. For example, a BASIC statement can be modified without the need to modify or to recompile the other statements.

   Another interesting feature of the close correspondence between intermediate representation and HLL program is that the source can be reconstructed more easily from the program representation. In (interpretive) interactive systems, the symbol table is generally still available which allows symbolic debugging.

Interpretive environments. The interpretive technique can also be used for other purposes than to implement a traditional programming language. In many interactive personal computer or workstation applications, the total time spent to obtain the solution of a given problem is only marginally influenced by the execution speed of the language processor. Aspects like interactivity and expressivity are of far greater importance (see section 1.3). These can be provided by the interpretive technique.

The method used in such systems is typically as follows: the input (query statements in database systems, equations and functions in spreadsheets, rules in expert systems) are incrementally compiled into a more suitable intermediate form, and held in memory. The execution process is performed by an interpreter scanning the input and generating a result. Thus the transformation process is done by a simple compiler (the outer-interpreter or parser) while the execution process is done by the actual (inner-) interpreter (the processor or engine). Hence, there is no principal difference between the execution method of interpretive (on-line) language implementations and interactive applications.

1.4.2 Aspects of microprocessor instruction sets

So far, we have used the term architecture to denote the way in which basic system building blocks are interconnected. The term can be used in another meaning, induced by the instruction set. Indeed, for the programmer, only those architectural aspects are relevant that can be observed or controlled through the execution of machine instructions. Some hidden aspects, e.g. some forms of parallel execution, or the physical bus width, have no observable effect (unless perhaps global performance). The architecture defined by the instruction set is often called the *instruction set architecture* (ISA).

Instruction sets have several important aspects, related to the ease of use (by humans or automatic translators), the compactness of program representation, and the ease and speed of execution. We shall now review some of these aspects.

Ease of use. Given the knowledge of the instruction set we can determine two characteristics: *regularity* and *completeness*.

The regularity of an instruction set is a characteristic that defies exceptions in the semantics and encoding of the instructions. More specifically, similar instructions should have similar behavior and should be allowed to appear in similar contexts. A number of examples will make this clear:

- an addition should affect the condition flags if the multiplication does;
- a division should be interruptable if the multiplication is;
- an addition of register operands or of memory operands should have the same opcode;
- any addressing mode should be allowed with any opcode, as far as this is still meaningful. This is often called *orthogonality*;
- the format of an addition should be the same of a multiplication (of similar operands).

This regularity is important mainly for the sake of the compiler [Wulf81]. Irregularities increase the complexity of the code generator, while comparable profits are not always achieved. Wirth [Wirt86] indicates that code generators of Modula-2 compilers for the Motorola MC68000 and the National NS32000 contain more lines than that of a Lilith system, by a factor of 2.54 and 1.37, respectively. In spite of

1.4. Bridging the Semantic Gap

the larger MC68000 code generator, the size of the generated code is 2.3 and 1.5, respectively, compared to that for the Lilith. This means the irregularity of the MC68000 instruction set implies not only a more complex code generator but also a higher code size.

A second important feature is completeness. While regularity facilitates code generation, the compilation process will still be hampered if the operations visible at the source language level are not available in the machine's instruction set. In such a case the HLL operations must be emulated by a sequence of machine instructions. A typical example of this are floating point operations.

Regularity and completeness make the task of automatic code generators easier. In the same way these characteristics also make manual programming at the machine level easier. A regular and complete machine language is less difficult to learn, to understand and to use. Of course, the manual, machine-level programming aspect is becoming less important.

The concepts of regularity and completeness mainly relate to the ease of programming. These characteristics may not be essential when seeking high execution speed or high code density.

Compactness of representation. The code density can be increased by the following techniques which often contradict the principle of regularity:

- **The use of implicit operand addressing.** Certain instructions are allowed to work only with particular registers. This eliminates the need for the explicit identification of the operand, leading to a higher code density. Attention must be paid to the possible need of additional instructions required to move the actual operands into the implied registers. *Stack architectures* or *zero address machines* are based on this principle: the top of stack is the implicit source/destination for the instructions. In this case POP and PUSH instructions are required to put the operands onto the stack. However, as the result is also pushed on the stack, the next instruction can be executed without the need for extra 'moving' operations.

- **Frequency based encoding.** Frequently occurring opcodes, formats, or operands may be represented by short bitstrings, while less frequent opcodes may be encoded using longer bitstrings. One can go very far in this direction: variable length codes (Huffman code) and block codes are well known examples. Such techniques may reduce the static representation size by 75% [Hehn76].

- **Combining opcode, operand and format fields.** Analysis of instruction sequences has revealed that small integers (e.g. 0, 1, 2) occur very frequently as operands. This has led to special opcodes for instructions using such operands [Stev79]. The INC instruction is a more compact encoding of an ADD 1 command.

- **Increasing the semantics of instructions.** Operations such as string comparison require a lot of instructions if there are no specific machine instructions for this task. In microcoded architectures, internal sequences of microinstructions emulate this task and are called by a single machine instruction. The execution of such operations typically takes up a considerable amount of cycles depending on the data (multi-cycle execution).

- **Complex addressing modes.** By using complex addressing modes in a single instruction, sophisticated computations of effective addresses can be specified. The alternative is to execute explicit instructions that actually compute the address. The former strategy improves code density again.

- **Context sensitive encoding.** The previous techniques can be applied to all instructions in a program. However, at each point in the execution, the set of meaningful instructions a microprocessor can encounter is only a subset of the entire instruction set [Fost71]. Hence, if the microprocessor has knowledge of the recent history of the process, the computation context, the encoding of the elements can be more compact. This principle can be applied to instructions as well as to data. Also, in procedural languages, variables have a restricted scope and at a certain place during execution the number of variables that can be reached is less than the total number of variables in a program. A compact, lexical encoding can be used to locate variables within a certain context [John71].

On the speed of execution, and CISCs vs. RISCs. We have already mentioned that the semantic gap is a fundamental cause of many inefficiencies. We have also reviewed the traditional ways of bridging the gap: compilation and interpretation. It is clear that the properties of the instruction set are crucial to obtain a fast execution of high level language programs. In CISC-style (Complex Instruction Set Computers) machines, one tries to fulfill this goal by decreasing the differences between high level language concepts and those found at the level of the executing machine. Typical CISC-style computers provide instructions similar to HLL operations such as DO-LOOP and string operations. The complex data structures available in high level language programs (arrays, lists, records), are supported by the CISC-style through complex addressing modes. The high level language concepts are adopted by CISC-style architectures at the expense of hardware complexity. Typically, the execution of complex instructions is controlled by means of microcoded routines. For example, the Motorola MC68000 contains two instruction levels: (1) machine instructions, which are interpreted by microcode

1.4. Bridging the Semantic Gap

instructions, and (2) microcode instructions, which are emulated by nano-code instructions [Tred88]. Hence, internally, the MC68000 is a two-level interpretive system. The same is true for the MC68020, where the microcode store is 30-bit wide and contains 34560 bits; the nano-code store is 74-bit wide and contains 50616 bits [Tred88].

Table 1.2 summarizes some typical characteristics of the CISC-style. No one doubts that the CISC evolution was stimulated by the progress in integrating capabilities: CAD-tools are available to handle complex structures [Tred88]. Moreover, the belief existed that the only way to speed up the execution of high level language programs was by narrowing the semantic gap.

Research at IBM (IBM801), Berkely University (RISC I) and Stanford University (MIPS) revealed that another approach could be followed to speed up high level language execution. Instead of raising the level of the instruction set of the machine, RISC (Reduced Instruction Set Computer) advocates propose to increase the execution speed of only the most time-consuming operations found in typical compiled high level language programs. It turns out that, of the rich CISC instruction sets, only a small fraction is frequently used. Hence, a point of difference with the CISC-style is the number of operations set up for direct support by hardware. In basic RISC processors, the number of the microprocessor instructions is rather low and they only perform simple operations such as move and addition (no multiplication nor string handling instructions). A consequence of the low number and the low level of the instructions is that these can be directly executed by hardware (hardwired control), which eliminates the need for microcode. This reduces the minimal instruction execution time of the machine. It also frees considerable space on the chip that can be used for other purposes, e.g. reducing the external bus bandwidth requirements. Typically, most RISC-like microprocessors fill the freed space with registers (up to 528 in the Pyramid) in order to increase execution speed further. This is only one possibility: other designs would benefit more from floating-point support or on-chip caches.

The restricted, low level instruction set implies that more complex or less frequent operations must be emulated by sequences of primitive instructions. The low level of the operations of RISC-style instructions allows an execution in one cycle. The other steps of instruction processing (fetch/decode, reading and writing of operands) are handled by other stages of a strongly pipelined computer. The RISC-style machine can be considered as a highly streamlined, pipelined architecture through which simple instructions are rushed. Characteristics of the RISC-style are given in Table 1.2.

As can be observed, not every computer can be strictly categorized in either the CISC or RISC class. Neither the number of instructions, nor their level are safe criteria. Therefore, it is better to talk about CISC-style and RISC-style just as with styles of historical buildings. Also, the RISC abbreviation should not be taken too

	CISC-style	RISC-style
Internal control mechanism	microcoded	hardwired
Execution time	multi-cycle	one cycle
Instruction formats	many, variable length	few, fixed length
Addressing modes	many	single or few
Operand sources	memory and/or registers	only from registers
Number of instructions	rather high	low
Code density	rather high	low
Registers	few (up to 16)	many (up to 528)
Instruction set	high level language oriented	only basic operations
Role of the compiler	translation	translation and optimization

Table 1.2
A comparison of RISC-style and CISC-style properties

literally: some people suggest a replacement of the adjective 'Reduced' by 'Regular' [Wirt87] or 'Streamlined' [Henn84].

There are two main weak points with RISCs [Henn84]: the required memory bandwidth, and the need for additional software tools. As explained above, the information per instruction bit in a RISC-style instruction is lower than that of a CISC-style one. Therefore, more instruction bits have to be transferred between microprocessor and instruction memory for constant program functionality. In [Davi87b], Davidson et al. indicate that, based on carefully designed experiments, the program representation size in a RISC-style is 2.5 times larger, when compared to a CISC-style one (VAX). This refers to static size and, of course, as the price per memory bit decreases (more rapidly so than microprocessors [Myer86]), this is not so important. However, the static size is directly related to the *dynamic size*: the amount of instruction bits to be fetched during the execution of a program. A less dense instruction encoding will result in a larger size of the working set. The same experiment ([Davi87b]) revealed that the required memory bandwidth in the RISC case is at least twice that of the CISC case. Similar figures are obtained in experiments discussed in [Flyn87].

To reduce the dynamic instruction size, instruction caches are used. For such caches the difference in the required instruction bandwidth between CISC and RISC like instruction sets has important consequences. In [Flyn87] Flynn et al. show that the instruction cache must be twice as large compared to the CISC case in order to achieve the same hit ratio. This illustrates the consequences of the encoding density in both styles.

The second problem deals with the required additional software tools, in partic-

1.4. Bridging the Semantic Gap

ular the code generators. The complexity of a code generator is mainly determined by the regularity and the orthogonality of the target instruction set [Wulf81]. Every implementation decision conflicting with one of these rules makes the compiler's task more difficult. In this sense, if a high level language construct can be implemented in more than one way, the code generators have to find out which one must be chosen (based on criteria such as code size and/or execution speed). This is often the case in CISC-like instruction sets which explains the complexity of code generators for complex instruction set architectures [Wirt86].

In contrast, the RISC-style, promoting simple primitive instructions, is liberated from such complications, which eases the task of a code generator. However, to profit from features of the RISC-style (e.g. delayed branch, pipelining), much more effort must be devoted to optimization. This, despite the simplicity of the instruction set, complicates the code generating task [Wirt87].

The traditional code optimization techniques such as peephole optimization, elimination of common subexpressions, and code motion, are all very useful in this respect. A more hardware related optimization is to reorder instruction sequences to minimize delays of off-chip memory references. Load instructions introduce a memory access delay which can be ignored if a useful instruction can be executed meanwhile. This cannot be done if the following instructions need the value of that load-instruction (data dependency). In the MIPS (Microprocessor without Interlocked Pipe Stages) it is the task of the compiler to ensure that data dependencies involve no delay. If this cannot be done a NOP instruction must be inserted. This strategy is an alternative to built-in hardware which detects and avoids interlocks (e.g. *scoreboarding*).

A similar optimization concerns the reduction of the penalty of branch instructions caused by the pipelining of instruction fetch, decoding, and execution. A useful instruction may be executed during the delay required to fill the pipeline with the target instruction of a jump (delayed branch). Again, this is the task of the compiler and, in worst case, a NOP instruction must be filled in the delay slot. In the case of the MIPS compiler, it is found that 21 % of the executed instructions occur during delay slots [Henn84] which underlines the requirement for this optimization.

In addition, an optimal utilization of the large number of registers found in many RISC-like microprocessors, requires sophisticated code from the compiler which also increases the compiler's complexity and execution time [Stal88].

1.4.3 Architectural techniques to bridge the semantic gap

In general purpose architectures, the RISC and CISC approaches indicate that bridging the semantic gap can be thoroughly influenced by suitable hardware instruction sets. Requiring that the instruction set be *general purpose*, i.e., that several high level languages can be compiled equally well into the instruction set,

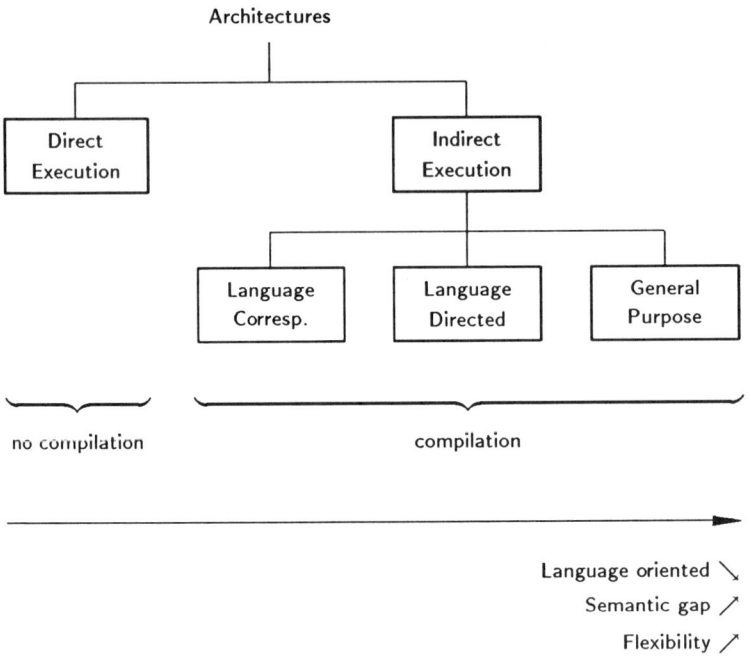

Figure 1.10
Language oriented computer architectures

severely limits the possibilities for direct hardware support. That this is indeed a limitation is illustrated by the performance attained by specialized coprocessors, e.g. numeric data processors. The performance ratios of a general purpose microprocessor and specialized coprocessor easily exceed 140 for numeric computations. It then comes as no surprise that several attempts have been made to bridge the semantic gap by means of specialized, dedicated hardware architectures. We shall now review some of these attempts (fig. 1.10). Our overview is inspired by classifications proposed in [Silb86,Myer82].

Direct execution architectures. A particular class of high level language implementations is formed by the Direct Execution Architectures (DEA). The concept implemented by these DEAs is that of interpretation in a strict sense. However, it is done by hardware. In this case, neither software compilation nor software interpretation is involved: the assembly language *is* the high level language, and

1.4. Bridging the Semantic Gap

the semantic gap does not exist.

Most of the architectures belonging to this class have remained in the prototype phase. At the university of Maryland a lot of effort was spent in this field [ChuA81]; therefore, this direction is also called the *University of Maryland Approach*. An example of a DEA is Pasdec [Silb86].

The organization of a DEA consists of a lexical processor, a control processor and a data processor [ChuA81]. The lexical processor performs an instruction by instruction encoding of the textual program representation into a token format. The control processor executes the resulting tokens corresponding to control flow, whereas the data processor executes the data flow tokens. In contrast to von Neumann architectures, code and data are kept in separate memories, and control flow and data flow are performed by separate processors. The data declarations are not 'compiled' but 'executed' by the data processor which builds an entry in a symbol table in an associative memory, records its type and reserves a number of memory cells for its value. The complex control processor has provisions for the execution of high level control structures. This approach has the following advantages above conventional systems [ChuA81]:

- The level of execution and that of programming are equal and, therefore, the programmer easily understands the execution of the program. This facilitates debugging and tracing. Moreover, as variables are not compiled, symbolic debugging is inherent to the environment.

- There is a syntactic and semantic checking at program entry, and not later on during compilation. The computer internally contains the constructs of the language and stores all information of the declared variables. In a compiling environment a certain time passes between programming in an editor and the messages during parsing.

- There is no compilation or other static program preparation. Consequently, no compiler, linker or loader are required.

Two main disadvantages are [Kavi82]

- **complex hardware.** There seems to be a direct correspondence between the complexity of the language and that of the supporting DEA hardware. Hence, the DEA hardware provides a measure for the high level language complexity. Compared to conventional machines the DEA hardware is very complex.

- **language dedicated hardware.** The DEA is oriented towards a single language and is, as a consequence, inflexible. Not only the syntax (compiler), but also the debugger and the execution unit (all in hardware) are oriented towards the single language.

Indirect execution architectures. In contrast to direct execution architectures, indirect execution architectures (IEA) reduce but do not completely eliminate the semantic gap. Hence, a compilation step is required with the IEAs. They reduce the semantic gap by orienting the instruction set architecture design towards one or more high level languages. Differences in the degree of orientation lead to several classes: language directed architectures, language correspondence architectures, and, of course, general purpose architectures.

Language directed architectures provide some constructs that facilitate HLL translation, whereas language corresponding architectures have their machine language level very close to that of the HLL. General purpose architectures primarily do not intend to reduce the semantic gap.

1. **Language directed architectures.** Language directed architectures possess constructs that are borrowed from one or more HLLs. In this way, the compiler can benefit from this and dispatch a HLL construct to the execution of a single or a few machine instructions. Examples of such constructs are: access protection, complex addressing modes, loop instructions, decrement and branch instructions, multiple operand instructions, array bound checking, string and bit operations, etc.

   Complex constructs consist of sequences of simple operations and, therefore, microcoding is a natural way to support them. Microcoded and complex processors such as the Motorola MC68020, National 32032, Zilog 80000 and DECs VLSI Vax are illustrative examples [Silb86]. The properties of this approach are:

   - The compiler must be aware of the constructs provided by the machine and must be able to exploit them. This increases compiler complexity [Wulf81]. Often, a machine construct is directly related to a high level language construct; the compiler is not able to match the machine construct with a sequence of source statements with corresponding semantics from the same or another language. This illustrates the inability of the compiler to exploit complex machine constructs.

   - The HLL constructs imply an increased complexity of the machines, with the known disadvantages of CISCs.

   - Advantageous is the execution speed is increased, since micro-instructions from fast control store define the primitive operations. Furthermore, this technique also reduces the required instruction bandwidth, as a lot of operations are encoded by a single instruction.

   - Often, constructs are oriented towards a single HLL and the computer hardware can not use a construct in a situation with very similar but

slightly different semantics. For example, a 'decrement and branch if not zero' is different from a 'branch if not zero and decrement'.
- The direct association of HLL constructs and machine instructions forces the compiler to use these instructions, which may prohibit optimizations. For example, a move of a string with length one may be performed by string instructions, while a read and write suffice.

2. **Language corresponding architectures.** Language corresponding architectures go one step further than language directed architectures, by raising the level of the complete machine language to that of the HLL. Ideally, there is a one-to-one correspondence between the two languages. The compiler 'translates' the source language into the machine representation. Note that in direct execution architectures, the translation is done only instruction by instruction; no machine language representation is stored. Silbey *et al.* distinguish between software translators (type A) and hardware translators (type B) [Silb86]. Examples of type A language correspondence architectures are the Scheme-79 chip [Suss81], the APL machine [Silb86], DELtran [Flyn83a] and the Lilith [Wirt81]. Type B language correspondence architectures are represented by the SYMBOL machine [Silb86].

Language correspondence architectures are similar to direct execution architectures, and differ from the latter only by the presence of a compilation phase. Hence, several direct execution architecture properties are also present here:

- easy debugging (one-to-one correspondence);
- small representation size;
- compilers with low complexity (translation);
- language oriented instruction set architecture (only flexibility with microcoded language correspondence architectures);
- hardware is very complex with type B language correspondence architectures.

The distinction between language directed architectures and general purpose architectures is not always clear. Examples are Motorola's MC68020 and Intel's 80386 which can be considered language directed to some extent. Of course, most of them still remain general purpose architectures by any reasonable criterion.

1.5 Conclusion

In this introductory chapter we have covered a lot of ground. We have very briefly reviewed the long history of computation support devices. This history has entered its modern phase in the early fifties, with the arrival of the first stored program computers. The introduction of semiconductor technology and the subsequent use of lithographical integration techniques has made the development of low-cost microprocessors possible. The same technological advances have allowed to build large and fast random access memories. As a whole, the hardware cost of computation has been reduced dramatically, and this evolution is still going on. However, some parts of contemporary microprocessor systems, such as raw processing power, are becoming cheaper and more powerful at a much faster rate then other parts, such as off-chip communication bandwidth.

As to the deployment of available computer hardware, we have sketched the evolution of computer programming languages. The existence of a large variety of high level languages is mainly caused by the desire for high expressiveness and a need for high levels of abstraction in several application fields. Historically, imperative languages were the first languages used to program machines; they are still the most widely used ones. Several other language paradigms have come into existence since then. Functional languages grew out of mathematics and tend to increase the programmer's productivity as well as the quality of the programs. Object oriented languages evolved from imperative languages and have the important characteristic of modularity and information hiding. Logic languages go one step further in programming than the former languages, as they allow the programmer to specify *what* must be done and not *how* the computer must do it. Such a programming style has a lot of promise, in particular in the growing field of software engineering and logic system design. In its current state, however, declarative programming has not matured sufficiently to allow a truly productive use. Application oriented languages existed even before 'languages' were used. They still remain important tools and enhance expressiveness in particular application areas.

Languages can be implemented on general purpose computer architectures in basically two different ways: through interpretation, and through compilation. Compiled implementations offer by far the greatest potential for fast execution, in particular on modern RISC processor architectures. However, compiled language implementations are non-interactive, and much more rigid than truly interpreted languages. They also pose stringent requirements on the bandwidth of the instruction path, and the optimizing properties of the compiler. Compiled implementations are static; compiled programs can not be altered dynamically (by themselves) or interactively (by the programmer). As many modern microprocessor applications rest on the dynamical and interactive nature of their implementation, it is no wonder that interpretive techniques are already widely used, and are still gaining importance every day.

2 A CLOSER LOOK AT INTERPRETATION

In the previous chapter we have briefly discussed the use of interpretation as a software means to bridge the semantic gap. The following advantages have already been mentioned: interpretive techniques help in providing the much desired interactivity in programming or application environments; porting a language implementation from one architecture to another is easier with interpretive implementations; interpretive techniques and their associated intermediate program representations allow a more dense encoding of high level language programs than either CISC or RISC machine instruction sets.

Of course, there is no such thing as a free lunch. A price must be paid to benefit from the advantages of interpretation: its execution speed is significantly lower than the execution speed of native code programs generated by an optimizing compiler.

Hence, whether or not to use the interpretive implementation technique is not always an easy decision, and often problem-specific arguments must be taken into account. Nevertheless there are a few trends in the evolution of microprocessors and their applications that affect the significance of interpretive techniques in a more general way:

- **Interactivity is becoming an increasingly important asset of many modern microcomputer applications.** Data-base environments (with interactive schema design and query interpretation), spreadsheet programs, word processors, and desktop publishing packages are typical examples of this evolution. Several language environments owe many of their properties to an interpretive implementation: BASIC, APL, FORTH, LISP, PROLOG, SMALLTALK, the ASYST[1] environment are just a few examples. In this context, Rosin has made the following remark [Rosi69]

  > [...] Although interpreters have traditionally been considered too inefficient to use for most applications, [...] the recent upsurge in interactive environments in which programs as well as data take on a dynamic structure has lead to a re-establishment of interpretation as a valid technique.

- **Raw processing power is becoming cheaper at a fast rate.** Often, using a more powerful processor to compensate the loss of speed due to interpretation is the cheapest way to benefit from the advantages of interpretation.

- **Bus bandwidth is becoming a more expensive resource relative to either memory size or processing power.** Using a cache can alleviate this problem to a large extent; it is even imperative with modern RISC processors. However, caches are complex and relatively expensive. In combination with

---

[1] ASYST is a trade mark of the McMillan Software Company; it is an interactive environment for the collection and processing of measurement data, and is based on a FORTH-like language.

caching, interpretation of a compact instruction set may provide a more cost-effective solution by keeping the caches small, or by further improving the bandwidth reduction achieved by the cache.

Hence there are several reasons why interpretation deserves close attention. That there is indeed much research being devoted to interpretation, also for reasons other than those listed above, will become clear in Section 2.3. There we give a brief bibliographical overview of research papers concerned with interpretation. But before doing this, we shall have a closer look at how interpretation is done using microprocessors. We shall limit ourselves to the interpretive implementation of high level languages. In Section 2.1 we discuss general aspects of intermediate program representations on which a classification can be based. To illustrate the concepts we give three concrete examples of intermediate languages in Section 2.2.

2.1 Intermediate Language Representations

Intermediate languages exist in a variety of forms, and so do their associated interpreters. In general we can say that intermediate instructions have semantics that are closer to the semantics used in the high level language than to those of machine instructions. As a consequence, the execution of an intermediate instruction necessarily involves the execution of a (short) sequence of native machine instructions.

2.1.1 The interpretive loop

The execution mechanism of most interpreters does not differ from the execution mechanism of von Neumann machines. The method consists of repeatedly executing the following steps:

1. locating the next intermediate instruction to be executed, retrieving and analyzing it; this involves:

   - reading and updating an (intermediate) program counter;
   - reading the contents of the intermediate instruction memory addressed by this program counter;
   - sectioning the intermediate instruction into different fields (format, opcode and operands);
   - storing those fields into a set of fixed locations, which act as an interface to the second step;
   - transferring control to the routine that corresponds to the opcode of the instruction just decoded (second step);

2.1. Intermediate Language Representations 49

2. executing the semantics that correspond to the analyzed intermediate instruction.

3. transferring control back to the instructions executing step 1.

Various names are in use to denote the above steps. Mallach calls the first step the *Do Interpretive Loop (DIL)* [Mall75]. Stankovic calls the operations corresponding to the first step *mapping actions* [Stan81], i.e., the mapping of a virtual instruction (and its parameters) onto the instruction sequence of the emulating machine. The operations of the second step are called *execution actions*. Step 3, the return from the second step to the first step, also belongs to the mapping actions. Other authors, concerned with the architectural level of microprocessors, would call the first step the *fetch/decode phase*, while the second step is the *execution phase*. The latter terminology does not explicitly take into account the parsing and analysis of the instructions, and the saving of the different fields into predefined interface cells.

Note that a part of the analyzing/parsing phase of the instruction can also be done by the corresponding interpreter routines (execution actions). The knowledge of the opcode suffices access the corresponding interpreter routines. Furthermore, the format and the number of operands are well related to the opcode and, therefore, the parsing and analyzing can be done more efficiently by the actual interpreter routine. Note also that it can be more appropriate to involve multiple decoding steps. The primary decoding step could then be centralized, whereas subsequent decoding steps could be distributed among the semantic routines. However, relegating the analyzing/parsing actions to the execution part increases the interpreter size, as instructions are duplicated among the interpreter routines. In microprogrammed implementations of interpreters, where the expensive control store is restricted, this may be a reason to opt for a single and common parsing of the instruction fields. We shall come back to these considerations in Chapter 3.

It is obvious that the mapping actions can cause a significant slowdown with respect to native code execution. Indeed, when executing native code, it is the *microprocessor hardware* that performs the (native code) mapping actions, mostly pipelined and in overlap with the execution of the previous instruction. As soon as a representation is used that differs from pure native code, direct execution by hardware is precluded. Several ways exist in which one can try to reconcile execution speed and more compact program representations. We shall now analyze some relevant aspects of intermediate representations. We take two views: the way in which individual intermediate instructions are represented, and the way in which programs are represented using the intermediate instructions. Table 2.1 provides a classification of some popular intermediate representations according to these criteria.

Intermediate Code	Corresponding HLL	Instruction Encoding	Program Structure
A-code	Ada [Domm]	token	sequential
Bytecode	Smalltalk [Kras83]	token	sequential
C-code	Chill [Samm82]	token	sequential
CVM-code	C [Davi87a]	token	sequential
DTC	Prolog [Kral87]	pointer	threaded
DTC	QuickBasic [Vose87]	pointer	threaded
G-code	Lazy ML [Thak86]	token	sequential
ITC	Snobol4, Spitbol [Dewa75,Dewa77]	pointer	threaded
ITC	Forth [Moor74]	pointer	threaded
ITC	Pascal [TheT82,Hell83]	pointer	threaded
M-code	Modula-2 [Wirt81]	token	sequential
Mesa-code	Mesa [John82,Swee82]	token	sequential
OPA-code	Pascal [Schu82]	token	sequential
O-code	BCPL [Rich71]	token	sequential
P-code	Pascal [Pemb82]	token	sequential
S-code	Scheme [Suss81]	token	linked list
SECD-code	Lispkit Lisp [Hend80]	token	linked list
Warren code	Prolog [Warr83]	token	sequential

Table 2.1
A classification of intermediate representations

2.1.2 The intermediate instruction encoding level

The encoding of an intermediate instruction must allow the interpretive engine to locate and execute the corresponding sequence of native instructions. The following encoding schemes offer different trade-offs between encoding compactness and execution speed:

1. **Subroutine encoding.** Each intermediate instruction is represented by a native code subroutine call (fig. 2.1):

    CALL Native_Sequence

    The interpreter consists of a collection of machine-level subroutines:

    Native_Sequence:
            <native instructions>
            RET

    One could say that the interpreter for this instruction encoding needs no mapping actions; alternatively, it would be equally correct to state that *the*

2.1. Intermediate Language Representations

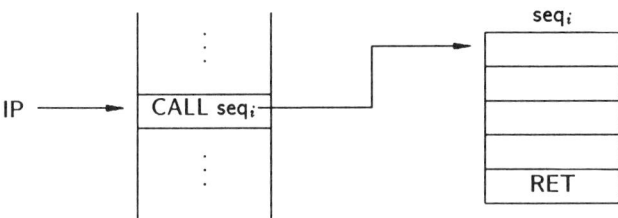

Figure 2.1
Subroutine encoding of intermediate instructions

mapping actions have been distributed into the program. Indeed, it are the CALL instructions that perform the mapping actions.

This interpretive technique allows a very fast execution, as the mapping actions (subroutine calls) are directly supported by the host machine. The method differs in no way from the use of subroutine libraries by native code compilers, except that compilers also use tailor-made inline macro expansion of frequently used short instruction sequences.

With subroutine encoding, compactness is not the main goal. It is rather low, in view of the explicit presence of the CALL opcodes, and the use of machine addresses (spanning the entire address range) to access primary native code sequences.

2. **Pointer based encoding.** To achieve a higher degree of compaction we identify the redundant bits in the subroutine representation. We note that the CALL opcode occurs frequently, and in a predictable way. Thus it can be removed. The resulting program representation is no longer directly executable, and requires extra mapping instructions. Removing the CALL opcodes implies that only subroutine calls were used in the intermediate representation (no mixing with non-CALL machine instructions allowed). The resulting intermediate instruction representation is a machine address, the operand of the former CALL instruction (fig. 2.2):

```
Native_Sequence
```

For its mapping actions, the interpreter now needs an intermediate program counter IP, pointing into the list of addresses. Thus, the native program counter is strictly separated from the intermediate program counter. A subroutine mechanism is no longer necessary, and the dispatching to the semantic

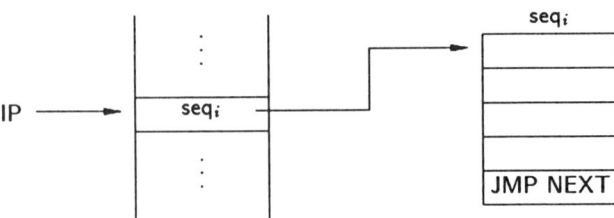

Figure 2.2
Pointer encoding of intermediate instructions

routines can be done using a faster JMP instruction. Per intermediate instruction (address), the equivalent of a memory indirect jump must be executed, and the program counter must be updated. Resuming the mapping actions can also be done using a JMP instruction.

```
Next:       <update IP>
Mapping:    JMP mem[IP]            ;memory indirect jump

Native_Sequence:
            <native instructions>
            JMP Next
```

The advantage is a more compact representation compared to the subroutine mechanism. The reduction in size depends mainly on the length of the CALL opcode.

3. **Tokenized encoding.** The representation size of pointer based encodings is lower than that of the subroutine code version. The next compaction step is based on the fact that, generally, the address space is much larger than the number of semantic instruction sequences. A space efficient encoding of N instruction names requires only $\lceil \log_2 N \rceil$ bits, where $\lceil x \rceil$ stands for the smallest integer not smaller than x. For example, 8 bits suffice to name 256 subroutines, independent of whether the address length of the emulating machine is 16 or 32 bits. Of course, there is no longer a direct correspondence between the address of the subroutine and the token, and a translation of the token is needed. A table lookup can be used to locate the native code sequence corresponding to the token (fig. 2.3). This table lookup introduces additional slowdown: the token must be loaded into a processor address register IR, and

2.1. Intermediate Language Representations

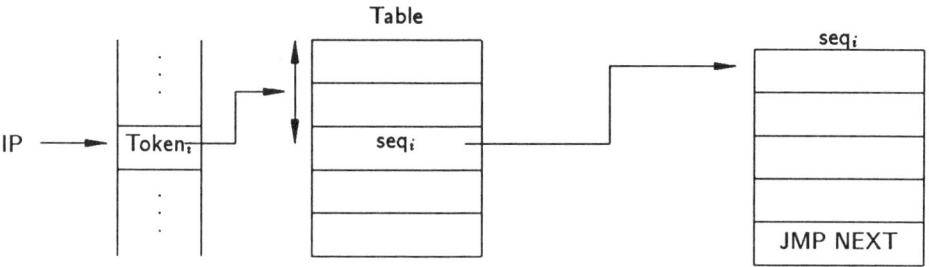

Figure 2.3
Tokenized encoding of intermediate instructions

converted into a dispatching table index. This implies an extension of the length of the token to the machine address length, and a proper scaling so as to index a list of machine addresses:

```
Next:      <update IP>
Mapping:   IR <- mem[IP]        ;load token indexed by IP
           <convert IR into index in Table>
           JMP Table[IR]        ;dispatch to native code sequence
                                 through memory indirect jump


Table:     ...                  ;indexed by scaled token
           Native_Sequence
           ...

Native_Sequence:
           <native instructions>
           JMP Next
```

2.1.3 The intermediate representation of program structures

Most well-written HLL programs exhibit a hierarchical structure. The use of structured control statements and subroutines allows the programmer to group primitive HLL language statements into *blocks*. A block has problem-oriented semantics that are not offered by individual statements. Blocks can be lexically nested in other blocks. A subroutine block can be dynamically invoked from inside several other blocks, just by mentioning its name. Thus, besides defining and naming semantic operations that surpass the basic language semantics, the subroutine mechanism also allows a compact representation of the HLL program. In fact, the compactness argument used in favor of intermediate instructions can also be used to advocate the use of subroutines.

It is desirable that the subroutine structure of the HLL program be retained at the intermediate level. Thus we face the question of how to do so in a way that takes our primary requirements, compactness of the representation and the execution speed, into account. Also other criteria are relevant when discussing the intermediate representation of programs:

- **the openness of the representation.** There is a great apparent similarity between grouping native machine instructions into intermediate instructions, and grouping intermediate instructions into (intermediate) subroutines. It is tempting to use *the same* mechanism to bind an instruction sequence to the name object that is used to access it. More precisely, the mapping technique used to locate the native code sequence, given the corresponding intermediate instruction, can be the same as the mapping technique used to locate the body of a subroutine, given the subroutine call. Besides offering a speed for the invocation of subroutines comparable to that of instruction mapping process, the uniformity of the representation leads to an *open* interpretive system. In the current context, openness means that there is no strict separation between interpreter-defined intermediate instructions and user-defined subroutines. Consequently, it is rather easy to add intermediate instructions to an existing interpreter, or to change existing intermediate instructions by overloading them. Without a uniform mapping mechanism, the extension of an interpreter with user-defined native code sequences is more involved.

- **the syntactical structure of the representation.**

  The intermediate program syntax defines the type of the interpretive engine that must execute it. For example, most intermediate languages allow the use of a *finite state machine* to execute the mapping actions. In such systems, the current intermediate instruction can be decoded using only a fixed amount of information about the instructions executed so far: the program representation is *regular*. However, one can also think of intermediate program representations which are even more compact, but which require a potentially unbounded amount of context information to decode the current instruction [Samm82]. *Context-free* program representations require a stack machine to perform the mapping actions.

  Similar observations can be made concerning the support of expression evaluation and subroutine calls. Most interpretive engines use explicit stacks to evaluate expressions (evaluation stack), to store local procedure variables

2.1. Intermediate Language Representations

(the environment stack), and to store procedure return information (control stack). The intermediate languages for such machines contain explicit instructions that control these stacks. They feature reverse polish stack machine code, stack marking and frame addressing instructions, and explicit CALL and RETURN instructions. On the other hand, some intermediate representations (e.g. of BASIC) do not use the reverse polish notation. Expressions are represented in infix notation, as they are at the source level. To evaluate these expressions, a hidden stack to store temporary results is required; again, the interpretive engine is no longer a finite state machine.

The intermediate program syntax can also be important for the ease with which the HLL program source can be reconstructed from its intermediate representation. This is an important asset for interactive programming environments. The reconstruction is feasible when the symbol table of user-defined symbols is at hand, and when the syntactical transformations performed by the outer interpreter (intermediate code compiler) can be inverted.

One way to classify intermediate program representations is based on their sequentiality or contiguity. This categorization is relevant for the way in which the intermediate program counter must be updated. We distinguish between three major classes: sequential allocation, threaded representations, and linked representations.

Sequential allocation. As with native code, intermediate instructions are expected to follow each other in a sequential fashion (fig. 2.4). The intermediate program counter is incremented by default; any deviation from the purely sequential thread of control must be effected by means of explicit control instructions (JMP, CALL, RETURN, etc). The target address operands of these instructions are often encoded in a way to provide compactness and independence of the position of the code in memory. When combined with tokenized instruction representation, the traditional intermediate language representations result: P-code, M-code, etc. This kind of representation is not open, because the token encoding is totally separate and independent of the encoding of intermediate instruction target addresses.

Threaded representations. In threaded representations, intermediate instructions are also stored in a predominantly sequential fashion. However, intermediate target addresses now use *the same* representation as the intermediate instruction proper. In this way a homogeneous pointer structure results (fig. 2.5). The entire program (including the interpreter semantic routines) consists of two kinds of sequences:

- sequences consisting only of (intermediate) subroutine-free machine code. These are called *primitives*.

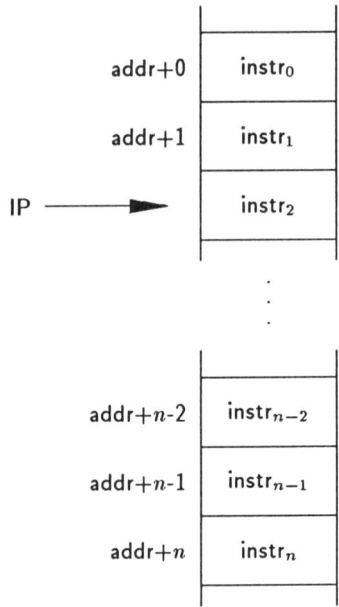

Figure 2.4
Sequential intermediate program representations

- sequences consisting only of references to other sequences. These are called *definitions* or *secondaries*. They are defined in terms of other definitions and/or primitives.

The execution of this intermediate representation consists of following the thread of control indicated by the pointers, and executing the machine code eventually found at the lowest level of the structure. The pointers used to denote both primitives and definitions can be represented using any of the representation methods mentioned above: subroutine encoding, pointer based, or tokenized. We have already mentioned that, in the case of subroutine encoding, part of the interpreter is distributed in the program representation, namely the CALL mapping actions. This is also possible when other representations of the primitives are used. Indeed, since the mapping mechanism is uniform, it follows that the execution of an intermediate subroutine call is identical to locating a primitive using its pointer representation. One can centralize the mapping code as a true primitive, or one can distribute copies of this code at the points where transfers of control take place. The distri-

2.1. Intermediate Language Representations

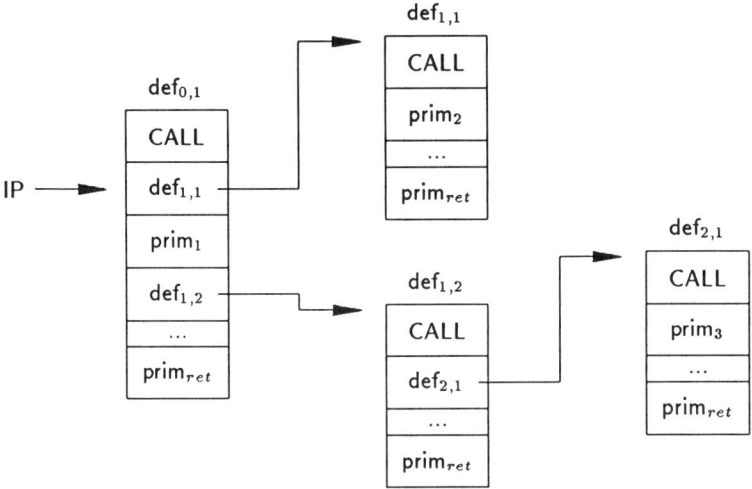

Figure 2.5
Threaded intermediate program representations

bution of the mapping code obviously leads to a larger program representation, but one level of indirection is removed from the access of all primitives. The version with central mapping is called *indirect*, the distributed mapping version is called *direct*. In combination with the method used for pointer encoding, one can distinguish between 5 types of threaded code. We shall present concrete representations of the different varieties of threaded code in the next section.

Threaded code is mostly used for the intermediate representation of FORTH programs, although this use is not exclusive: for example, on the DEC PDP-11, threaded code has been used to represent FORTRAN-IV programs. More recent examples include languages like PASCAL, PROLOG, and BASIC (see Table 2.1).

Linked representations. In linked representations, no sequential storage is used: all program elements are linked by means of pointers (fig. 2.6). The intermediate program counter is updated by traversing the linked program structure. Note that the presence of the links not only increases the static program size, but also the dynamic size. The links must effectively be read from memory to update the program counter. Linked representations are very interesting to represent objects of variable size, and to support interactive program development without having to copy big chunks of memory. Furthermore, a uniform representation of intermediate program code, and the data it operates on is, among others, very interesting to represent

Figure 2.6
Linked intermediate program representations

functional programs: functions (or the intermediate code to evaluate them) can be represented and treated as if they were data. Whereas most intermediate program representations imply an evaluation by means of imperative, von Neumann type interpretive engines, the linked program representation is particularly suited to support the evaluation of functional programs by means of the *graph rewriting* mechanism. Here, the evaluation of a functional expression, represented by a linked data structure, is performed by repeatedly replacing ('rewriting') parts of the linked structure by simpler but equivalent parts, until no further replacements are possible.

2.1.4 On the space/time trade-off of intermediate representations

The intermediate program representations analyzed so far offer different solutions of the space/time trade-off: the more compact a representation is, the more difficult it is to execute, and hence the slower the execution will be. This trade-off may be put in a broader perspective. One might raise the question as to which kind of representation provides an optimal solution. This question has been studied thoroughly at Stanford's Computer Systems Laboratory from the mid-seventies thru the mid-eighties.

About 'Ideal' intermediate representations. The result of the work of the Stanford team is known as the 'Directly Executable Language' or DEL approach [Flyn80,Hoev74,Flyn83a]. To preclude any misunderstandings, the approach does not involve systems where no compilation is required to execute a program (the so-called Maryland approach). Therefore, instead of 'DEL' the term 'Direct Correspondence Architecture' (DCA) is also used [Wake87].

The goals of the DCA approach are the minimization of the static program size, the dynamic instruction count, and the required data memory bandwidth. The DELtran experiment [Flyn83a] seeks an 'optimal' instruction set architecture to represent Fortran programs. In [Hoev74], Hoevel has shown analytically that, under certain architectural and technological conditions, the interpretive execution of an intermediate representation minimizes a space-time measure. The extreme cases, a direct execution of the source representation, and the execution of native code, are in general not optimal in Hoevel's sense. The *source representation* is

2.1. Intermediate Language Representations

not ideal because, for example, symbolic names can be replaced by a more space efficient binary encoding. Also, assigning a value to a symbolic name requires more operations compared to a case where a memory cell (address) is allocated for that variable. Similarly, *the native code representation* often does not minimize space-time measures either. For example, the execution of some important HLL operations require several machine instructions. This sequence could be replaced by a more appropriate instruction, which reduces the representation size.

Hoevel considered microprogrammed systems with a hierarchical storage consisting of a large, slow-access memory (main store) and a small, fast-access memory (writable control store). The control store is assumed to be too small to contain the entire program. Hoevel analytically showed that, for a range of technological parameters such as memory speed, bus width, and instruction compactness, the interpretation of a compactly encoded program representation minimizes a space-time criterion when the small interpreter program is held in control store and the compact program representation resides in main store. The alternative forms of execution do not use an intermediate representation. They require that the program be stored in directly executable machine code (in main store, because of its size). The first alternative is the direct execution from main store, the second uses the control store as a cache for the main store. The 'ideal' representation clearly lies somewhere between the HLL source and the machine language.

The DCA-approach has been discussed and elaborated further in [Flyn84,Flyn85, Wake87]. It is based on two concepts: (1) transformationally complete instruction format sets, and (2) the contour model. A *transformationally complete format set* is a set of instruction formats with which all HLL program constructs can be represented in a nonredundant way [Flyn85]. An example of a redundancy in instructions is the following. A three address instruction representing X:= X + Y contains two identical operand specifications and could be replaced by a two operand instruction of the form X Y +, with a format field indicating the correct semantics. By designing a limited set of similar formats, the representation size can be reduced and the information per instruction bit can be increased. Furthermore, the corresponding code generator is less complex. Flynn argues that about 30 formats are required.

Johnson's *contour model* [John71] is based on the limited scope of identifiers (variables, procedures) in HLL programs. This means that, at each point during the execution, the number of reachable operands is limited and can be represented by a binary encoding which is much more space efficient than a full address of a variable, for example a lexical address. At the entry of each block in a block structured language program a descriptor table (contour) is constructed. In each contour an entry is included which provides all information necessary to access that variable. This mechanism allows a more space efficient encoding of the operands.

The DIL approach. Another approach to construct 'ideal' intermediate representations with similar goals (reduction of representation size and execution time) in mind is described in [Bose83,Bose84]. Starting from a formally specified HLL (syntax and semantics) a systematic process is described constructing a Directly Interpretable Language (DIL) which increases the space-time efficiency. The process is iterative, and consists of applying incremental transformations to the definition of the HLL, so as to obtain a definition of an intermediate representation (a DIL). The language definitions consist of a BNF syntax definition and a semi-formal definition of the semantics.

The definition of the newly derived DIL is evaluated using some metrics, and are based on HLL statistics. One starts with a set of possible ('canonic') transformation steps. The optimization process iteratively determines the best combination of transformation steps that optimizes the values returned by the metrics.

In this process, two elements are important: the set of transformations and the set of space/time metrics. Each transformation has a positive or negative effect on one or more metrics. By choosing different subsets of transformations, different DILs can be constructed. Examples of transformations are [Bose83,Bose84]:

- **space-efficient encodings.** The encoding of terminal grammar symbols using a variable length code, such as the frequency based (Huffman-like) or syntax based codes;

- **the factorization of actions/attributes.** Sequences of instructions using the same opcode are replaced by the opcode followed by the sequence of the operands. The opcode now acts as a list head. For example, the sequence PUSH A PUSH B PUSH C ADD ADD could be replaced by PUSH A B C ADD 2.

- **state attribute factorization.** Sequences of operations in equal mode (e.g. integer arithmetic, 32-bit real computation) are replaced by an instruction specifying the mode (integer, 32-bit real) followed by instructions with mode-independent opcode (addition, multiplication). This allows generic (polymorphic) operations The semantic routines are determined based on the mode most recently used, and the current opcode;

- **operator semantics that minimize stack height variation.** The standard postfix representation of an expression such as A - B / C in a stack based architecture is A B C / -. Its dynamic stack depth variation is larger than that of B / C -' A, where -' denotes *reverse subtraction*, i.e., subtraction with the arguments exchanged;

- **simplification of operators.** Commonly used sequences of operations are replaced by a single operation;

2.1. Intermediate Language Representations

Each DIL evaluation metric quantifies an aspect of space-time efficiency of the interpretive execution of the DIL representation of a program. Examples are [Bose83,Bose84]:

- **the static code size:** the number of code bits allocated by the DIL representation;
- **the dynamic code size:** the number of DIL bits transferred during the execution;
- **the dynamic data value:** the number of bits allocated on a run-time stack at a given instant;
- **the total number of memory instruction references.** This is a technology independent measure of the total execution time.

For further details we refer to [Bose83] and [Bose84].

On the relevance of the space-time trade-off. Hoevel has developed his analysis [Hoev74] in the context of the computer technology of the early seventies. Machines were microprogrammable, with fast but very expensive semiconductor memory in control store, and slower but less expensive core memory technology to be used as main memory. Relatively speaking, memories were more expensive than they are today, and any development which would reduce both the static and the dynamic size of a program was highly welcome. With current semiconductor memory, things are different. Big memories have become very cheap, and processors have 32-bit addressing ranges.

Trying to keep static program sizes low is no longer considered an important contribution. Similarly, with the current breed of CISC microprocessors, the speed disparity between main and local memories is not very high, and can be bridged with current cache technology. On this type of technology, Hoevel's analysis identifies the use of data and instruction caches as the fastest and cheapest way to execute HLL programs. Interpretation is always slower than native code execution, and one should have a good reason, other than raw execution speed, to use it.

Is this situation permanent? In order to answer this question, let us briefly look at the technological evolution in the years to come. De Man [DeMa89] predicts that by 1995, in CMOS technology the speed disparity between on-chip memory and bulk off-chip memory will again increase to a factor of well over 10. The on-chip memory size is restricted by the available chip area. Typical CMOS die sizes are expected to be 2 cm^2, and both processor logic and cache size compete for this area. Taking into account the differences in achievable densities for both parts, the future chip may be divided between the parts according to the following amounts: $x \times 1200K$ transistors for processor and coprocessor logic, and $(1-x) \times 110$

Kbytes of on-chip static memory, with x the partitioning factor. A reasonable size estimate for the on-chip memory is 4 to 32 Kbytes, with an access time under 4 ns. Bulk memory will consist of 8 Mbit dynamic RAMs with access times between 40 and 80 ns. The speed disparities between on-chip and off-chip memories, and the limitations imposed on the size of the on-chip memory take on more extreme forms in Gallium Arsenide technology [Fura 88].

For a re-assessment of Hoevel's analysis in the new context, we assume that the total execution time is dominated by the time required to fetch the machine instructions. This assumption is quite acceptable in the context of contemporary RISC architectures with strongly pipelined von Neumann-type and Harvard-type microprocessors. We compute the fetch time for each of the methods involved during the execution of a program with a dynamic instruction size of n words. A word has the width of the instruction bus; we assume that all the busses have equal width (e.g., 32 bits). All times are expressed as multiples of the processor cycle time. With

- M the external memory cycle time;
- C the compaction achieved by the intermediate representation;
- S the relative slowdown caused by interpretation;
- F_n the (instruction) cache miss rate for the direct execution of native code;
- F_i the (data) cache miss rate for intermediate instructions fetched during interpretation;
- n the dynamic program size;

we obtain the following results. In the case of direct execution from external memory, the total fetch time is simply given by the product of the memory cycle time and the dynamic program size,

$$N_D = nM.$$

In the case of direct execution using the on-chip instruction cache, the program is executed mainly from the cache. We assume that the (on-chip) cache is accessed within one processor cycle. Only in the case of a cache miss, the extra penalty of a main memory access must be paid. We find

$$N_C = n(1 - F_n) + nF_n M.$$

Finally, in the case of interpretive execution from on-chip memory, we obtain

$$N_I = nS + \frac{n}{C}(1 - F_i + F_i M).$$

From these equations we can draw the following conclusions:

- Caching is faster than direct execution as soon as $M > 1$ (i.e., always).

2.1. Intermediate Language Representations

- Interpretation is faster than direct execution as soon as

$$M > \frac{CS + 1 - F_i}{C - F_i},$$

which, for very small F_i, reduces to

$$M > S + 1/C.$$

That is, the interpretive slowdown must be smaller than the slowdown caused by accessing external memory.

- Interpretation is faster than caching if

$$1 - F_n + F_n M > S + \frac{1 - F_i + F_i M}{C},$$

or

$$M > \frac{1 - F_i + CS - C(1 - F_n)}{CF_n - F_i},$$

provided that $F_i < F_n C$, i.e., that the intermediate instruction bandwidth from external memory is lower than the comparable native instruction bandwidth.

So as to obtain realistic figures from these equations we consider typical values of the parameters valid for current technology. From [Smit82,Smit85] we obtain a typical relation between the cache size k and the miss rate F:

$$F = 0.2k^{-0.5},$$

were k is expressed in kilobytes. With an on-chip memory of 4 Kbytes, which is also sufficiently large to hold an interpreter, the miss ratio F_n equals 10%. When using interpretation, a small fraction of the on-chip memory can also be used as a (data) cache for intermediate instructions. Due to the compaction factor, low miss ratios can be obtained even with very small caches. Then, with some reasonable values like $M = 10$, $C = 5$, $S = 4$, and $F_i = F_n = 0.1$, we obtain

$$N_I = 2.30 N_C.$$

That is, the initial interpretive slowdown $S = 4$, which would have been recorded in a cache-less system, has been reduced to 2.3. At the same time the external memory (instruction) traffic of the interpretive implementation is only 5% of that of the direct execution case. In order to achieve equal performance with the above parameters, the external memory speed disparity M must equal 41. While this value will probably not be achieved by CMOS, the current values for GaAs point in this direction [Fura 88].

The low residual instruction bandwidth of interpretive implementation will not saturate the external memory bus, since it was assumed that even the residual rate in the direct execution case does not. It may then be interesting to attach *more than one* interpretive processor to the same memory. One so obtains a shared memory type multiprocessor which executes its code *directly* from the shared memory. Such a setup may be interesting for two reasons:

1. A delicate problem with many small-scale multiprocessors is that of an efficient resource utilization. To fully utilize the available processing power, a form of *dynamic load sharing* is needed, in which tasks can migrate from one processing element to another. Full dynamic load sharing can be done with modest requirements on fast memory if the code is stored centrally. Otherwise, the total amount of fast memory in the system increases as the *square* of the number of processors, since the local memory of each processor is assumed to grow with the total system size [Kirr84];

2. In a von Neumann machine, no program can be executed faster than it can be fetched from memory. With an interpretive execution, the effective information rate at bus saturation is higher than in the native code case, since intermediate instructions contain much more information than the low-level native code instructions. Consequently, the multi-interpreter solution will provide a higher total execution speed from the external memory than any native code solution.

The authors have studied the use of interpretive techniques in this context. Multi-interpreter realizations of CHILL [VanC84] and MODULA-2 [VanC86,VanC88] were made, clearly indicating the feasibility of the approach.

2.2 Examples of Intermediate Languages

In this section we shall present three concrete examples of intermediate languages and their associated instruction set architectures, one for each major class identified in the previous section. Since they have all been published elsewhere, we shall not attempt to give complete descriptions. Rather, we shall limit ourselves to a presentation of the essential features of each of the examples, and provide the references to the publications that contain complete descriptions.

2.2.1 MODULA-2 and M-code

The high level programming language MODULA-2 was designed by Wirth as a successor of PASCAL [Wirt82]. Intended to serve as a vehicle to teach structured programming concepts, PASCAL was deliberately kept simple. As a result, it lacks essential properties needed to allow sound software engineering of large applications, for example separate compilation. Nearly every practical implementation of PASCAL contains ad hoc extensions to remedy this situation. However, ad hoc extensions severely limit the portability of programs, and even may obscure or obviate the original intentions of the language. In an attempt to eliminate much of these problems, MODULA-2 was developed, offering a module concept cleanly separating interface definitions from their implementations. The module concept supports separate compilation, and provides version control of previously compiled modules to enforce consistency. The module concept is also used to define the interface with the operating system (I/O), greatly enhancing code portability, even to other operating systems. This module concept was later inherited by languages like ADA.

MODULA-2 provides an embryonic form of concurrency, allowing the development of concurrent programs. The basic built-in concurrency primitives are the **PROCESS** type and the **NEWPROCESS** procedure, coroutining support by means of the **TRANSFER** operation, and mutual exclusion by means of *priority modules.*

Besides the high level language proper, Wirth has also defined M-code, an intermediate language to represent MODULA-2 programs. This intermediate language was used to implement MODULA-2 on the personal computer Lilith, a bitsliced microprogrammable architecture [Wirt81]. The M-code interpreter on the Lilith was microcoded. Since then, MODULA-2 has become available on a large variety of machines and operating systems, mostly with a *compiled* implementation, although implementations based on software interpretation of M-code are also commercially available [Modu84].

M-code is a typical and well-documented example of tokenized, sequentially stored intermediate code. Tokens are eight bits wide, allowing the use of 256 intermediate instructions. Escape instructions have been provided, so that specific infrequently used extensions to the intermediate language are possible. The instruction set architecture of the M-machine, and the precise semantics of the intermediate instructions are defined by means of a MODULA-2 program.

In the M-machine, the modularity of the MODULA-2 program remains visible (fig. 2.7). In fact, modules can be linked dynamically when loaded, and inter-module references always contain the module number. The static representation of a module consists of a code frame, containing the M-code representation of the procedures defined in the module; and of a data frame, containing the statically allocated data of the module. These are the variables defined in the module which are not local to a procedure. The data frame of a module contains a pointer to its code frame. The code frame itself begins with a dispatching table of code-frame relative pointers to procedure entries of the module. Thus, procedures of the current module can be accessed solely by their numbers. System-wide, the addresses of all

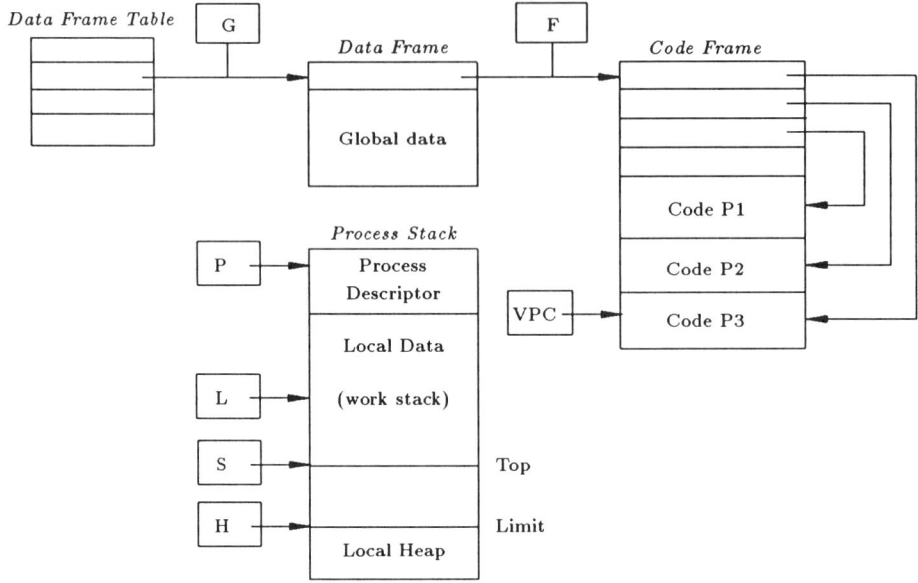

Figure 2.7
The architecture of the M-machine

module data frames are stored in the data frame table (DFT). The DFT resides at a fixed location in memory. Inter-module data references use the module number to obtain the location of the data frame, and then use a data frame-relative offset to access the data. Inter-module procedure calls also use the module number to locate the data frame. Then the code frame pointer and the procedure number are used to locate the procedure entry point in the code frame.

In the M-code representation of a concurrent MODULA-2 program, each process is represented by a separate stack frame, used to store local procedure variables and subroutine return information. At the bottom of each process stack frame, a fixed amount of space is reserved to store the Process descriptor and the processor state when a coroutine TRANSFER is made to another process. The stack frames can be reached through variables of type POINTER TO PROCESS. The creation and allocation of these variables is the responsibility of the programmer.

The M-machine is a finite state machine; it contains the following registers:

- **The G register.** This register points to the data frame of the current module;

- **The F register.** This register points to the code frame of the current module;

2.2. Examples of Intermediate Languages

- **The P register.** This register points to the stack frame of the current process;
- **The L register.** This register points to the current stack mark. Local variables and procedure parameters are addressed relative to this pointer;
- **The S register.** This register points to the current top of the stack;
- **The H register.** This register points to the base of the heap. The heap is a contiguous memory area allocated at the end of the stack frame;
- **The M register.** This register holds the current interrupt mask; it is used to control the mutual exclusion in priority modules;
- **The VPC register.** This is the virtual program counter;
- **The expression stack.** The expression stack is a fixed length stack of sixteen word locations. M-code uses a reverse polish syntax to evaluate expressions, and the expression stack is used for that purpose. Procedure parameters and result values are also passed on the expression stack.

The M-machine has *word addressability*: all address expressions and pointer values have word resolution. Individual bytes cannot be pointed at, and special instructions exist to access bytes in a packed byte array. The word length is implementation dependent; both 16 and 32-bit implementations exist. Word addressability improves the portability of the environment to systems with different word lengths. However, the interpreter is responsible for the scaling of pointer values to the byte-address resolution present in nearly all microprocessor systems.

Consider the implementation module of the following short MODULA-2 program fragment.

```
MODULE Fact;

FROM Terminal IMPORT WriteString, WriteInt, WriteLn;

VAR I : INTEGER;

PROCEDURE Factorial(X : INTEGER) : INTEGER;
BEGIN IF X <= 1
        THEN RETURN(1)
        ELSE RETURN(Factorial(X-1)*X)
      END
END Factorial;

BEGIN FOR I:=1 TO 5 DO
```

```
            WriteString("The factorial of ");
            WriteInt(I,4);
            WriteString(" is ");
            WriteInt(Factorial(I),4);
            WriteLn
        END;
END Fact.
```

The intermediate M-code representation of this MODULA-2 program is shown below, in a symbolic form. The example assumes a 16-bit word length, and little-endian representation of literal values[2].

```
LEM HexDecode   version 4.9.86
input file: fact.OBJ

codekey     = 0003
module name:  Fact
datasize    = 0010
key           B255 02D6 83A4          ; this is the module key
                                      ; used for version control
import  InOut               is # 001 (1)  key is AE81 0299 332C
        Fact                is # 002 (2)  key is B255 02D6 83A4

data, relative to G
0001:   0000
0002:   0000

procedure Factorial # 001 (1) at 0004 bytes relative to F
code at F + 0002 words
word byte opcode     mnemonics
0002 0004 0EB        ENTR   001        ; reserve space for parameter
0003 0006 034        SLW4              ; store parameter
0003 0007 024        LLW4              ; value of X
0004 0008 001        LI1               ; the constant 1
0004 0009 0CB        LEQ               ; compare
0005 000A 01A        JPFC   [005] -> 0010
                                       ; take jump if X > 1
```

---

[2]although pointer values are independent of the word length, literal values are not. The compiler generates unsigned and signed integer values and double-word floating point literals in the M-code instruction stream. The compiler-generated format of the representations of these quantities may require runtime transformations to the native format of the host. Only a modification of the compiler may eliminate this overhead.

2.2. Examples of Intermediate Languages

```
0006 000C 001       LI1                    ; else return value 1
0006 000D 0EC       RTN                    ; return with result on stack
0007 000E 01B       JPF    [008] -> 0017
0008 0010 024       LLW4                   ; value of X
0008 0011 001       LI1                    ; constant 1
0009 0012 0D9       SUB                    ; compute X-1
0009 0013 0F1       CL1                    ; call self recursively
000A 0014 024       LLW4                   ; value of X
000A 0015 0DA       MUL                    ; compute result
000B 0016 0EC       RTN                    ; return with result on stack
000B 0017 009       LI9                    ; error code traps
000C 0018 0C4       TRAP
000C 0019 0DE       NOP
```

procedure Fact # 000 (0) at 001A bytes relative to F
                                                            ; main block is procedure #0
data, relative to G   ; string constants are stored
0004: STRING "The factorial of ",0 ; in data frame
data, relative to G
000D: STRING " is ",0

```
code at F + 000D words
word byte opcode    mnemonics
000D 001A 0EB       ENTR   000             ; no space for local variables
000E 001C 015       LGA    001             ; test module initialization
000F 001E 094       TS
000F 001F 01A       JPFC   [002] -> 0022
0010 0021 0EC       RTN
0011 0022 015       LGA    004
0012 0024 052       SGW2
0012 0025 0ED       CX     001 000         ; initialize external module
0014 0028 015       LGA    003             ; the address of I
0015 002A 001       LI1                    ; the bounds of the FOR loop
0015 002B 005       LI5
0016 002C 0C0       FOR1   000 [0021] -> 004F
0018 0030 042       LGW2                   ; address of "The ..."
0018 0031 010       LIB    010             ; string length
0019 0033 0ED       CX     001 008         ; ext. procedure WriteString
001B 0036 043       LGW3                   ; the value of I
001B 0037 004       LI4                    ; number of digits
001C 0038 0ED       CX     001 00D         ; ext. procedure WriteInt
```

```
001D 003B 042      LGW2
001E 003C 016      LSA    009             ; address of " is "
001F 003E 003      LI3                    ; string length
001F 003F 0ED      CX     001 008         ; ext. procedure WriteString
0021 0042 043      LGW3                   ; value of I
0021 0043 0F1      CL1                    ; local procedure #1
0022 0044 004      LI4                    ; number of digits
0022 0045 0ED      CX     001 00D         ; ext. procedure WriteInt
0024 0048 0ED      CX     001 006         ; ext. procedure WriteLn
0025 004B 0C1      FOR2   001 [FFE3] -> 0030
                                          ; test loop termination
0027 004F 0EC      RTN
fixups at 0049 0046 0040 0039 0034 0026
                                          ; places where module
                                          ; numbers should be
                                          ; corrected by linker
end decode
```

We now present an implementation of an M-code interpreter on the Intel i8086. The implementation uses a 16-bit word length and a little-endian number representation. Since the i8086 has only a limited number of registers, and a far from orthogonal instruction set, considerable attention must be paid to how the M-machine registers and expression stack are mapped onto the resources of the i8086. This situation is further aggravated by the fact that an efficient implementation of the instruction fetch/decode actions requires the allocation of some processor registers, which are then unavailable for the representation of M-machine registers. In our example we have used the following mapping:

- the code frame is mapped onto the processor data segment (the F pointer is mapped onto the DS segment register). The data frame is mapped onto the processor extra segment (the G pointer is mapped onto the ES segment register). The interpreter itself obviously needs the code segment (CS segment register).

- the expression stack is mapped onto the native processor stack (SS segment register);

- the virtual program counter is mapped onto the SI index register. The 32-bit pair DS:SI then provides the full addressing range of the i8086. The LODSB instruction provides a fast autoincrement loading of the next M-code byte into the AL register.

2.2. Examples of Intermediate Languages

- the L register is mapped onto the BP register, since the latter can be used as the default index register into the processor stack segment.

- the other M-machine registers are mapped onto memory variables at fixed locations in the processor stack segment. This allows us to keep the frequently used M-machine resources and the interpreter code in a limited amount of zero-wait state memory (the processor stack and code segments), while the program representation and its data reside in larger, but slower dynamic memory. The 8086 AX, BX, CX, DX and DI registers are used to hold temporary values during the execution of the interpreter.

The resulting code then looks as follows:

```
; ************** M-code interpreter mapping actions ***********

FETCH_NEXT: LODS   DS:PROG_BYTE    ; Fetch next token
            CBW                    ; Convert to table index
            MOV    DI,AX           ; DI and AX are used as
            SHL    DI,1            ; interface registers
            JMP    CS:WORD PTR Table[DI]
                                   ; dispatch to semantic routine

; ************* Token decoding table *************************

Table:      DW     LIx   ; Token = 0
            DW     LIx   ; Token = 1
            ...
            DW     JPBC  ; Token = 28
            ...
            DW     LLWx  ; Token = 36
            DW     LLWx  ; Token = 37
            ...
            DW     LGWx  ; Token = 66
            DW     LGWx  ; Token = 67
            ...

; ************* Some semantic routines ***********************

; OH .. OFH: (*LI0 - LI15 load immediate*)  push(IR MOD 16) |
```

```
LIx:            PUSH            AX              ; note use of AX
                                                ; as interface reg.
                JMP             FETCH_NEXT

; 1CH: (*JPBC   jump backward conditional*)
;       IF pop() = 0 THEN VPC := VPC - next() ELSE INC(VPC) END  |

JPBC:           POP             DX
                TEST            DX,DX
                JNZ             NoJmp0          ; ELSE
                MOV             AL,DS:[SI]      ; THEN
                SUB             SI,AX           ; note here AH=0
                JMP             FETCH_NEXT
NoJmp0:         INC             SI
                JMP             FETCH_NEXT

; 24H .. 2FH: (*LLW4-LLW15       load local word*)
;       push(stk[L + (IR MOD 16)])  |

LLWx:           AND             DI,01FH         ;DI is interface reg
                MOV             DX,ES:[BP][DI]
                PUSH            DX
                JMP             FETCH_NEXT

; 42H .. 4F: (*LGW2 - LGW15   load global word*)
;       push(stk[G + IR MOD 16 ])  |

LGWx:           AND             AL,0FH
                ADD             AX,SS:G
                MOV             DI,AX
                SHL             DI,1
                MOV             DX,ES:[DI]
                PUSH            DX
                JMP             FETCH_NEXT
```

2.2.2 FORTH and threaded code

The first publications about FORTH date from the early 1970s [Moor74]. FORTH is a rather unusual, yet powerful and simple language [Moor80]. It was intended to fill in the need for high-performance and powerful software development tools in

2.2. Examples of Intermediate Languages

real world application environments. Forth claims to improve software productivity by providing:

- a flexible bottom-up implementation method;
- extensive use of subroutines;
- step-by-step testing possibilities;
- powerful debugging capabilities;
- advanced interactivity.

Originally, FORTH was used mainly in process control environments (astronomy, medical environments) [Ball84]. Later on, it became a popular and widespread programming environment in small-size systems. Currently, it is also a base for the implementation of other languages and applications [Gree86]. Some authors discuss FORTH's suitability for artificial intelligence applications [Carr86] and [Arno86].

A complete FORTH environment allows to program at the FORTH-level, as well as at the assembly-level and at the meta-level. Such a system is based on a set of built-in assembly routines, *primitives*, which are specified in FORTH standards such as FORTH79 and FORTH83. Using these primitives *definitions* are built. Both primitives and definitions (also called *words*) can be used to build other definitions.

As to its syntax, FORTH is unconventional. The FORTH engine is a stack machine which is driven by programs in postfix notation. This syntax allows an easy and invertible translation from FORTH-level definitions to an intermediate, also stack-based, machine. Parameter passing between words occurs through the *data stack*. Named variables can be created and statically allocated by means of explicit instructions. Mentioning the name of such a variable in a program is equivalent to the call of an argumentless function that returns the value of the variable on the data stack. Let us look at a simple FORTH example. Assume that the following primitives are present in the environment:

- `DUP`, duplicating the top of stack;
- `SWAP`, swapping the two top of stack elements;
- `LIT`, pushing a literal on the stack;
- `*`, multiplying two top of stack elements;
- `+`, adds two top of stack elements.

Then the definition

```
: SQUARE DUP * ;
```

creates a function which squares the top of stack element. The symbol ':' denotes the start of a definition, ';' terminates the definition. The sequence DUP * forms the body. Similarly, the definitions

```
: 5* 5 * ;
: FUNC SQUARE SWAP SQUARE 5* + ;
```

define a word 5* multiplying the top of stack element by 5, and a word FUNC implementing a function $f(x,y) = x^2 + 5y^2$ of the top elements of the stack, respectively. In order to invoke and test the definition 5* it suffices to interactively enter the following string:

```
7 5* .
```

which pushes 7 on the stack, executes the routine 5* and views and pops the resulting top of stack element, the value 35.

The FORTH environment can be called an open system for several reasons:

- a program is built by extending the set of available words (primitives and/or definitions) until, eventually, a word is constructed that represents the entire program.

- application dependent primitives can be added, e.g.,. multiprocessing primitives [Wijn89].

- a FORTH system can be tailored towards one's needs: not only can lacking words be added; unnecessary words can also be discarded (FORGET). The meta-level facilities allow the modification of standard FORTH conventions.

- the optimization process can occur gradually: frequently used but slowly-executing may be replaced by hand-coded primitives. In some implementations, user-created definitions can even be assembled into new primitives by built-in utilities.

- the extending and tailoring capabilities are significantly enhanced by *defining words* and *compiling words* [Moor80]. Their meaning and use is beyond the scope of this book.

A FORTH implementation in Indirect Threaded Code. From the above discussion it is clear that threaded code is well suited to represent FORTH programs at an intermediate level. The threaded code interpretive engine contains the following data structures (fig. 2.8):

- the *data stack*, used in precisely the same way as FORTH does. The data stack pointer DSP points to the top element;

2.2. Examples of Intermediate Languages

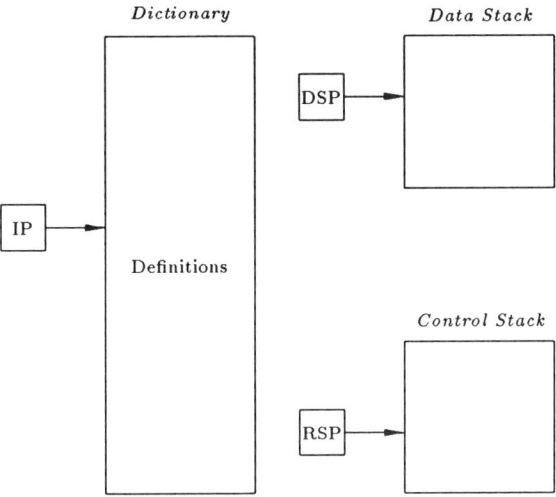

Figure 2.8
The architecture of a threaded code machine

- the *control stack*, used to store return information during the traversal of the threaded program structure. The return stack pointer RSP points to the top element;

- the *dictionary*, which holds all definitions. The instruction pointer IP points to the current word;

- the *primitives area*, which holds the native code primitives. This area, in fact, contains the semantic part of the interpreter.

We shall now illustrate the implementation of an indirect version of pointer-based threaded code called *Indirect Threaded Code* (ITC). Each pointer within the representation of the body points indirectly to executable machine code. The interpreter mapping actions can be executed by a few very simple routines. Executing a FORTH definition is nothing else than traversing the program tree, where the primitives are leaves and the definitions are intermediate nodes. The NEXT routine chains sequential words within a definition. The CALL primitive, representing the start ':' of a definition, saves the current value of IP on the control stack, descends one level in the program tree and prepares the execution of this definition. The RETURN primitive, representing the end ';' of a definition, ascends one level and resumes the execution of the calling definition from the control stack.

The following use of processor resources can be made to implement indirect threaded code on the Intel 8086:

- both the data and control stacks are mapped onto the processor stack segment (segment register SS). The data stack pointer DSP is mapped onto the machine stack pointer SP; the control stack pointer is mapped onto the default stack indexing register BP.

- the dictionary is mapped onto the processor data segment (segment register DS). The instruction pointer IP is mapped onto the auto-incrementing index register SI. The sequential fetch of intermediate instructions can then be done using the LODSW instruction.

- the primitives and the native code for the interpreter mapping actions are stored in the processor code segment (segment register CS).

In systems with a visible memory hierarchy, it is wise to allocate both stacks and the native code areas (CS and SS in the example) in fast memory, while the dictionary containing the program definition may reside in large but slower memory. With these conventions, the basic interpreter mapping actions can be implemented as follows:

```
; ASSUME THE FOLLOWING REGISTER ALLOCATION :
;        VIRTUAL REGISTER      8086 REGISTER
;              IP              DS:SI   Virtual Instruction Pointer
;              WA              DS:BX   Word Address Register
;              DSP             SS:SP   Data Stack Pointer
;              RSP             SS:BP   Return Stack Pointer

INITIALIZATION:

; initialize stack registers
            MOV BP,0            ; Top of control stack
            MOV SP,OFFSET TOP_DATA_STACK
                                ; Top of data stack
; initialize program counter
            MOV SI,OFFSET PROGRAM_START
                                ; Start from FUNC
            JMP NEXT            ; start interpretation

; routines for parsing the ITC representation

CALLCode:   INC BX              ; WA <-- WA+1
```

2.2. Examples of Intermediate Languages

```
                    INC BX
                    DEC BP              ; PUSH IP on control stack
                    DEC BP
                    MOV [BP],SI
                    MOV SI,BX           ; IP <-- WA
NEXT:               LODSW               ; Fetch intermediate instruction
                                        ; and increment IP
                    MOV BX,AX           ; use as index
                    JMP WORD PTR DS:[BX] ; Jump to primitive indirectly

RETURNCode:         MOV SI,[BP]         ; POP IP from control stack
                    INC BP
                    INC BP
                    JMP NEXT
```

The primitives of the FORTH environment are the following:

```
; Duplicate      ( n -- n n )    , duplicates top of stack value
DUPCode:          POP AX
                  PUSH AX
                  PUSH AX
                  JMP NEXT

; Multiply       ( n1 n2 -- n1*n2 ), multiplies two top of stack values
MULCode:          POP AX
                  POP DX
                  IMUL DX
                  PUSH AX
                  JMP NEXT

; Swap           ( n1 n2 -- n2 n1 )  , swaps two top of stack values
SWAPCode:         POP AX
                  POP DX
                  PUSH AX
                  PUSH DX
                  JMP NEXT

; LIT            ( -- n )  ,  pushes literal on the stack
LITCode:          LODSW
                  PUSH AX
                  JMP NEXT
```

```
; add            ( n1 n2 -- n1+n2 )  , adds two top of stack values
ADDCode:         POP AX
                 POP DX
                 ADD DX,AX
                 PUSH DX
                 JMP NEXT
```

Finally, the program itself has the following symbolic representation. Note that, since we are talking about *indirect* threaded code, intermediate instructions such as DUP are indirect pointers to primitives. They all point to locations containing direct addresses, such as DUPcode. The only exception is the CALL operation: it points directly to its native code sequence (see also Section 2.1.2).

```
BEGIN_CODE:
; Direct pointers to primitives
DUP:             DW DUPCode
MUL:             DW MULCode
SWAP:            DW SWAPCode
LIT:             DW LITCode
ADD:             DW ADDCode
RETURN:          DW RETURNCode

; Indirect pointers used in definitions (except for CALL)
; Square         ( n -- n^2 ) , multiplies top of stack with itself
SQUARE:          DW CALLCode
                 DW DUP
                 DW MUL
                 DW RETURN

; Multiply by 5  ( n -- 5*n ) , multiplies top of stack by 5
FIVEMUL:         DW CALLCode
                 DW LIT
                 DW 5
                 DW MUL
                 DW RETURN

; Function       ( n1 n2 -- 5*n1^2+n2^2 )   , computes FUNC(x,y)
FUNC:            DW CALLCode
                 DW SQUARE
                 DW SWAP
                 DW SQUARE
```

2.2. Examples of Intermediate Languages

```
                    DW FIVEMUL
                    DW ADD
                    DW RETURN

PROGRAM_START:      DW FUNC
```

Other Threaded Code varieties. An alternative to ITC is *Direct Threaded Code* (DTC). Here, each intermediate instruction used in a definition points *directly* to executable code. As a consequence, the CALL primitive must be expanded at the beginning of each definition representation. This threaded code variety clearly increases the representation size when compared to ITC, but allows a faster chaining of the words during execution. An 8086 implementation of the mapping instructions of a direct threaded code version is as follows:

```
; ASSUME THE FOLLOWING REGISTER ALLOCATION :
;         VIRTUAL REGISTER        8086 REGISTER
;               IP                DS:SI   Virtual Instruction Pointer
;               DSP               SS:SP   Data Stack Pointer
;               RSP               SS:BP   Return Stack Pointer

INITIALIZATION:

; initialize stack registers
                MOV BP,0                ; Top of control stack
                MOV SP,OFFSET TOP_DATA_STACK
                                        ; Top of data stack
; initialize program counter
                MOV SI,OFFSET PROGRAM_START
                                        ; Start from FUNC
                JMP NEXT                ; start interpretation

; routines for parsing the DTC representation

NEXT:           LODSW                   ; Fetch intermediate instruction
                                        ; and increment IP
RUN:            JMP AX                  ; Jump to primitive directly

RETURNCode:     MOV SI,[BP]             ; POP IP from control stack
                INC BP
                INC BP
                JMP NEXT
```

The representation of the primitives is the same as in the ITC case, while the program representation now includes the code for the CALL operation:

```
; Macro implementing call prologue in definitions
CALL            MACRO
                DEC BP          ; PUSH IP
                DEC BP
                MOV [BP],SI
                MOV SI,OFFSET LAB_&&&& ; addr. of first instruction
                JMP NEXT
LAB_&&&&
                MEND

BEGIN_CODE:

; Direct pointers used in definitions
; Square         ( n -- n^2 ) , multiplies top of stack with itself
SQUARE:         CALL            ; this code is expanded in-line
                DW DUPCode
                DW MULCode
                DW RETURNCode

; Multiply by 5  ( n -- 5*n ) , multiplies top of stack by 5
FIVEMUL:        CALL
                DW LITCode
                DW 5
                DW MULCode
                DW RETURNCode

; Function       ( n1 n2 -- 5*n1^2+n2^2 )  , computes FUNC(x,y)
FUNC:           CALL
                DW SQUARE
                DW SWAPCode
                DW SQUARE
                DW FIVEMUL
                DW ADDCode
                DW RETURNCode

PROGRAM_START:  DW FUNC
```

2.2. Examples of Intermediate Languages

In systems where the logical address space is much larger than the number of defined or built-in words, its is more space efficient to tokenize the instruction representation. This leads to *Direct Token Threaded Code* (DTTC) and *Indirect Token Threaded Code* (ITTC) as tokenized versions of DTC and ITC, respectively. In this case, a translation table determines the relation between the token and the corresponding machine addresses. Tokenized varieties are more space efficient than the pointer-based varieties but are slower (table lookup). Note that a DTTC representation not using any lower-level definitions (only 1 **CALL** and 1 **RETURN**) is identical to sequential token representations such as M-code. Consequently, their primitive interpreter operations (fetch/decode) are equal. The following code fragment shows the 8086 implementation of indirect token threaded code mapping actions:

```
; ASSUME THE FOLLOWING REGISTER ALLOCATION :
;         VIRTUAL REGISTER        8086 REGISTER
;               IP                DS:SI   Virtual Instruction Pointer
;               WA                DS:BX   Word Address Register
;               DSP               SS:SP   Data Stack Pointer
;               RSP               SS:BP   Return Stack Pointer

INITIALIZATION:

; initialize stack registers
            MOV BP,0                ; Top of control stack
            MOV SP,OFFSET TOP_DATA_STACK
                                    ; Top of data stack
; initialize program counter
            MOV SI,OFFSET PROGRAM_START
                                    ; Start from FUNC
            JMP NEXT                ; start interpretation

; routines for parsing the ITC representation

CALLCode:   INC BX                  ; WA <-- WA+1
            DEC BP                  ; PUSH IP on control stack
            DEC BP
            MOV [BP],SI
            MOV SI,BX               ; IP <-- WA
NEXT:       LODSB                   ; Fetch indirect token
                                    ; and increment IP
            CBW                     ; convert to table index
```

```
                MOV DI,AX
                SHL DI,1

                MOV BX,Table[DI]    ; translated token
                                    ; use to fetch direct token
                MOV AL,BYTE PTR [BX]
                CBW                 ; convert to table index
                MOV DI,AX
                SHL DI,1
                JMP DS:Table[DI]    ; Jump to primitive

RETURNCode:     MOV SI,[BP]         ; POP IP from control stack
                INC BP
                INC BP
                JMP NEXT
```

The code now consists of indirect tokens, which refer to tokens leading to the actual code. As with pointer-based indirect threaded code, only the CALL token is direct.

```
BEGIN_CODE:

; Token translation table

Table:          DW CALLCode         ; CALLCtoken     = 0
                DW RETURN           ; RETURNToken    = 1
                DW DUP              ; DUPToken       = 2
                DW LIT              ; LITToken       = 3
                DW MUL              ; MULToken       = 4
                DW SWAP             ; SWAPToken      = 5
                DW ADD              ; ADDToken       = 6
                DW SQUARE           ; SQUAREToken    = 7
                DW FIVEMUL          ; FIVEMULToken   = 8
                DW FUNC             ; FUNCToken      = 9
                DW RETURNCode       ; RETURNCToken   = 10
                DW DUPCode          ; DUPCToken      = 11
                DW MULCode          ; MULCToken      = 12
                DW SWAPCode         ; SWAPCToken     = 13
                DW LITCode          ; LITCToken      = 14
                DW ADDCode          ; ADDCToken      = 15

; Direct tokens for primitives
```

2.2. Examples of Intermediate Languages

```
RETURN:         DB RETURNCToken
DUP:            DB DUPCToken
LIT:            DB LITCToken
MUL:            DB MULCToken
SWAP:           DB SWAPCToken
ADD:            DB ADDCToken

; Indirect tokens are used in definitions (except for CALL)

; Square         ( n -- n^2 ) , multiplies top of stack with itself
SQUARE:         DB CALLCToken      ; Direct token
                DB DUPToken        ; Indirect token
                DB MULToken
                DB RETURNToken

; Multiply by 5  ( n -- 5*n ) , multiplies top of stack by 5
FIVEMUL:        DB CALLCToken
                DB LITToken
                DW 5
                DB MULToken
                DB RETURNToken

; Function       ( n1 n2 -- 5*n1^2+n2^2 )   , computes FUNC(x,y)
FUNC:           DB CALLCToken
                DB SQUAREToken
                DB SWAPToken
                DB SQUAREToken
                DB FIVEMULToken
                DB ADDToken
                DB RETURNToken

PROGRAM_START:  DB FUNCToken
```

Threaded code varieties are also discussed in [Ritt80,Kogg82,Brak82b,Brak82a, Deba87]. As table 1.9 indicates, some space/time efficient implementations of languages such as BASIC and PROLOG also use threaded code techniques. The simplicity and uniformity of FORTH and of its corresponding threaded code invited several implementors to design high-performance FORTH oriented machines. Examples of microcoded machines are described in [Wada82,Dums83,Haye87,Gold85] and hardware controlled processors in [Burs86].

2.2.3 Lispkit LISP and SECD-code

Lispkit LISP [Hend80] is a purely functional language (it has no-side effects). It is very similar to 'real LISP', but it is quite simple and well-suited for quick implementation and study.

The differences only appear in minor details. In [Hend80], Henderson presents this LISP variant and also describes the SECD-architecture as the corresponding virtual machine. Note that there is a large resemblance between Scheme-79 [Suss81] and the SECD-machine, both with respect to architectural design as well as to implementation strategy.

Lispkit LISP. A functional program consists of *objects*; *functions*, transforming objects into objects; and *higher-order functions*, combining functions and/or objects to construct new functions. The objects, traditionally called *Symbolic Expressions* (S-expressions) are indivisible (*atoms*), and are of two kinds. Numeric atoms correspond to numbers and symbolic atoms are represented by character strings starting with a letter. NIL is a special symbolic atom playing an important role when dealing with list-structures. Non-atomic S-expressions (or *lists*) are described by the following definition: *if* A *and* B *are S-expressions then the dotted-pair denoted by* (A.B) *is also an S-expression*.

The notation for a dotted pair is often shortened in the following way: (A.(B.C)) into (A B.C), (A.NIL) into (A), and (A.(B.NIL)) into (A B). As is usually done in LISP, both programs and data are represented by lists [McCa60].

The following code fragment shows the Lispkit LISP implementation of the function APPEND, which concatenates two lists.

```
(LETREC APPEND
    (APPEND LAMBDA (X Y)
        (IF (EQ X (QUOTE NIL)) Y
            (CONS (CAR X) (APPEND(CDR X) Y) ) ) ) )
```

The LETREC APPEND group defines a recursive function with name APPEND. The body of the function declares two arguments X and Y and the implementation of the function. If the first argument is the empty list NIL the second argument Y is the result; otherwise, the result is the concatenation of the first element of X and the result of the APPEND function applied to the remaining part of X and Y. In this way the APPEND function is called recursively.

Lispkit LISP implementation and the SECD-machine. In [Hend80], it is shown how a Lispkit LISP program is compiled into an SECD-machine representation. The SECD-machine is an abstract machine originally proposed by Landin [Land63]. It has only 4 registers and 21 instructions. Each letter in the acronym SECD stands for one of the four registers (fig. 2.9):

2.2. Examples of Intermediate Languages

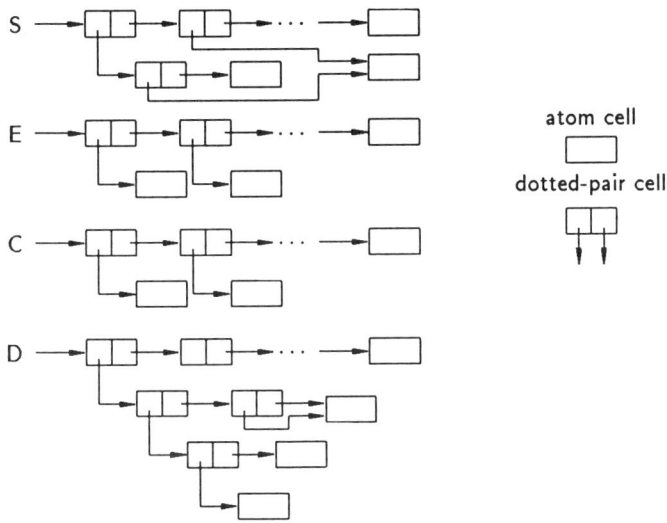

Figure 2.9
The data structure of the SECD intermediate LISP engine

- the S-register points to the *stack*, holding the intermediate results during expression evaluation (data stack);

- the E-register determines the *environment* (context) defining the variables accessible by a function, and the values bound to them.

- the C-register acts as an instruction pointer to the *control list* holding the SECD-instructions;

- the D-register is a stack, *dump*, saving values of the registers when a new function is called.

All structures (stack, environment, control list and dump) are S-expressions. The state of the machine during a function evaluation is determined by the values of the S, E, C, and D registers and the structures pointed to by them. The execution of each SECD-instruction causes a transformation of the old SECD values into a new set of values. In the SECD machine, memory consists of a set of cells. There are three kinds of cells: number cells containing a number, symbol cells containing a symbol and dotted-pair cells grouping two cell pointers. The operation *car* on an dotted-pair cell returns its first pointer and the operation *cdr* returns its second pointer. During the operation of the SECD-machine, cells are created and other cells get unreferenced. Therefore, a memory management process must provide free cells when needed and collect unreferenced cells (garbage). A description of such memory management algorithms is beyond the scope of this book.

A compiler, also written in Lispkit LISP, compiles a list representation with the Lispkit LISP source (containing dotted-pair cells and symbol cells) into a list representing the corresponding intermediate code. Figure 2.10 shows the representation of the APPEND program. Each virtual instruction (SECD instruction) is represented by a token residing in a number cell. These number cells are linked together in a list representation using dotted-pair cells. Hence, we have a token representation of the intermediate instructions chained by a list structure.

The interpreter fetches each virtual SECD-instruction and performs the corresponding semantics. Except for the chaining of SECD-codes the interpreter mechanism is identical to that of the M-machine: a table lookup followed by a dispatching to the corresponding interpreter routine. The code fragment below gives the 8086 interpreter routines for some SECD-instructions.

```
; ******** 8086 SECD INTERPRETER :   CONSTANT DEFINITIONS *******

; cell structure

car     EQU 0   ; Offset of cell car pointer
cdr     EQU 2   ; Offset of cell cdr pointer
tag     EQU 4   ; Offset of cell tag

;tag values

Iscons      EQU 0
Isnumber    EQU 1
Issymbol    EQU 2

;register usage

S       EQU SI
E       EQU BX
C       EQU BP
D       EQU CX

; *************** INTERPRETER CODE ***************************

init_SECD_registers:
```

2.2. Examples of Intermediate Languages

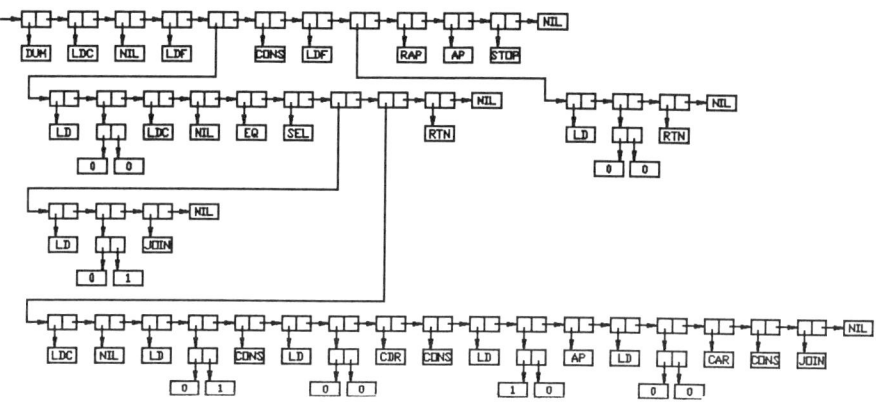

```
( DUM LDC NIL LDF
    ( LD (0.0) LDC NIL EQ SEL
            ( LD (0.1) JOIN )
            ( LDC NIL LD (0.1) CONS LD (0.0) CDR CONS
                    LD (1.0) AP LD (0.0) CAR CONS JOIN )
      RTN )
  CONS LDF ( LD (0.0) RTN ) RAP AP STOP )
```

Figure 2.10
Intermediate representation of the APPEND function on the SECD machine

```
        CALL    CrconsS         ; create Stack cell
        MOV WORD  PTR DS:[S+car],offset Args
                                ; car points to arguments
        MOV WORD  PTR DS:[S+cdr],offset Nil
                                ; bottom element
        MOV E,offset Nil        ; environment NIL
        MOV C,offset Fn         ; C points to function
        MOV D,offset Nil        ; dump NIL

; ***************** MAPPING ACTIONS **************************
```

```
FETCH:  MOV  DI,DS:[C+car]       ; fetch car pointer to token
        MOV  DI,[DI]             ; get actual token
NEXT:   MOV  C,[C+cdr]           ; update program counter :c := cdr(c)
DECODE: SHL  DI,1                ; convert token to table index
        JMP  WORD  PTR CS:Table[DI]

; ************** INTERPRETER DISPATCHING TABLE *****************

Table:  DW   error
        DW   LDCode              ; LD   1
        DW   LDCCode             ; LDC  2
             ...
        DW   ADDCode             ; ADD  15
             ...
        DW   STOPCode            ; STOP 21

; ************** SOME SEMANTIC ROUTINES **********************

; LD, load :
; w:=e;     for i:= 1 to value(car(car(c))) do w:=cdr(w);
; w:=car(w); for i:= 1 to value(cdr(car(c))) do w:=cdr(w);
; w:=car(w); s:=cons(w,s); c:=cdr(c);

LDCode: MOV  AX,D                ; save old D value
        MOV  DI,DS:[C+car]       ; CX:= value(car(car(c)))
        MOV  DI,DS:[DI+car]
        MOV  CX,[DI]
        MOV  DI,E                ; w:=e
        CMP  CX,1
        JL   ld_1
loop_1: MOV  DI,DS:[DI+cdr]      ; w:=cdr(w)
        LOOPNZ  loop_1
ld_1:   MOV  DX,DS:[DI+car]      ; w:=car(w)
        MOV  DI,DS:[C+car]       ; CX:=value(cdr(car(c)))
        MOV  DI,DS:[DI+cdr]
        MOV  CX,[DI]
        MOV  DI,DX               ; w
        CMP  CX,1
        JL   ld_2
loop_2: MOV  DI,DS:[DI+cdr]      ; w:=cdr(w)
```

2.2. Examples of Intermediate Languages

```
        LOOPNZ  loop_2
ld_2:   MOV   DX,DS:[DI+car]    ; w:=car(w)
        CALL  CrconsDI          ; s:=cons(w,s)
        MOV   DS:[DI+car],DX
        MOV   DS:[DI+cdr],S
        MOV   S,DI
        MOV   D,AX              ; restore D value
        MOV   C,DS:[C+cdr]      ; c:=cdr(c)
        JMP   FETCH

; LDC, load constant:
; s:=cons(car(c),s); c:=cdr(c)

LDCCode:
        MOV   DI,DS:[C+car]     ; s:=cons(car(c),s)
        MOV   DX,S
        CALL  CrconsS           ; create cons cell pointed to by S
        MOV   DS:[S+car],DI
        MOV   DS:[S+cdr],DX
        MOV   C,[C+cdr]         ; c:=cdr(c)
        JMP   FETCH

; ADD, addition of top stack items
; s:=cons(number(value(car(cdr(s)))+value(car(s))),cdr(cdr(s)));

ADDCode:
        MOV   DI,DS:[S+car]     ; AX:=value(car(s))
        MOV   AX,DS:[DI]
        MOV   S,DS:[S+cdr]      ; AX:=AX+value(car(cdr(s)))
        MOV   DI,DS:[S+car]
        ADD   AX,DS:[DI]
        MOV   DX,DS:[S+cdr]     ; DX:=cdr(cdr(s))
        Crnumber AX,DI          ; macro creates number cells with value
                                ;   AX and pointed to by DI
        CALL  CrconsS           ; s:=cons(ival..+ival...,cdr(cdr(s)))
        MOV   DS:[S+car],DI     ; pointer to number cell
        MOV   DS:[S+cdr],DX     ; rest of stack
        JMP   FETCH
```

2.3 Bibliographical Notes on Interpretation

So far we have already indicated some points of interest associated with interpretive techniques. It comes as no surprise that many more reasons exist to use some or another form of interpretation to fulfill a goal other than raw processing speed. Table 2.2 shows a classification of some of the published research works. This classification is based on the context in which interpretive techniques were used by the authors.

Extensibility. The capability to extend a language facilitates software development. Extension allows the system designer to tailor his system towards his needs of that moment. Extensibility is used in different meanings in the literature. In a strict sense, extensibility implies the ability to modify and extend the semantics of the built-in language elements. Overlaying keywords in ADA, and modifying the primitives in FORTH are examples of strict language extension. In the weakest sense, the ability to create abstractions in subroutines can also be called extensibility, although this statement is admittedly void, as virtually all languages provide the subroutine mechanism.

With extensible languages the program size grows logarithmically with the program complexity instead if linearly in the case of non-extensible languages [Sach83]. Often, extensibility requires interactivity: it is preferable to define and test the extensions quickly. In [Notk87] it is described how extensibility can be achieved through interpretive techniques: *the extension interpreter.* The approach is based on call arbitration, dynamic linking and multilanguage calls. The call arbitration mechanism maps a procedure name and context onto a procedure implementation for execution (mapping actions). The system-wide extension mechanism considers extensions defined through compiled as well as through interpreted languages. In order to give both the equal appearance to the user compiled extensions are dynamically linked at calling time. Calls between different languages are supported through an advanced remote procedure call technique (taking into account differences in data representation and data transfer). In this way, the extension interpreter provides and handles extensions expressed in interpreted as well as in compiled languages.

In [Brak82a] and [Harr80] Forth's extensibility in a monolingual environment (Forth) is described. Forth provides mechanisms to define primitives in terms of native instructions, to construct definitions in terms of primitives and other definitions. The ability to modify the primitives from within the Forth environment is a true form of extensibility. Similar possibilities are found in SMALLTALK, where objects are defined in terms of objects and in LISP, where functions are expressed in terms of functions.

In [Bhuj83] a program is defined using an instruction set which is based on

2.3. Bibliographical Notes on Interpretation

Context	References
extensibility	[Notk87], [Bhuj83], [Brak82a], [Harr80]
debugging/testing	[Chas87], [Offu87]
interactivity and flexibility	[Harr87], [Sach83], [Jona86], [Park83], [Feue], [Phil78]
space/time efficiency	[Pitt87], [Clar87b], [Flyn78], [Bell73], [Dewa75], [Bose84], [Bose83], [Flyn83a], [Hoev74]
space efficiency	[Mark80], [Fras84], [Fost71]
interpreter generation	[Kosk87], [Srid86], [Raus78]
portability	[Mira87], [Hell83], [Tayl84], [Tane82], [Davi87a], [Wall87]
robustness	[Lepp86]
education	[Kels], [McMi87], [DeBo88]
simplicity of compilation process	[Schu82], [Wirt86], [TheT82]
accuracy of computations	[Boeh87]
tools for program analysis	[Sked87], [Crag83]
speedup through result caching	[Kari87], [Stan81], [Nort83], [Luqu88]
language description and definition	[Cohe85], [McCa60], [Wirt81]
principles of interpretation	[Cord87], [Klin81], [Brak82b], [Hoff83], [Flyn80], [Mall75], [Ritt80], [Bell73], [Dewa75], [Kogg82]
implementation of evaluation mechanisms	[O'ba87], [Faus87], [Bark87], [Dewa77], [Robi87], [Furn87], [Week86], [Glas85], [Cive87a], [Davi87a], [Gree86], [Vose87], [Yama81], [Hart88], [Chun78], [Cast88], [Patt84], [Sked87]
hardware supporting interpretation	[Flyn83b], [Gum86], [Koop86], [Wiln72], [Pier83], [Posa79], [Laws71], [VonP83], [Harl86], [Kers81], [Wilk84], [Noji86], [Coop88], [Atki87], [DeBl86]

Table 2.2
An overview of research papers dealing with interpretation

software requirements (time, space) and which is not limited by the supporting machine. Only a fraction of the instruction set is directly supported by the hardware, the rest is not. When a non-supported instruction is encountered, a trap (a GAP) is invoked to transfer its execution to an interrupt handler that emulates its semantics using supported instructions. The trap is used to switch from native mode to interpreted mode and the interrupt handler is a true interpreter program.

Debugging and testing. Interpreters have full control over the execution of an intermediate program. Enlarging the basic interpretive actions with possibilities to observe the execution allows the easier modification of program sources, the monitoring of variables, program tracing, individual testing of modules and reversible execution.

In [Chas87] these techniques are used during the execution of part of a large, computationally intensive program. The remainder of the program is executed in native mode. In this way the enhanced debugging facilities are used at the places where needed without penalizing the execution time for the other parts of the program. In [Offu87] *mutation analysis* is used to test software systems. Mutation analysis investigates the quality of test data by imposing the data onto slightly modified versions (mutants) of a particular program. The testing of each mutant requires a compilation to the machine language. To reduce this step the original program is compiled into a high-level intermediate code and the mutation is done at the intermediate level. In this system the interpreter executes the intermediate representation, allows the mutation of a program and monitors program behavior.

Interactivity and flexibility. We have already mentioned the significance of interactivity in modern computer applications: it improves productivity in software development and makes programming easier for non-experienced users. Besides the languages and environments mentioned earlier in this book, the following publications describe the use of interpretive techniques to support interactivity. In [Harr87], an interpreter is described to implement a document generating language intended for use by lawyers, law students, and paralegal staff. A What-You-See-Is-What-You-Get (WYSIWIG) version is presented, which simplifies the formatting process. In such interactive systems speed is not of primary importance, since considerable time is spent waiting for the user's actions.

In [Sach83] the implementation of the Forth based language STOIC is described. It offers enhancements convenient for user interaction, error checking, file handling and text editing. An interpreted C language environment is described in [Feue]. Its major goal is to reduce software development cost. Differences with compiled C environments are: a short editing/running cycle, more error checking at runtime instead of at compile-time, more control on program execution, and better debugging facilities.

Interpretive execution provides more flexibility than direct execution; in [Phil78]

2.3. Bibliographical Notes on Interpretation

it is shown how an interpretive system may be tailored towards the needs found in laboratories where programs are continually being modified. The hierarchical structure of threaded code is found extremely useful in these environments.

Space/time efficiency. We have already discussed the attempts to construct 'ideal' intermediate languages: the DEL approach [Flyn78,Hoev74,Flyn83a] and the DIL approach [Bose84,Bose83]. Other authors discuss the principles of threaded code [Bell73,Dewa75]. Interpretive techniques can also be used in other ways to improve the space/time efficiency of computer applications. In [Pitt87], Pittman makes a comparison of the space/time efficiencies offered by machine level representations, threaded code varieties, and variable length representations, respectively. He proposes a hybrid representation scheme consisting of a compact intermediate representation for infrequently used parts of a program, and fast machine code for the remainder. In fact this is exactly what is done in some variants of threaded code.

In [Clar87b], the representation size and the execution time of a syntax directed editor are compared. The editor consists of a small number of primitive editing actions, which are represented by machine code, and an intermediate representation encoding the actions. This interpretive approach is compared to the native code implementation of similar editors.

Space efficiency. Although the recent developments in memory technology have made mere program representation size a relatively unimportant issue, it is interesting to note how interpretation has been used in this context. In [Fost71], Foster presents a case for 'conditional interpretation of opcodes'. There is significant correlation between successive instructions. It is intuitively clear that the correlation between instructions in compiled code will be higher than that of hand-coded programs. One can reduce this redundancy in machine instruction sequences by keeping the identification of the most recently executed instruction(s) in some memory of the mapping process, and using this information to identify the next instruction. Instructions can now be encoded with a reduced number of bits. The interpretation of each instruction is conditional to the previous instruction.

In [Fras84] the representation size is reduced by replacing repeated closed instruction sequences by subroutine calls and a unique representation of the subroutine body (procedure abstraction). In fact, the presented compiler produces a linear instruction stream akin to subroutine threaded code. Together with a code compression technique (cross jumping), the encoding scheme gives an average space reduction of 7%, with an increase of the execution time of only 5%.

This method of procedure abstraction is applied until only subroutines are left in [Mark80] (pure one level deep subroutine threaded code). Then the linear sequence of call instructions is transformed into a compact representation only using addresses (direct threaded code). At run time, this representation is interpreted.

The experiments showed a code compaction of 15%, at the expense of a 15% hike in execution time.

The generation of interpreters for specific languages. In [Srid86], a technique is described to generate microcode for interpretation from the language definition. The inputs are a BNF description of a language and a definition of its semantics in terms of the available hardware semantics. The output is a sequence of microcode instructions to be loaded into a microprogrammable machine. In [Kosk87], a system TOOLS (Translator for Object Oriented Language Specification) is described. It allows to compile a language specification into an interpreter program. It is suitable for fast prototyping in experimental implementations of small languages.

In contrast to these *language based* interpreter generators, [Raus78] presents a *program dependent* interpreter. After analysis of the program, intermediate instructions are composed with corresponding interpreter routines.

Portability. There are several ways in which portability can be achieved using interpretive techniques. There are the high level language implementations described in equal or other high level languages. Examples are a C interpreter written in C, based on a virtual C machine [Davi87a], and a Smalltalk interpreter written in C, based on a Smalltalk virtual machine [Mira87].

Other ways use intermediate representations. [Hell83] describes a Pascal implementation based on indirect threaded code and implemented in MINIMAL (Machine Independent Macro Assembly Language); [Tayl84] gives a simple virtual machine for the Pascal language and [Tane82] illustrates a virtual machine for algebraic languages. In [Wall87], intermediate languages are proposed for RISC target systems in order to hide hardware related aspects.

Robustness. In [Lepp86], Leppala shows how memories and system resources can be protected by using interpretive techniques. Each reference to memory or other system resources is performed by the interpreter, which is assumed to be reliable. This is a good alternative to a more expensive forms of reliability provided by extensive redundancy of hardware.

Computer science education. In educational environments, software exercises are often more feasible than hardware exercises. If it is the aim to teach the structure and operation of a conventional architecture, a software interpreter is a suitable tool. The students may have full control of the hardware model and the architectural parameters. Examples are [Kels] and [McMi87]. When sufficiently open interpretive environments are used, also other aspects of computer science can be covered: compiler design, concurrency, program behavior, etc. [DeBo88].

Simplifying the code generating part of compilers. Virtual machines are closer to high level languages than general purpose machines are. Therefore, using a well chosen and high level language directed intermediate representation eases code generation. In [Wirt86], Wirth quantitatively demonstrates the dependency of the simplicity of the code generator on the target instruction set architecture. He indicates that the code generators for the NS32000 and the MC68000 microprocessors are larger than the code generator for the M-machine by factors of 1.37 and 2.54, respectively. For similar reasons [Schu82] presents a virtual architecture to execute Pascal-like languages. In [TheT82], intermediate representations (threaded code varieties and P-code) are used to represent Pascal programs.

Accuracy of numerical computation. During native code execution, the representation of real numbers is determined by the hardware architecture. In some cases this causes precision problems, as a result of the limited length of the representation. Boehm proposes to use an interpreter which replaces all floating point operations with operations on *constructive real numbers* [Boeh87]. Constructive real numbers are rules for computing an arbitrarily precise approximation for a real number.

Tools for program analysis. During direct execution only the results of the computation and its execution time can be observed by the user. Interpretive execution is well suited for gathering information easily. In [Sked87] an interpretive environment is presented aimed at the analysis of the compilation of applicative languages. Another approach is to use interpretive environments as simulation tools. In [Crag83] it is shown how a LISP environment can be used both as an executable specification language and as a simulator during the design of an instruction set.

Speedup through result caching. In the software development cycle, considerable time is spent on small modifications and on rerunning the program. In such cases the main part of the program will produce the same results as it did previously; only the modified parts will produce different results. To shorten the turnaround time incremental compilation and incremental re-execution can be applied as presented in [Kari87]. So as to support incremental re-execution, the programming environment has to store a lot of detailed information between different runs. An interpreter takes care of gathering the information and the selection of those parts that must be executed again. Depending on the program and the modifications, savings in execution time of up to 90% are observed.

In [Nort83] *adaptive interpretation* is presented. Interpretation is called adaptive if the performance of an instruction sequence can be improved during a subsequent execution due to information gathered previously. This is used in the case of complex instruction sets [Nort83]. In complex multioperand instructions a lot of operations must be done before the actual operation can be performed (e.g., address calculation). In the case of native execution these suboperations are performed each time the instructions are executed, even if the operand addresses are the same as during the previous execution. The virtual addresses of the operands are cached together with control information. In this way, at the next execution, the operand addresses are taken from cache and the suboperations are no longer performed. In the experiments presented improvements are achieved by a factor of almost 3. Similar techniques (caching of partial results) are also used in the case of functional languages (results of functions are cached and reused immediately when the same function is called in an identical context and with identical operands. Note that result caching can be performed by hardware as well as by software, i.e., an interpreter.

In [Stan81] and [Luqu88], the technique of *virtual migration* is described as a means to speedup program execution. Virtual migration is used in multi-level interpretive systems. The mechanism consists of moving instructions from higher levels (selected by observation), possibly at run-time, to lower levels of the hierarchy. As the interpretive overhead increases towards higher levels of software this technique contributes to the overall speedup.

Description and definition of high level languages. Describing the semantics of a high level language can be done efficiently and accurately by implementing an interpreter. Examples are Lisp interpreters [McCa60], M-code interpreters [Wirt81] and Prolog (meta)interpreters [Cohe85]. To define the syntax of a language, an outer interpreter or a BNF description suffices.

Principles of interpretation. In [Hoff83] interpretive systems are classified according to the number of structural levels they contain. Others discuss the interpretive process in a concrete way [Mall75] or in a more generalized manner [Flyn80]. In [Cord87] a systematic design method of interactive interpretive systems is presented. The design is divided into a user interface and an executing engine which communicate through a database. Finally, several papers describe characteristics and varieties of threaded code [Bell73,Dewa75,Brak82b,Klin81,Ritt80,Kogg82].

Implementation of alternative evaluation mechanisms. The way in which today's computer systems operate conforms to the principles of Babbage and von Neumann (step by step execution of algorithms). Direct execution does not leave freedom to modify this evaluation mechanism. Consequently, the evaluation and implementation of other evaluation mechanisms must be done through software. Interpretation provides great freedom in implementing evaluation algorithms, or models of computation. Typical examples are Prolog evaluations [Bark87,Week86, Cive87a,Davi87a,Yama81], reduction mechanisms [Hart88,Cast88], applicative evaluations [Glas85,Furn87,Robi87], backtracking in expression evaluation [O'ba87], data-flow systems [Patt84], demand driven control [Faus87], extensive run-time checking and conversion [Dewa77], complex operation [Gree86] and special languages [Sked87,Chun78].

Hardware supporting interpretation. Aimed at the elimination of the slowdown caused by interpretation, microprogrammable architectures supporting interpretation have been developed. In the academic world these systems are used for their flexibility in providing a test bed for experiments. In commercial applications these architectures are used for their speed in supporting unusual or foreign evaluation techniques.

Well known examples are Emmy [Flyn83b], the Burroughs B1700 [Wiln72], the Dorado [Pier83], the Dragon [Atki87] and Rekursiv [Harl86]. Other microprogrammable machines are described in [Koop86,Laws71,VonP83,Kers81,Wilk84], and [Noji86,Coop88]. Proposals for hardware supporting interpretation are user microprogrammable microprocessors [Koop86], special emulation modes in existing machines [Gum86], microprocessor based interpretive engines [Posa79] and hardware units to support subfunctions of interpreters (e.g. pattern matching) [DeBl86].

2.4 Conclusion

In this chapter we have had a brief look into the basic properties of intermediate language representations and their associated interpreters. From this analysis it has become clear that the interpretive execution of high level language programs offers an extra degree of freedom in providing an appropriate answer to the space/time tradeoff of an application.

We have briefly digressed into the DEL and DIL approaches, which pose the more general question of optimal program representation. The analytical arguments developed by Hoevel indicate that the interpretation of intermediate program representations is the fastest way to execute large programs on the microprogrammable computer architectures of the early seventies. Since then, the technological evolution has made Hoevel's arguments obsolete. Interpretation is slower than direct native code execution. However, the latest technological evolutions create a renewed interest in Hoevel's arguments. The presence of a limited amount of on-chip memory, which is an order of magnitude faster than off-chip bulk memory is similar to the conditions investigated by Hoevel. It turns out that the relative slow-down caused by interpretation is significantly reduced, or, in some extreme technological cases, completely eliminated through the intelligent use of on-chip memory. The resulting lower instruction access rate to external memory is an additional benefit which, in turn, can be used in an interesting way.

To illustrate the above rather abstract concepts, we have analysed a few concrete examples of intermediate representations and their associated interpreters. Finally, we have presented the reader with a survey of the contexts in which interpretation has been used as an instrumental technique. Even in the limited amount of space devoted to this survey, the great interest in interpretive techniques has become apparent.

3 OPTIMIZING INTERPRETIVE EXECUTION

The overall performance of an interpretive system strongly depends on the properties of both the intermediate architecture implied by the program representation and the actual architecture of the interpretive engine. In earlier days, interpretive engines were microprogrammable machines, and interpreters were microcoded. The underlying hardware structure was optimized towards interpretation. This situation offered an almost ideal compromise between the advantages and drawbacks of interpretation. However, since the introduction of low-cost microprocessors, the situation has changed thoroughly. Except for bitsliced components, microprocessor architectures are not oriented towards fast interpretation of intermediate instruction sets; direct execution of compiler-generated native code is the true goal. It then comes as no surprise that, on general purpose microprocessor architectures, interpretation is significantly slower than the execution of native code programs. This unfortunate situation is only partially compensated by the fact that microprocessor computing power has indeed become very cheap. It is definitely worthwhile to speedup interpretive execution on general purpose microprocessor architectures as much as possible; this chapter deals with precisely this goal. First, we shall look into the reasons why interpretive execution is slow on contemporary microprocessors. Then we shall try to remedy this situation, and analyze several programming techniques than can somewhat lessen the interpretive burden.

3.1 Why are Interpreters Slow?

Consider the following experiment: the *same* high level language program is compiled into an intermediate representation and interpreted on one hand, and compiled into native code and directly executed on the other. Such an experiment is possible with several HLLs, e.g., with MODULA-2. One observes a specific value for the slowdown S, the ratio of the interpretive and direct execution times. The observed value of S obviously depends on several factors, including the properties of the intermediate representation, the mere fact that interpretation is used, and the architectural dissimilarities between the intermediate machine and the interpretive engine. We shall now discuss these factors one by one.

3.1.1 The effect of the intermediate representation

In the previous chapter we have observed that, frequently, the intermediate machine exhibits a stack architecture. There are several reasons for this. First, a stack machine is an almost ideal target architecture to generate code for. Compilers often use stack oriented internal intermediate representations. The code generating part of such a compiler can be kept simple. Second, the interpreter implementing a stack machine has a very simple internal structure; operators only apply to the stack, and need not be concerned with operand addresses. Only data transfer instructions need operand addresses. The entire state of the interpreter is contained in explicit data structures: registers, stack, memory. No additional state memory is required between the execution of intermediate instructions. Consequently, interpreters for such intermediate languages tend to be very simple and small; a few Kbytes is a typical size. Thus choosing a stack architecture as the intermediate architecture has definite advantages. However, several modern compiler optimization techniques are not applicable on stack architectures. For example, a stack architecture inhibits the compiler to generate code exploiting data locality on the CPU, as it would for a register architecture. Indeed, once an object has been popped of the stack, it no longer resides in the CPU; there is no way to reuse it, unless by pushing it on the stack again. In contrast, on a register architecture, the compiler can keep track of the validity of the register contents *after* is was used. If appropriate, the contents of a register can be used later on, without the necessity to reload it from memory.

A second aspect of the intermediate program representation is *the semantic level* of its primitives [Klin81]. Increasing this level will increase the number of semantically useful machine instructions per intermediate instruction. Provided that the mapping actions do not grow in the same proportion as the semantic actions do, the overall interpreter efficiency will improve. Typical examples of rather low-level intermediate languages are basic M-code and P-code. Languages like APL and ASYST, providing primitives for complex operations on arrays, allow intermediate primitives with very high semantic contents. The same holds for the Warren's intermediate WAM code for PROLOG, or for PostScript.

In this chapter we consider the choice of the intermediate language fixed; it cannot be altered by the implementor of the interpreter. Only its *use* can offer a certain degree of freedom. It should be kept in mind, though, that an appropriate choice of the intermediate language (and a good, optimizing compiler for it), can greatly influence the global performance of an interpretive system.

3.1.2 The interpretive overhead

We have already identified the major cause of interpretive overhead: the interpreter mapping actions. In the previous chapter we have identified the nature of these actions:

1. fetching and decoding the next intermediate instruction;

2. updating the intermediate program counter;

3. fetching any literal operands, either as part of the intermediate opcode, or as subsequent bytes or words in the intermediate instruction stream;

4. storing these literal data in locations which provide a uniform interface to the semantic routines;

3.1. Why are Interpreters Slow?

5. transferring control the appropriate semantic routine;

6. returning control to the mapping actions after the termination of the semantic routine.

Often, literal operands that are not already included in the intermediate opcode are read by the semantic routines. This does not mean, however, that reading the intermediate literals should not be considered as a form of overhead. Indeed, in native code, literals can be *directly* used by the instruction in which they appear. In an interpreter, the use of program literals involves the intervention of extra load instructions and the occupation of a data register.

It is very difficult to define a clear-cut separation between the instructions that should be considered pure interpretive overhead, and operations that perform semantically useful actions. Besides the direct overhead caused by their presence, mapping actions can have an *indirect effect* on the performance of the semantic actions. For example, literals in the intermediate instruction stream *never* appear as literals in the semantic interpreter routines. They are always loaded into an interfacing register, so as to allow a *generic* encoding of the semantic actions. Generic code tends to be slower than tailor-made code. The question then arises as to whether this extra slowdown is caused by the mapping actions, or by the semantic actions proper.

The interpreter mapping actions can be characterized in two ways: in an absolute way, counting the number of cycles needed to perform them; and in a relative way, by means of the ratio of the execution time of the mapping actions T_m to the total execution time, consisting of the mapping actions T_m and the semantic actions T_s. We shall call the ratio

$$\tau = \frac{T_m}{T_s + T_m}$$

the *interpretive overhead*. In a way, the measures T_m and T_s characterize the global performance of the interpretive engine, and could be used to compare microprocessor architectures. The interpretive overhead τ is more interesting, since it characterizes how good the microprocessor is at interpretation.

The above measures can be determined for the execution of an entire program, by classifying and counting machine instructions. Alternatively, one can calculate the measures for each individual intermediate instruction, and then compute an average of the values obtained using an appropriate *intermediate instruction mix*.

Clearly, the interpretive overhead depends on both the semantic level of the intermediate language and the properties of the interpretive engine.

Figure 3.1 shows the interpretive overhead for the interpretation of M-code on different architectures, as a function of the mapping time T_m. The overhead ratio is computed for the 10 most frequently occurring M-codes, according to a dynamic analysis of intermediate instructions of MODULA-2 programs [Blom87]. These

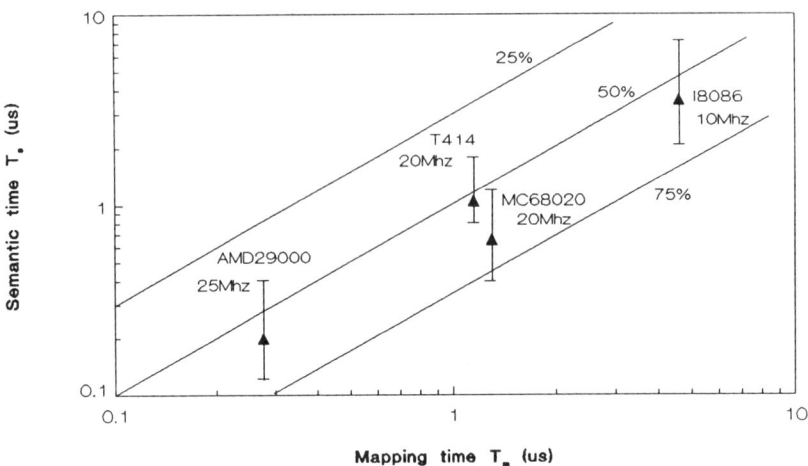

Figure 3.1
The interpretive overhead of M-code on various processors

10 M-codes represent over 35 % of the total number of dynamically encountered intermediate instructions. While a noticeable (although not unexpected) difference exists between the absolute figures, it appears that the overhead ratio is roughly independent of the interpreting machine: it varies between 52% and 66%. As the architecture, technology and the instruction sets of the involved microprocessors vary widely, this result suggests that the interpretive overhead could be considered as a characteristic of the intermediate language.

So as to illustrate the slowdown of the interpretive execution with respect to direct execution of compiled programs, we have timed the execution of the widely used Eratosthenes' Sieve benchmark, which counts the number of primes smaller than a given integer [Gilb83]. Figures 3.2 and 3.3 show listings of this program.

Table 3.1 shows the relative execution times of different modes of execution. For the MODULA-2 version of the Sieve, the interpretive and compiled executions are compared. The native code compilers used where the Logitech v3.01 (1987) and the Topspeed v1.12 (Jensen & Partners, 1988). The M-code compilers were the university of Hamburg v02 (1983) and the Modula Corporation v1.10 multipass compilers. The M-code compilers are based on Wirth's original PDP-11 implementation v.M22. The M-code interpreters used were the optimized LEM[1] interpreter, written by the authors, and the Modula Corporation M-code interpreter for the IBM PC. The FORTH versions used were the HS/FORTH Rev. 3.8 (Harvard Softworks, 1986), and the public domain IBMF83 (Laxen & Perry, 1984).

---

[1]LEM is an acronym for Laboratory of Electronics and Metrology.

3.1. Why are Interpreters Slow?

```
( Eratosthenes' Prime Number Sieve program in Forth )
( by Jim Gilbreath, BYTE Sept. 1981 p. 190 )

decimal              ( assume decimal source-representation for
                       numbers )
8190 constant size   ( create a constant 'size' with value 8190 )
0 variable IsPrime   ( create a variable 'IsPrime' serving as an
                       array base )
size allot           ( allocate 'size' bytes in that array
'IsPrime' )

: do-prime           ( define a word with name 'do-prime' )
  IsPrime size 1 fill ( fill 'size' bytes from address 'IsPrime'
                       with value 1 )
    0                ( counter := 0)
    size 0 do        ( perform 'do-loop' size times starting from 0)
        IsPrime I + c@        ( get IsPrime[i] )
        if I dup + 3 + dup    ( if IsPrime[i] then prime:= 2i+3)
            I +               ( k := prime+i  )
            begin dup size <            ( while k < size do )
            while 0 over IsPrime + c!   ( IsPrime[k] := false)
                  over +                ( k := prime + k )
            repeat                      ( end-while )
            drop                        ( drop k )
            drop                        ( drop prime )
            1+                          ( counter := counter+1)
        then                            ( end-if )
    loop                                ( end-do )
. ." primes " ;      ( output counter, output string 'primes' )
```

Figure 3.2
The Sieve Benchmark in FORTH

```
MODULE Primes;
(*$T-*)

FROM  InOut    IMPORT WriteInt;
  CONST  size = 8190;
  VAR    IsPrime           : ARRAY [0..size-1] OF BOOLEAN;
         i,j,k,prime,counter : INTEGER;
BEGIN
    counter := 0 ;
    FOR j := 0 TO size-1 DO
      IsPrime[j] := TRUE ;
    END;
    FOR j := 0 TO size-1 DO
      IF IsPrime[j] THEN
        prime := j + j + 3 ;
        k := j + prime ;
        WHILE k < size DO
          IsPrime[ k ] := FALSE ;
          k := k + prime ;
        END ;
        counter := counter + 1 ;
      END ;
    END;
    WriteInt(counter,5);
END Primes.(*$T+*)
```

Figure 3.3
The Sieve Benchmark in MODULA-2

The results are striking: the non-optimized interpretive M-code implementation is up to 30 times slower than the well-optimized native code implementation. Note also the difference between the two native code compilers. Beside the actual total execution time, we have also compared the semantically useful execution time T_s observed during the interpretive execution, and the total native execution time. Even then large slowdown factors remain. As observed earlier, the residual difference between these numbers is due to the quality of compiler, the lack of optimization caused by the intermediate language, and the less efficient generic semantic actions of the interpreter routines.

3.1. Why are Interpreters Slow?

Implementation	Relative Execution Time	
	Total	Semantic
TopSpeed (Native)	1.00	1.00
Logitech (Native)	3.50	3.50
LEM (Interpretive)	15.33	6.54
Mod. Corp. (Interpretive)	30.68	17.00
HS/FORTH (Interpretive)	10.63	4.07
IBMF83 (Interpretive)	15.95	4.70

Table 3.1
The interpretive slowdown of the Sieve benchmark on the i8086

Interpretive execution makes other use of the microprocessor resources than does the execution of compiled programs. While certain machine instructions encountered during the execution of compiled programs are rarely used during interpretation, other machine instructions occur more frequently. Some differences are:

- **More mapping related instructions.** Instructions which are normally considered uncommon can be found in the hand coded and frequently occurring fetch/decode sequence. An example is the i8086 CBW (convert byte to word) instruction, which pads an M-code byte to a word. Other instructions have to do with the mapping problem. The instructions realizing the mapping are used very frequently. Typical examples are shift, masking and padding instructions. A special case is formed by the JMP instruction. Jumps are needed to implement HLL control constructs (Do-Loop, Repeat-Until, While-Do, If-Then-Else). In compiled programs, they appear in the code as native JMP instructions. When compiled into intermediate code, they appear at the intermediate level. Jumps at the intermediate level do not give rise to machine-level jumps directly, since the virtual program counter is kept in a register and updated by explicit data-path instructions. Native JMP instructions all originate from within the interpreter. The mapping actions are responsible for at least one jump instruction for each intermediate instruction.

  As a result, the relative dynamic frequency of machine jumps during the interpretive execution is almost independent of the program. For M-code interpreters, jumps make up typically about 16% of the total instruction stream. Nearly all jumps encountered are taken. In compiled native code programs, the dynamic frequency of jumps depends mainly on the complexity of the inner program loop, i.e., the number of non-jump instructions between jumps. As soon as this number is larger than 6 (which is likely to happen in programs with non-trivial inner loops, or with compilers that badly optimize sequential code between jumps), the jump frequency of an interpretive execution will be higher.

- **More complex addressing modes.** The mapping actions of an interpreter involve the register indirect fetch of the intermediate instruction, the (auto)increment of the intermediate program counter, and the register or memory indirect jump to the semantic routine. Intermediate literals are fetched using the same mechanism. In compiled code operand addresses are often direct, using literal offsets. The generic nature of interpreter routines requires the use of more complex, register based addressing modes, so as to allow the run-time calculation of the effective address without the use of literals.

- **More move operations.** The same mechanisms that cause the increased use of complex addressing modes also cause the number of move operations to and from registers to be relatively high. An obvious example is the intermediate instruction fetch, using an explicit move. In compiled programs the instructions are loaded by the hardware, rather than by explicit instructions. The number of move operations also increases when virtual registers are mapped onto memory cells, or when using an intermediate stack machine architecture.

- **Less HLL related instructions.** In the case of interpretation the instruction set is restricted to that of the virtual machine. Generally, the virtual machine will provide instructions very close to the high level language constructs. However, the *machine* instructions related to high level language will typically not be useful for the support of the virtual architecture. Take, for instance, the support of the FOR-NEXT in M-code. While the MC68020 and i8086 both have a Decrement-and-Branch-instruction, the M-code instructions FOR1 and FOR2, implementing the MODULA-2 FOR-NEXT loop, cannot benefit from this instruction. The same holds true for native stack marking instructions, supporting the execution of block structured languages. If the allocation and control stacks are separate, or if the structure of the intermediate stack mark differs from the one implied by the native stack mark instruction, other (slower) instructions must be used.

3.1.3 The architectural gap

The term *architectural gap* refers to the gap between the emulated architecture and the emulating architecture. A representative measure of the size of this gap is the number of cycles required to interpret a particular intermediate instruction sequence. In the case of a small architectural gap the fetch, decoding, and execution phases can be executed in a small number of cycles (ideally 1 cycle for each phase).

3.1. Why are Interpreters Slow?

The larger the architectural gap, the higher the number of cycles required for interpretation. In this context, Flynn distinguishes between *well-mapped* and *partially mapped* configurations [Flyn80,Flyn84]. Well-mapped host-image pairs allow the execution of each phase in one cycle. Partially mapped host/image pairs require more than one cycle, because of the mismatching. The architectural support for the different phases can be so large that their execution can occur in an overlapped way. This is called an overlapped host. If the textual order of the intermediate instructions does not correspond to the their order of execution, transparency is lost. Such a configuration provides even more hardware support for interpretation and is called a 'confluent machine' [Flyn84].

General purpose microprocessors are far from well-mapped according to Flynn's definition. A few of the more notable mismappings are the following.

General machine architecture. Contemporary general purpose microprocessor architectures are register machines, with widely varying numbers of registers. The virtual machine architectures implied by intermediate representations are typically stack machines, often with some extra registers. The mapping of the virtual resources onto the real resources of the microprocessor strongly affects the interpretive performance.

Data and instruction path widths. The mismatching between the widths of the instruction and/or data path of the virtual machine on one hand, and that of the host machine on the other, may penalize the emulation speed considerably. For example, the emulation of a 12 bit machine on a byte-wide host machine requires masking and padding operations to load and store intermediate-level data. The extension of the 12 bit instructions to 16 bits would involve less overhead. This requires a modification of the code generator (compiler or outer-interpreter). The elements likely to be modified are literals (immediate values) and displacements (offsets to target instructions).

Data representations. A problem arises when the data representations of the virtual machine do not correspond with those of the emulating machine, even, if the widths of the data-paths are the same. A well-known problem is little-endian[2] versus big-endian representations of integers. The resolution of address objects, word versus byte pointers, is another source of overhead. Also with reals, problems exist. For example, the real number format of the M-machine does not correspond to that found in an 8086/8087 machine. The overhead induced by this kind of mismatching can only be eliminated through the modification of the code generator.

Another cause of possible mismatching concerns data structures. For example, basic elements in typical LISP machines (tags, linked lists) find no equivalent in

---

[2] in the little-endian representation of integers, the least significant bytes occupy the locations with the lower addresses.

the data structures of microprocessors. Operations on such data types require an excessive number of instructions.

3.2 Interpreter Optimization Techniques

We shall now present and analyze a few programming techniques to improve the performance of microprocessor-based interpreters. From what we saw in the previous section, the mere fact that an interpreter is used is responsible for the largest fraction of the interpretive slowdown. Short of doing away with interpretation all together, there is no programming technique which can remedy this situation completely. Nevertheless, we have identified some points affecting the interpretive performance for which some freedom is left in their implementation. We shall now review these, and report on their effects.

3.2.1 Improvements at the intermediate language level

While it is true that, in most cases, the intermediate language should be considered fixed, there are some ways in which *the use* of the language can significantly improve the speed of interpretation. The main idea is to increase the semantic level of the interpretive routines without increasing the mapping overhead. How can this be done without changing the language? There are a few possibilities.

First, in interpretive environments for open languages such as FORTH, it is possible to extend the set of primitives with new ones. The interpretive overhead needed to invoke the new primitives is the same as for the existing ones. A careful, application-oriented choice of the new primitives can significantly increase the global execution speed of the application. Of course, it is often not easy to choose the new primitives, as their effect depends on the statistical behavior of the program. The program statistics must be collected before a decision can be made. Note that the interpretive technique can be very useful in collecting this information. Second, in intermediate languages which provide *escape* instructions, the interpreter can be extended with specific semantic routines. An example of this technique can be found in M-code. This intermediate language offers several escape prefixes: FFCT, Floating Function, allowing the addition of complex numeric functions such as trigonometric operations, and SYS, System Call, allowing the addition of system related functions. Furthermore, the MODULA-2 compiler allows to invoke these escape instructions by means of in-line M-code instructions in the implementation part of a module using the semantic operations. The definition part of the module offers a standard MODULA-2 access to the rest of the application, and hides the implementation details. It is clear that this mechanism is neither as flexible, nor as efficient as the one above, since the extension of the interpreter cannot be accomplished from within the environment. However, the technique can be very effective, as shown by

3.2. Interpreter Optimization Techniques

Language	Program Segment	Execution mode	Time (relative)
MODULA-2	VAR A,B : ARRAY[1..1024] OF REAL;	native:	
	C : REAL;	TopSpeed	1.00
	I : CARDINAL;	Logitech	1.74
	...	interpretive:	
	C:=0.0;	LEM	3.26
		Mod. Corp.	7.33
	FOR I:=1 TO 1024 DO		
	C:=C+A[I]*B[I]		
	END;		
MODULA-2	FROM MatOps IMPORT InnerProduct;	extended interpretive LEM	0.60
	VAR A,B : ARRAY[1..1024] OF REAL;		
	C : REAL;		
	...		
	C:=InnerProduct(A,B);		
ASYST	REAL DIM[1024] ARRAY A	interpretive	1.95
	REAL DIM[1024] ARRAY B		
	REAL SCALAR C		
	...		
	A B << * | + >> C :=		

Table 3.2
The effect of raising the semantic level of intermediate instructions

the example below.

Consider the implementation of matrix operations, e.g., the inner product. Table 3.2 shows program fragments for this operation in MODULA-2 and in ASYST. The FORTH-like ASYST environment offers a large set of matrix primitives, among which the inner product. In MODULA-2, five implementations were compared: the first two were compiled to native i8086 code using the TopSpeed and Logitech native code MODULA-2 compilers; the third and the fourth were compiled into M-code and interpreted using the LEM and Modula Corporation interpreters; and finally, for the fifth implementation a **FFCT** escape was used to augment the LEM interpreter with an inner product function **InnerProduct**.

It is interesting to observe that the interpretive slowdown is not very large for any of the interpretive implementations. This is a result of the fact that scalar floating point operations are already semantically complex operations. Note also how an increase of the level of the primitives to matrix operations lowers the interpretive overhead. In the case of M-code, the execution time even drops below that of the native code case: the programmer who has hand-coded the primitive has done a far better job than the compiler. Of course, one might argue that similar improvements are also possible with compiled implementations, by improving the efficiency of the run time library used by the compiler. The rather anomalous result of the extended M-code example will then be reduced to normal proportions. At any rate, raising the semantic level of the primitives will *reduce* the speed disparity that exists between interpreted and compiled implementations.

3.2.2 Reducing the interpretive overhead

Usually, an interpreter program is a relatively small program (2K bytes for FORTH, 4K bytes for MODULA-2). If the execution speed must be maximized, hand optimization is manageable. In this section we shall discuss some software techniques to speed up the mapping process on microprocessor systems. We shall concentrate on two issues: the usage of host microprocessor resources in the mapping process, and the placement of the mapping instructions in the interpreter program.

The optimal use of host resources for the mapping operations. From the examples in the previous chapter it has become clear that great care must be taken in allocating basic resources of the host machine to the different stages of the interpretive loop. Small savings in the mapping actions can result in significant savings in the total execution time. It is difficult to state general rules for obtaining a good resource allocation, since the best policy obviously depends on both the intermediate architecture and the host architecture. However, a few principles can be formulated:

- The virtual program counter should be kept in a register which allows the use of the addressing mode needed for the instruction fetch and the efficient updating of the program counter value. On CISC architectures, this means that the virtual program counter should be kept in an address register. For intermediate languages with sequential representation, this address register should also be autoincrementing. The use of the DS:SI register pair together with the LODSB instruction in the i8086 M-code interpreter is a typical example of this principle.

- With tokenized program representations, the use of a dispatching table cannot be avoided. To index this table, an appropriate CISC addressing mode should be used. The overhead to convert the intermediate instruction token to an index into the dispatching table should be kept as low as possible. The use of a *scaled index*[3], as possible e.g. in the Motorola 68020, is advantageous.

---

[3] during its use, a scaled index is automatically multiplied by the size of the elements pointed at. Thus no additional token-to-word pointer conversions are needed.

3.2. Interpreter Optimization Techniques

- When the intermediate opcode also contains the literal operand of the instruction, one could provide tailored copies of the corresponding semantic routines. These routines can use a literal representation of the operand without the need for additional operand extraction or conversion instructions. However, in some cases, it might be advantageous *not* to follow this general technique. For example, in M-code, the intermediate instruction LI 5 is represented by the byte 05H. The fetch phase thus leaves *the operand itself* in a processor register. Using this register is faster than reading the operand as a literal, and only one semantic routine should be provided for an entire class of similar instructions.

Code reorganization of the mapping instructions. In a naive implementation of an interpreter, the mapping instructions are centralized in one location. These instructions end with the *decoding jump* to the proper semantic routine. Each semantic routine ends with a jump back to the mapping instructions. Thus two jump instructions are associated with the execution of an intermediate instruction. On processor architectures without suitable handling of jumps, the frequent flushings of the instruction prefetch pipeline can cause significant overhead.

Since on most processors the mapping instructions take only a few instructions, it is quite feasible to *end each semantic routine with them*, rather than keeping them central. This will eliminate one jump from the interpretive overhead. Obviously, replicating the mapping instructions a number of times increases the size of the interpreter. In view of the values obtained for the interpretive overhead, one can expect a growth by a factor of around 2, which still keeps the interpreter size modest. Figure 3.4 illustrates the gain obtained by coding the fetch/decode routines in-line in some 8086-based threaded code interpreters executing the FORTH version of the Sieve benchmark.

This figure also provides some information on the effect of keeping word entries (pointers) aligned on word boundaries. In pointer-based encodings, word alignment affects the entire intermediate program representation. In tokenized versions, alignment only affects the token translation tables. The combined effect of in-line mapping and pointer alignment yields a speedup of up to 29% for direct threaded code, but only of 16% for indirect token threaded code. The latter comes as no surprise, in view of the complexity of the mapping actions for indirect threaded code.

3.2.3 Bridging the architectural gap

As observed in the previous section, intermediate architectures are often biased towards easy compilation (M-code). Stack machines are preferred target architectures, or may already be implied by the language itself (FORTH, ASYST). In other cases, the intermediate architecture reflects an unusual computational model (e.g.,

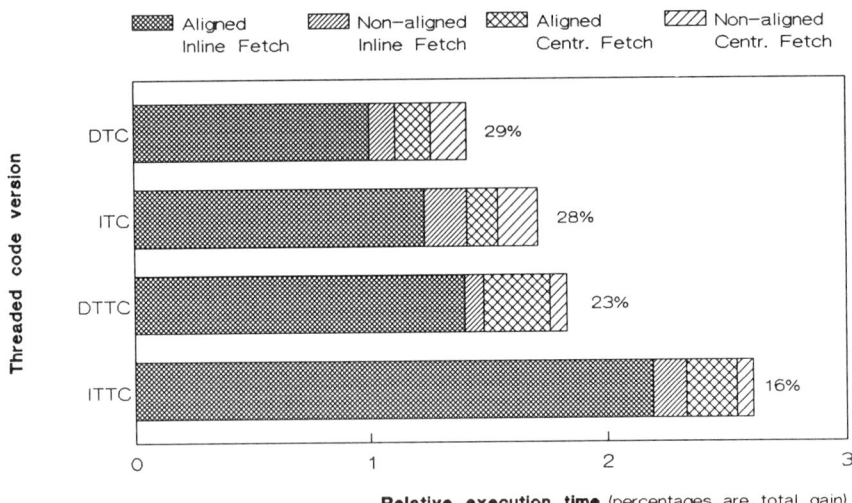

Figure 3.4
The effect of in-line mapping instructions and pointer alignment in i8086 threaded code FORTH implementations

S-expressions in Lispkit LISP). Contemporary general purpose microprocessors are neither pure stack machines, nor list processing engines. The resulting architectural gap must be bridged dynamically, i.e., at run time. Furthermore, the choice of an intermediate architecture often precludes code optimization techniques used on the host architecture. The resulting interpretive slowdown cannot be eliminated through a clever use of interpretive techniques.

Nevertheless, some gain can be achieved by an intelligent bridging of the architectural gap between the intermediate and host architectures. The techniques we are about to describe concern the mapping of a stack architecture onto a register architecture, the exploitation of parallelism on the host architecture, and the synergy between caches and interpreters.

Top of stack optimization. In a naive implementation of a stack machine architecture on a register machine, the intermediate stack is mapped onto host memory. When done properly, the intermediate PUSH and POP instructions are mapped on

3.2. Interpreter Optimization Techniques

appropriate native host instructions, e.g., the native PUSH and POP instructions. Operations involve the top element(s) of the stack. In order to perform these operations, the host machine must transfer these operands to processor registers, perform the operations, and write the result back to the top of the stack. For example, the intermediate ADD instruction in the FORTH interpreter of Chapter 2 is executed as follows:

```
POP   AX
POP   BX
ADD   AX,BX
PUSH  AX
```

It is clear that this mode of operation not only causes a steep increase of the number of data transfers between the host and its stack memory, but also in the number of semantic instructions that must be executed. These transfers and instructions are simply not present in well-optimized native code.

Measurements of the behavior of stack machines [Blom87,Stal88] indicate that the short term stack depth variations are predominantly shallow. One can characterize the stack depth variation by the lengths of the successive uninterrupted sequences ('runs') of depth increases or decreases. Sequences that modify the stack depth by more than 3 units are rare. Figure 3.5 shows the statistics of the stack depth variation observed in a collection of interpreted MODULA-2 programs. This collection contains both computationally intensive programs and control-intensive programs. The resulting statistics are rather insensitive to the kind of program that is executed.

The shallowness of the stack depth variations suggests that a significant reduction of the data transfers (and the associated instructions) between the stack top and the host registers can be obtained by keeping the top stack elements in *just a few* processor registers. Data are only transferred to and from memory when the processor registers are all occupied or empty, respectively. This technique has been used extensively in hardware stack machines such as the HP3000, and is also used on modern RISCs like the Am29000.

The problem with software interpreters is that the exploitation of this technique requires the runtime management of data flow to and from the external memory. At all times, the interpreter must know in which register the stack top resides, or, equivalently, how many registers are occupied. Let us call this information the *stack state*. With one register, there are only two states: *occupied* and *free*. With n registers, up to 2^n states of occupation are possible; one can limit this number to $n+1$ provided that the registers are ordered such that the occupation of a register implies the occupation of all lower registers. For example, when three registers R_1, R_2, R_3 are used and the occupation of a register is denoted by 1, the four stack states are $000, 100, 110, 111$.

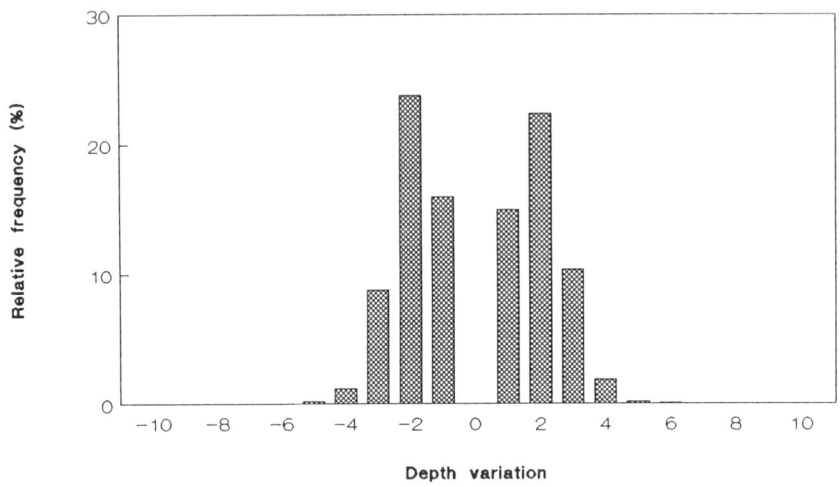

Figure 3.5
Statistics of the depth variations of the M-machine expression stack

The actual instructions to be executed obviously depend on the stack state. Furthermore, the stack state must be maintained by the interpreter. When the use and maintenance of the stack state is done by additional explicit machine instructions, an additional slowdown is incurred which might wipe out the potential gain achieved by the optimization. A technique is needed to use and update the stack state preferably *without* executing additional instructions.

One clever way of doing this is to keep the stack state *in the program counter of the host*. That is, at each point in the interpreter one assumes a certain state of the stack, and codes the semantic routines accordingly. Of course, one can no longer use a single central fetch/decoding routine, since jumping to it would erase all information concerning the stack state. At least as many copies of the fetch/decoding routine are required as there are stack states. At the entry of a semantic routine, the stack state is known. The semantic routine itself modifies the stack state in a predefined way. Thus, the stack state at the exit of the semantic routine is known, and the appropriate fetch routine can be selected, either by jumping to it or by coding it in-line.

Because of the duplication of the semantic routines and the mapping actions with their associated dispatching tables, the size of the interpreter grows dramatically.

3.2. Interpreter Optimization Techniques

To implement a one register optimization the size doubles, for a two-register optimization it triples. However, things are not as bad as they appear at first sight. In the first place, some situations cannot occur during the execution of a correct intermediate program. For example, in the M-machine, before the start of a FOR loop, the state of the expression stack is always known: it only contains the loop parameters, and these were loaded onto an empty stack. In this case, only one semantic routine is needed. Secondly, for a large fraction of the intermediate instructions, code may be shared without the introduction of jump or other instructions. For example, the semantic routine for a given intermediate instruction corresponding to the state 'top of stack in memory' is equal to that corresponding to the state 'top of stack in register', preceded by an instruction moving the stack top into the register.

Note that the technique of keeping the stack state in the program counter is also applicable in the absence of decoding tables. For example, in indirect threaded code, each primitive now starts with $n + 1$ pointers, one for each stack state. The memory indirect jump through the intermediate instruction uses an additional offset representing the stack state:

```
; Two-register top of stack optimization of i8086 ITC interpreter

; Registers are DX and CX, and are filled in this order.

; *************** mapping actions *************************


NEXT0:  LODSW               ; fetch phase for empty registers
        MOV     BX,AX
        JMP     [BX]

NEXT1:  LODSW               ; fetch phase for DX in use
        MOV     BX,AX
        JMP     [BX+2]

NEXT2:  LODSW               ; fetch phase for DX and CX in use
        MOV     BX,AX
        JMP     [BX+4]

; *************** some primitives ************************


; add   (n1 n2 -- n1+n2) , add top stack elements
```

```
ADD:    DW    ADD0
        DW    ADD1
        DW    ADD2
ADD0:   POP   DX           ; both registers empty, load DX
ADD1:   POP   CX           ; CX empty, load it
ADD2:   ADD   DX,CX        ; perform addition, result in DX
        JMP   NEXT1        ; may also code NEXT1 in-line

; litt ( -- n ), push literal on stack

LIT:    DW    LIT0
        DW    LIT1
        DW    LIT2
LIT0:   LODSW              ; load literal in AX
        MOV   DX,AX        ; transfer to DX
        JMP   NEXT1
LIT2:   PUSH  DX           ; both DX and CX full : free CX
        MOV   DX,CX
LIT1:   LODSW              ; CX free : load literal into CX
        MOV   CX,AX        ; now CX and DX are both in use
        JMP   NEXT2
```

The extra offset needed in the decoding jump causes a slight slowdown of the mapping actions, but this slowdown is largely compensated by the improved semantic actions. Observe the amount of code sharing possible between the semantic routines for different stack states.

In direct threaded code, top of stack optimization is also possible. It can be accomplished by using an extra literal offset in the register or memory indirect decoding jump. Since the jump directly leads to executable code, the offset used depends on the size of the semantic routines. In fact, no code sharing is possible, and the interpreter size increases linearly with n.

Figure 3.6 gives an idea of the speed gain achieved by this kind of top of stack optimization. Observe the strong reduction of the data traffic to and from the stack memory, as well as of the semantic execution time. The global speedup is rather modest.

Another kind of stack optimization, applicable to numeric coprocessors or numeric data processors (NDP), is *lazy operand fetching*. The idea is the following. Most NDPs allow both zero-address operations (stack machine) and one-address operations. That is, in order to compute the product **A*B**, the NDP can use the instructions

3.2. Interpreter Optimization Techniques

```
FLOAD A
FMUL  B
```

rather than the pure stack machine code

```
FLOAD A
FLOAD B
FMUL
```

The one-address sequence executes faster. This sequence of NDP operations can be generated dynamically from pure intermediate stack machine code by delaying the use of a floating point operand until it is actually needed. Only the *effective address* of the operand is evaluated and saved in a register:

```
intermediate   interpreter actions
code

PUSH A    -->  compute effective address of A and keep
               in register;
PUSH B    -->  issue FLOAD using register;
               compute effective address of B and keep
               in register;
MUL       -->  issue FMUL using register;
```

Note that this techniques does not use the NDP at all for simple assignments like `A:=B`. The assignment is reduced to a memory to memory move. Generalizations using several address registers are possible.

The exploitation of parallelism in the host. In contemporary microprocessor systems a variety of coprocessors can be used in the data path to speed up specific tasks. Examples are coprocessors speeding up numeric calculations (NDPs), graphics, memory management, and block data transfers. Such coprocessors are either activated by specific coprocessor instructions which appear in the CPU's native instruction stream, or by instructions explicitly executed by the CPU. Once activated, the coprocessor can proceed independently and in parallel with the CPU. Before the next coprocessor instruction can be issued, the CPU must verify whether the previous coprocessor operation has terminated. In the next chapter we shall give a more detailed description of the relation between the CPU and datapath coprocessors. Compiler-generated code seldom or poorly exploits the potential parallelism between the CPU and the coprocessor. This is due in part to the absence of useful instructions that could be performed by the CPU during the operation of the coprocessor because of data dependencies, but also in part to an inappropriate optimization level of the compiler. Now consider the case of interpretive execution.

Chapter 3. OPTIMIZING INTERPRETIVE EXECUTION

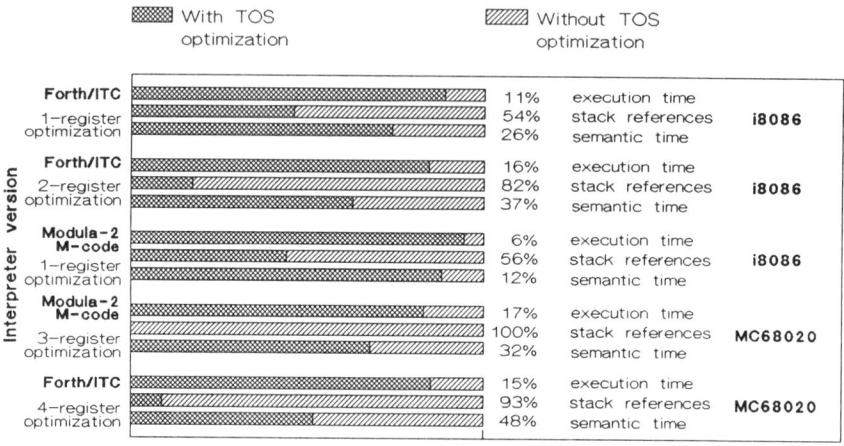

Figure 3.6
Improvements achieved by top of stack optimization

The coprocessor instructions are part of the semantic routines executing intermediate instructions. The result of the last coprocessor operation executed in a semantic routine will not be needed until the semantic routine of the next intermediate instruction is executed. This means that the mapping actions needed to locate the next semantic routine can be executed by the CPU without having to wait for the coprocessor. Truly parallel operation of the CPU and its coprocessor is possible in an interpretive environment. This parallelism can reduce the interpretive slowdown significantly. Figure 3.7 illustrates the idea by means of the interpretive execution of the following MODULA-2 program fragment

```
VAR a,b,c : REAL;

LOOP
    a:=(b*c)/(c-d)
END;
```

3.2. Interpreter Optimization Techniques

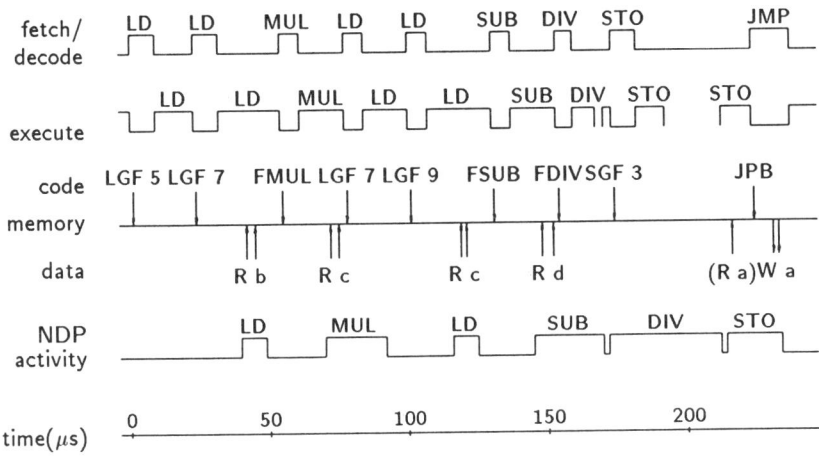

Figure 3.7
Parallel operation of CPU and NDP during interpretation

This fragment is compiled into the following M-code sequence[4]

```
0006 000D 011    LGF    005
0007 000F 011    LGF    007
0008 0011 09A    FMUL
0009 0012 011    LGF    007
000A 0014 011    LGF    009
000B 0016 099    FSUB
000B 0017 09B    FDIV
000C 0018 08C    SGF    003
000D 001A 01D    JPB    [00E] -> 000D
```

It can be seen from figure 3.7 that there is an effective degree of parallelism between the CPU and the NDP. The CPU has to wait for the NDP only at one point: after the division, before it can store the result in the variable **a**. One can also observe that the coprocessor is active during more than 60% of the time. This implies that the slowdown of the interpretive execution of this MODULA-2 fragment is less than 1.67 with respect to the best possible native code implementation.

A similar form of parallelism can be found in modern RISCs. These processors

---

[4] the example does not quite use Wirth's definition of M-code. In order to allow an efficient utilization of a numerical coprocessor, the authors have extended M-code with specific LGF and SGF instructions to load and store real operands, instead of using the corresponding operations for double-word operands.

are strongly pipelined. In order to avoid frequent breaks in the pipeline traffic, a technique called delayed branch is used, which allows the further use of the current pipeline contents until the new instructions or data are present. Optimizing compilers for RISCs exploit these properties to a large degree. Since interpreters are hand coded, they can exploit this microscopic form of parallelism even better.

We now give a few examples of the exploitation of microscopic RISC parallelism. The examples are based on the Am29000 RISC.

- overlapped memory references Reading or writing off-chip memory takes more than one pipeline stage delay. It pays to follow a memory-reference instruction by instructions that do not depend on the data being read from external memory. Interpreters offer numerous occasions to do this.

- delayed branch In microprocessors with delayed branching, the instruction *following* the jump instruction is executed, whether or not the jump is taken. If no useful instruction can be found to fill this delay slot a NOP must be inserted. Interpreters feature an abundance of jumps that can benefit from the delayed branch optimization.

- delayed effects of internal registers The manipulation of certain internal registers in pipelined systems delays the execution of instructions that explicitly or implicitly use these registers. Examples are the internal stack pointer and the processor status register in the Am29000. At least one clock must pass between the modification of the stack pointer and the accessibility of the top of stack element. Again, useful instructions must be inserted to minimize wasted clock cycles.

The above optimization techniques amount to reordering the instructions without changing the program semantics. An optimizing compiler can use a large scope in which instructions can be reordered. In general, the scope extends over sequences of instructions free of jumps (or calls), e.g. the body of a loop. In the case of an interpreter, the optimization scope is limited to a semantic routine and the fetch/decode routine immediately following it. This suggests that the gains achievable by reordering instructions is relatively small in interpreters. On the other hand, the code generator is a human expert who, most likely, can go further in the optimization process. The following code fragment from an Am29000 M-code interpreter illustrates how the instructions of a semantic routine and the subsequent fetch/decode routine can be completely intertwined. The fetch/decode instructions are marked with an asterisk. Note that intertwining is impossible with intermediate jumps.

```
;NOTE:     Register use    M-machine registers are referred to
;                          by their proper name
```

3.2. Interpreter Optimization Techniques

```
;                       lr01 : top of stack element
;                       SP : expression stack pointer (gr1)
;                       gr46 contains base address of dispatching
;                       table/4 (long word addresses)
;
; Load 0 on expression stack
;
LI0:    load    byte,gr50,VPC       ; * load next M-code
        add     SP,SP,4             ;   update stack pointer
        exbyte  gr50,gr50,gr46      ; * extract M-code from word
        sll     gr6c,gr50,2         ; * convert to byte index
        load    word,gr66,gr6c      ; * load address from table
        add     lr01,gr68,0         ;   load 0 on stack
        jmpi    gr66                ; * jump to address
        add     VPC,VPC,1           ; * update VPC
;
;load local word #4 on expression stack
;
LLW4:   load    byte,gr50,VPC       ; * load next M-code
        add     SP,SP,4             ;   update stack pointer
        add     gr63,L,4<<2         ;   compute operand address
        exbyte  gr50,gr50,gr46      ; * extract M-code from word
        load    word,lr01,gr63      ;   get operand
        sll     gr6c,gr50,2         ; * convert to byte index
        load    word,gr66,gr6c      ; * load address from table
        jmpi    gr66                ; * jump to address
        add     VPC,VPC,1           ; * update VPC
;
; jump backward unconditionally
;
JPB:    load    byte,gr61,VPC       ;   load jump offset
        exbyte  gr61,gr61,gr68      ;   extract from word
        sub     VPC,VPC,gr61        ;   perform jmp
```

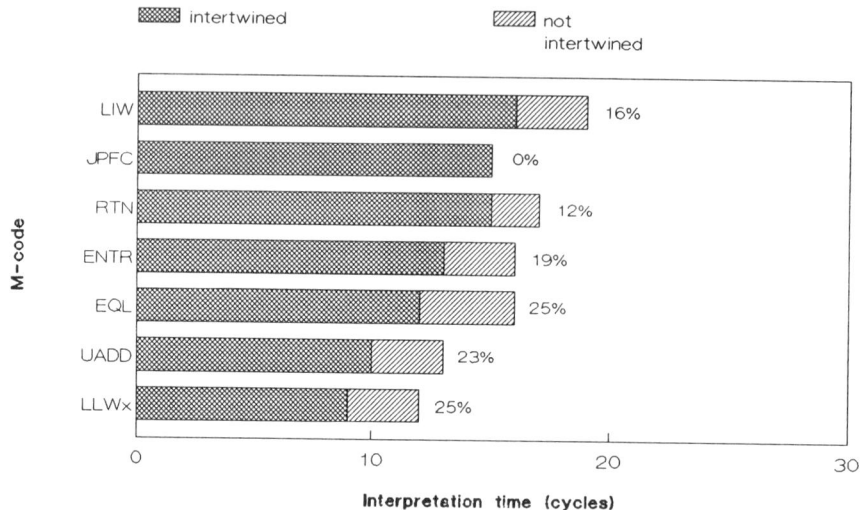

Figure 3.8
Speedup obtained by intertwining the semantic and fetch/decode operations for some M-codes on the Am29000 processor

```
              load    byte,gr50,VPC       ; * load next M-code
              exbyte  gr50,gr50,gr46      ; * extract M-code from
      word
              sll     gr6c,gr50,2         ; * convert to byte index

              load    word,gr66,gr6c      ; * load address from
      table
              jmpi    gr66                ; * jump to address
              add     VPC,VPC,1           ; * update VPC
```

The speedup obtained by the exploitation of microscopic parallelism on the Am29000 is shown in fig. 3.8.

Interpretation and caches. The advantage of an instruction cache depends on its hitrate, which, in turn, depends heavily on the locality of the program. Instruction sequences containing small loops typically exhibit a high locality. The body of a small loop can be kept in cache, and the CPU can execute with a 100%

hit rate. The hit rate drops sharply when the cache size is too small to hold the entire working set of the program. With respect to the instruction cache, only the size and locality of the *interpreter* are relevant, not the locality of intermediate program. When the interpreter does not fit entirely in the cache, the hitrate of interpretive execution may be smaller than that of native execution. For example, consider a FOR-loop of size 40 bytes. The corresponding intermediate program may take only 10 bytes, but the corresponding number of interpreter instructions may have a size of well over 200 bytes. For a small cache, this results in a lower cache effectiveness. In this case it may be better to 'train' the cache with the most frequently used instruction sequences of the interpreter, e.g. the fetch/decode and semantic routines of the most frequent intermediate instructions. The instruction cache can be frozen after the training sequence.

Data caches can also be used to reduce the bus occupation caused by intermediate code accesses. Even small caches can have a dramatic effect on the residual intermediate instruction rate. There are two reasons for this:

- In the case of a tokenized intermediate representation, several intermediate instructions fit into one machine word. Even without the use of a cache it is possible to fetch one wordful of intermediate instructions, and keep them in a processor register until they have all been executed. However, the extra instructions needed to manage this software caching process might make the approach useless. A true hardware cache provides this function automatically. When interpreting an 8-bit token representation on a 32-bit architecture, this form of grouped access alone reduces the number of code accesses by a factor of 4.

- Intermediate representations, in particular tokenized representations, are compact. This results in high hit rates, even for very small caches. In this respect, Fig. 3.9 shows the simulated hit rate of a few M-code programs. In this figure, appl3 and appl4 refer to applications that make heavy use of subroutines (in fact, appl3 is the M-code compiler itself). The other traces appl1 and appl2 were taken from a real-time control application. It turns out that, even with caches as small as 16 words, hit rates of over 80% can be achieved. The high initial hit rates of 50% to 70% are caused by the grouped access of M-code bytes.

3.3 Conclusion

In this chapter we have looked into the possibilities of improving the interpretive process by using clever programming techniques. Several techniques have been identified which can lead to faster interpreters: raising the semantic level of the

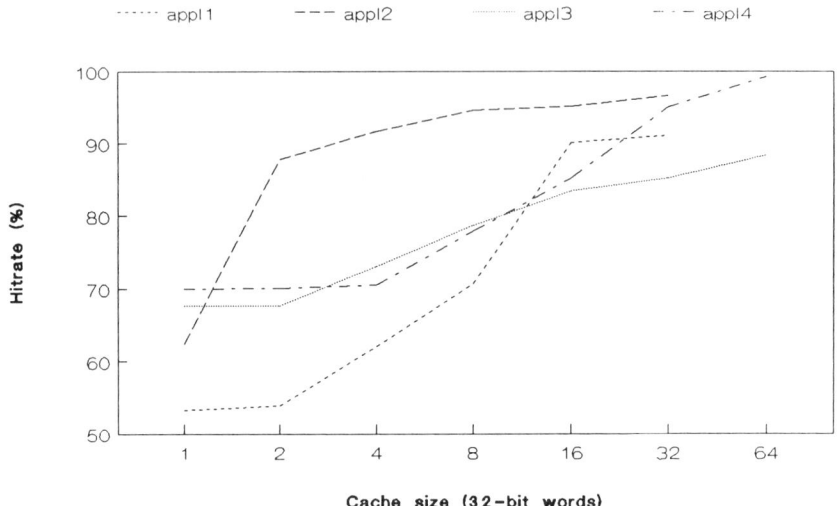

Figure 3.9
The effectiveness of a small M-code cache

primitives, reducing the interpretive overhead by optimizing the mapping actions, using registers for top of stack optimization, and exploiting various forms of microscopic parallelism available in today's microprocessors. A combination of these optimization techniques applied to an i8086-based M-code interpreter has yielded a speed improvement by a factor[5] of 2; the Laxen & Perry V2.1.0 FORTH interpreter was improved by a factor of 1.6 on the Sieve benchmark.

Although such a gain is definitely worthwhile, it does not do away with the interpretive slowdown. Even after optimization, a considerable speed disparity is observed between the execution of programs compiled into native code, and programs compiled into interpreted intermediate code. In order to substantially reduce the interpretive overhead, while retaining the advantages of interpretation, the interpretive slowdown must be attacked at its very root: the mapping actions and the generic nature of the code. Pure programming techniques will not suffice; extra hardware might provide a solution. In the following chapter we shall elaborate on such an approach.

---

[5] This global speed improvement has been observed between the commercially available Modula Corporation M-code interpreter and the optimized LEM M-code interpreter written by the authors.

4 INTERPRETIVE COPROCESSORS

General purpose microprocessors owe much of their popularity to their excellent cost/performance ratio, which results from mass production. Microprocessors can be mass produced because they are universal components, that is, components by means of which *every* Turing solvable problem can be solved, provided a sufficient amount of memory (and time !) is available. A drawback of this general purpose nature is that, for *specific* tasks, microprocessors seldom offer the fastest possible solution. Almost always can a problem be solved faster using dedicated hardware. In some application fields, the use of *coprocessors* can circumvent the drawbacks associated with the general purpose nature of microprocessors. Perhaps the most widely known application of dedicated coprocessors is the acceleration of floating point computations, using numeric data processors (NDPs). Other examples of coprocessor applications are the support of bitmap manipulations on graphics displays, communications, intelligent I/O and bulk data transfers using direct memory access (DMA). Sometimes, memory management chips are also called coprocessors. Coprocessors can be an extremely cost-effective addition to a microprocessor system. For example, an NDP such as the i8087 speeds up individual floating point operations by a factor that ranges between 75 and 540. Although the global speedup of an application obviously depends on the intensity of the use of the coprocessor, one can say that computationally intensive programs are accelerated by an order of magnitude. Note that an NDP typically costs less than about one-tenth of the entire microprocessor system.

In this chapter we look into the possibility of accelerating the interpretive process by means of coprocessors. It turns out that it is indeed possible to speed up interpretation significantly with the addition of only a very modest amount of hardware. However, the relationship between the interpretive coprocessor and the CPU differs strongly from what is found in traditional coprocessors: the interpretive coprocessor is active in the instruction path, rather than in the data path. For that reason, we also call interpretive coprocessors *instruction path coprocessors*. Before we discuss the concept of instruction path coprocessors, we shall briefly describe the relationship between traditional coprocessors and the CPU. We proceed with the presentation of two concrete instruction path coprocessor prototypes, and end the chapter with an analysis of their performance.

4.1 Data Path Coprocessors

During the evolution of microprocessor systems, several of the above operations have become eligible for speedup using dedicated hardware. To be eligible, an operation must satisfy a few criteria:

1. the operation must be time-consuming on general purpose machines;

2. it must occur frequently, so that the total time spent on this kind of operation is a large fraction of the total execution time;

3. it must allow significant speedup by means of relatively simple hardware.

To some extent, the operations mentioned above satisfy these criteria, although coprocessors are not always simple. For example, the i8087 NDP contains approximately 100,000 transistors, whereas the i8086 CPU only has some 30,000. This large complexity is justified by the large speedup that can be obtained.

In this monograph we shall use the term *coprocessor* to designate a chip (or part of it) that is very tightly coupled to the CPU, and that speeds up a particular part of the task executed by the microprocessor system. Concurrent operation between the coprocessor and the CPU is not necessary, although it is useful to obtain an additional speed gain. The coprocessor must use the same physical and logical environment as the CPU (same clock signal and bus protocol). This is a point of difference with peripheral units. We could say that, hierarchically, the coprocessor resides between the CPU and a peripheral unit. In a logical sense, the coprocessor depends on the CPU, not on a peripheral unit.

In the personal computer world, boards speeding up particular operations are also called coprocessors. In fact they are processing elements of a heterogeneous multiprocessor. We suggest to call them *slave processors, booster boards*, or *accelerator boards*. Peripheral control units act as an interface between the CPU and its I/O devices. In a strict sense we do not consider them coprocessors either.

4.1.1 A classification of coprocessor interfaces

In order to perform its task, a coprocessor must be fed with appropriate instructions, and must synchronize its operation with that of the CPU. The task of a coprocessor can be strongly intertwined with the task executed by the CPU. A typical example are floating point operations in a computationally intensive program. This strong dependence is reflected in the embedding of coprocessor instructions in the CPU instruction stream. Other coprocessor applications are much less tightly coupled with the CPU's task, and have a separate, independent instruction stream.

Coprocessor activation schemes

We can distinguish among three major methods according to which the coprocessor obtains its instructions; they can be used to group coprocessors in the following classes:

1. Peripheral coprocessors;

2. Spying coprocessors;

4.1. Data Path Coprocessors

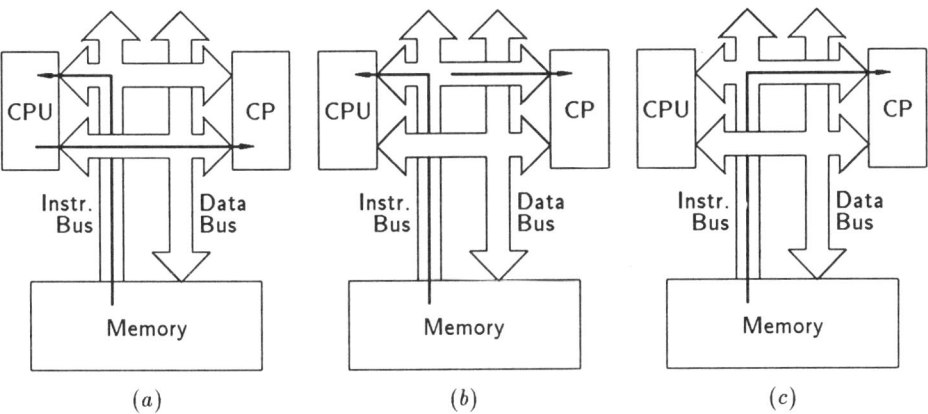

Figure 4.1
Instruction flow to data path coprocessors: (a) peripheral coprocessor; (b) spying coprocessor; (c) independent coprocessor

3. Independent coprocessors.

We shall now describe each of them briefly.

Peripheral coprocessors. Typical examples of this class are Motorola's numerical coprocessor MC68881, and Intel's DMA coprocessor i8237. A peripheral coprocessor acts as a slave of the CPU: Fig. 4.1(a). In order to pass instructions and parameters to a peripheral coprocessor, the CPU executes a sequence of data transfers to the memory, I/O, or coprocessor space. The last transfer of a sequence typically contains an activation command to start the coprocessor. There are two common procedures to accomplish such data transfers: through a sequence of explicit CPU instructions, as with the Intel 8237 DMA controller, or through a single specialized CPU instruction resulting in a complex dialog with the coprocessor, as with the MC68881. In the first case it is the responsibility of the user (programmer or software library) to correctly activate the coprocessor, while in the latter case the manufacturer has implemented the programming and activation sequence in microcode once and for all. Note that only the first method is used in RISCs.

Spying coprocessors. The peripheral coprocessor MC68881 is activated through the explicit execution of a single instruction by the CPU. This process can be accelerated if the coprocessor reacts on the mere *fetching* of this instruction by the CPU: Fig. 4.1(b). This method is implemented by Intel's numerical coprocessor i8087, which eavesdrops on the instruction fetches of the i8086 CPU. Whenever the fetched instruction starts with the specific ESC bit pattern, the coprocessor starts the corresponding execution immediately without further intervention of the CPU. The CPU itself ignores the ESC instruction, performs the effective address calculation of the operand (if any), reads the first word of the operand, and moves on to the next instruction. The coprocessor grabs the effective operand address computed by the CPU and, if needed, also the first word of the operand. Any further data transfers are executed by the coprocessor in an autonomous way.

Independent coprocessors. The two above coprocessor types obtain their instructions through an intervention of the CPU. The third type of coprocessor, shown in Fig. 4.1(c), is independent of the CPU. It is responsible for its own instruction fetches. These instructions may reside in the CPU's memory space, or in a separate memory space. Only in the first case is the memory bus shared, which requires provisions for bus arbitration. Independent coprocessors are suited for the simultaneous execution of loosely coupled tasks. This closely resembles true shared-memory multiprocessing. However, only one environment (memory, control logic) is shared by both processors. The Intel i8089 is a typical independent DMA I/O coprocessor.

Coprocessor Synchronization

So far, we have analyzed how the coprocessor obtains its instructions. The synchronization between the CPU and its coprocessor is equally important. There are two synchronization epochs: one at the beginning of the coprocessor activity, and one at the end.

The coprocessor has to know when to become active. For the first two coprocessor types this is very easy. The coprocessor is triggered by a transfer executed by the CPU. In the case of independent coprocessors it is slightly more involved: there are two processors, and two separate instruction streams. The CPU can signal the coprocessor by means of a data transfer to shared memory. This data transfer is distinct from the transfers needed to initialize the coprocessor. Once the coprocessor has finished its task, it can notify the CPU in three ways:

1. it can modify one of its status registers polled by the CPU;

2. it can modify the level on an output line directly observed by the CPU;

3. it may interrupt the CPU.

Polling of registers. A common way to synchronize the CPU and its coprocessor is to reserve a register in coprocessor space through which the status of the coprocessor can be observed. After activation of the coprocessor, the microprocessor repeatedly polls this register to determine the termination of the coprocessor operation. This mechanism thus requires that one or more data transfers be executed by the CPU. Again, these transfers can be the result of a sequence of separate CPU instructions, or part of a single CPU instruction.

Observing a dedicated output signal. While polling a coprocessor status register, the system memory bus is needed to execute the data transfers. This may cause bus contention when other devices need the bus (e.g. DMA controllers), and the polling period is limited to the bus cycle time. If the coprocessor has a dedicated status output signal, which can be observed by the CPU through a corresponding input signal, no bus cycles are required. The bus remains free, and polling can be done at a much higher rate. This is the case with the i8086/8087 configuration. When executing the WAIT instruction, the i8086 samples its TEST line which is connected to the BUSY line of the i8087.

Using interrupts. In both previous techniques, the CPU is directly involved in the detection of termination. This works fine when the coprocessor operations execute relatively quickly, i.e., in the time span needed to execute a few CPU instructions. In the case of time-consuming coprocessor instructions it is more efficient to allow the CPU to work concurrently. This is possible if synchronization is done by means of an interrupt. Now, the coprocessor must actively signal its termination by interrupting the CPU. The latter enters an interrupt handler which spells out the appropriate actions. This way of synchronization is commonly used with DMA coprocessors. A DMA operation may involve large amounts of data; the transfer speed often depends on an external device.

Although, in principle, any of the above activation methods can be combined with any of the synchronization methods, not all combinations occur in practice. The following combinations are commonly found: CPUs polling registers of peripheral coprocessors, CPUs testing hardware signals of spying coprocessors, and independent coprocessors signaling their termination by means of an interrupt.

4.2 Instruction Path Coprocessors: the Concept

The coprocessors described in the previous section are all located in the *datapath* of the CPU. By this we mean that the coprocessor helps *executing* instructions; it is of no assistance in obtaining instructions from memory, or decoding them. As we saw in the previous chapters, low-level interpretive systems devote the larger part of their execution time to the mapping of intermediate instructions. Each of the instructions constituting the mapping actions is simple, and can be executed by the CPU very quickly. Having these instructions executed by a traditional datapath coprocessor would not provide significant acceleration, since the communication between the CPU and the coprocessor is relatively slow. Consequently, another type of coprocessor support must be envisaged. This coprocessor must assist the CPU in executing the time-consuming intermediate instruction mapping actions. The result of the mapping actions, the identification of the semantic instructions to be executed, must be communicated to the CPU. The time scale on which all this must happen is smaller than the time scale used with traditional NDPs. Other methods for communication and synchronization are called for.

In order to fix ideas, let us again look at the operations required to execute the mapping actions.

The fetch operations. The time spent on acquiring the next intermediate instruction depends on the intermediate program representation. In Chapter 2, we have identified the following representation forms:

- **Sequential representations.** This is the case with most 'traditional' intermediate representations like P-code or M-code, or even languages like BASIC. It is also the simplest case. It suffices to read the memory contents pointed to by a virtual program counter. After incrementing the program counter, a new instruction can be fetched. Transfers of control are executed by reloading the virtual program counter, i.e., they are executed in the data path.

- **Threaded representations.** Threaded code is predominantly sequential, and thus offers the same difficulties as sequential representations. The uniformity of the representation simplifies the fetch operations when transfers of control are performed at the intermediate level, such as calls or jumps. Indirect threaded representations require many memory-indirect accesses.

- **Linked representations.** The intermediate instructions are elements of a linked list, and need not be placed contiguously in memory. This is the case with, for example, SECD-code. In this case one or more memory references are required to acquire an intermediate instruction, and to update the virtual program counter. Memory-indirect accesses are used frequently.

The decoding operations. The complexity of the decoding actions depends on the encoding of the intermediate instructions. We have identified two true intermediate representations:

- **Pointer-based representations.** The intermediate instruction takes the form of a machine address. This address is the indirect or direct address of the corresponding semantic routine. The decoding time is minimal, but the representation is somewhat wasteful.

- **Tokenized representations.** The instructions are tokens, i.e., highly compact encodings of the names of intermediate instructions. A translation is

4.2. Instruction Path Coprocessors: the Concept

necessary to obtain the start address of the semantic routine. Usually this is done by reading the contents of a dispatching table indexed by the token.

Decoding an intermediate instruction can be done either totally independent of the state of execution (context), or depending on it. When using the intermediate instruction as the effective address of the semantic routine, or when using only one dispatching table solely indexed with the instruction token, the decoding is independent of the context. On the other hand, the top of stack optimization technique analyzed in the previous chapter requires a decoding dependent on the stack state.

Another example of context-dependent decoding is the decoding of long instruction words, for instance when variable length bitstreams are used such as Huffman coding. Multiple decoding steps are needed to decode the entire instruction, each using a different decoding context.

In the top of stack optimization and variable length cases, the number of states is bounded: a finite state machine suffices to maintain the decoding state. One can easily think of program representations in which the decoding process actually needs a stack machine.

The more complex any of these suboperations is, the more it is justified to support it by hardware. In our discussion we will concentrate on simple intermediate representations. Therefore, we shall try to support the entire fetch/decode process. A first step in this direction is the *prefetch engine*.

4.2.1 The prefetch engine

Prefetch queues are used in microprocessors to decouple the native instruction fetch, decoding and execution. This technique can also be applied when fetching intermediate instructions. The prefetch unit contains the virtual program counter, and fetches intermediate instructions concurrently with the execution of the CPU. When the CPU starts the execution of an intermediate instruction, it obtains this intermediate instruction from a memory mapped register in the prefetch engine.

For complex fetch processes, a simple prefetch engine can significantly reduce the fetch-time compared to its software equivalent. However, for simple fetch processes the gain would not be significant: directly accessing the intermediate program takes as much time as accessing the prefetch engine, although some gain may result from the fact that a CPU register is freed. In such cases, it is worthwhile to also perform the decoding step in the prefetch engine. When the mapping time T_m is of the same order of magnitude as the semantic time T_s, such a coprocessor could at least double the execution speed. Note that now the prefetch engine must distinguish between intermediate opcodes and intermediate literal operands. Alternatively, it must present both the translated and raw intermediate bit patterns to the CPU. By context, the latter can distinguish between instructions and literals, and can select the proper prefetch engine register. The prefetch engine is simple; yet, it can yield a considerable speedup. Internally, it contains the following components:

1. A fetching subunit, consisting of bus arbitration logic, an address register VPC, an input data register, a memory control signal generator;

2. A decoding subunit, consisting of a decoding table that contains the start addresses of the interpreter routines, a table lookup mechanism, and either a primitive parser of intermediate instructions to determine their lengths and numbers of operands, or an additional direct output path always bypassing the table lookup;

3. An output register AR or output queue to hold the starting addresses of the semantic routines, and possibly a second output register LR to pass untranslated bit patterns.

Fig. 4.2 shows a possible configuration of a prefetch engine in a microprocessor environment. After initialization of its intermediate program counter VPC, the engine fetches intermediate instruction bytes, decodes them internally and outputs the start address of the corresponding interpreter routine to the address register AR which is memory-mapped in the CPU address space. Untranslated intermediate bit patterns are simultaneously output to the literal register LR. During the interpretation process, the CPU accesses the corresponding interpreter routine by executing the memory-indirect jump JMP [AR] through the coprocessor register AR. A semantic routine needing a literal obtains it from the memory-mapped LR register. Emptying either the AR or LR register will cause additional fetches to be executed. A write operation to the VPC register, i.e., an intermediate jump, will flush the current contents of the AR and LR registers. The communication between the CPU and the prefetch engine is done by means of shared memory; their synchronization rests on the basic synchronization mechanism between the CPU and memory. This means that reading an empty AR register will simply block the CPU.

We can immediately identify a few prominent features of the prefetch engine:

- The prefetch engine autonomously fetches intermediate instructions; to do so it behaves like a DMA device.

- The prefetch engine decodes the fetched instructions and determines the starting address of the corresponding interpreter routine. When communicating its result to the CPU, it behaves like a passive data memory.

- The total fetch/decoding overhead has been reduced to a memory indirect jump. For microprocessors with a large jump penalization the speed gain achieved may be relatively small. In the case of direct threaded code the

4.2. Instruction Path Coprocessors: the Concept

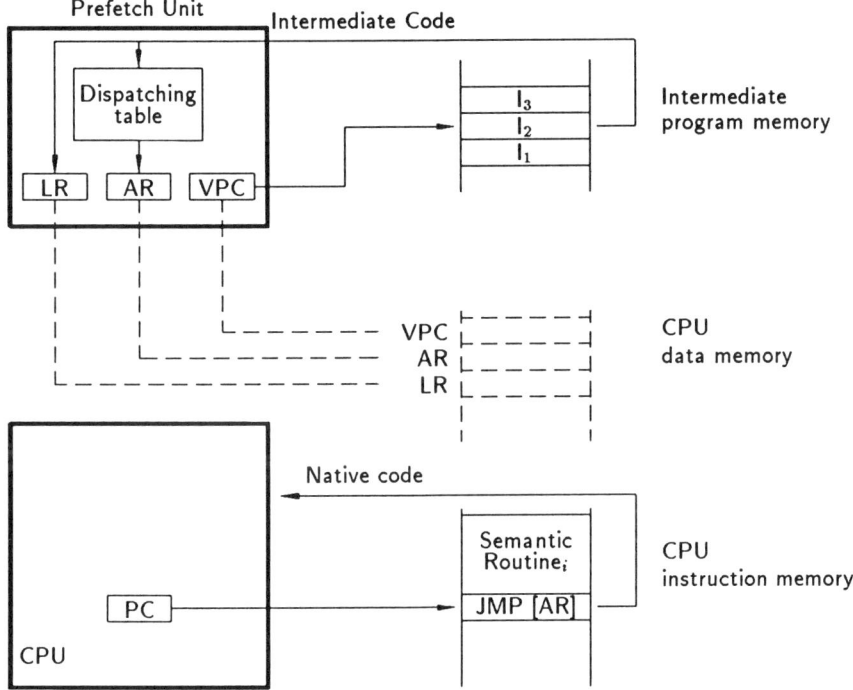

Figure 4.2
The instruction flow and data flow in a prefetch engine type interpretive coprocessor

decoding process is minimal and the speedup caused by the prefetch engine is restricted to the concurrent retrieval of intermediate instructions.

- The prefetch engine only provides the starting addresses of the semantic routines. The latter remain largely generic in nature. For example, literal operands in the intermediate instruction stream must still be fetched by instructions in the semantic routines. The only difference with software interpretation is that the literals now must be fetched from the prefetch engine.

Note that the prefetch engine is still located in the data path. The memory indirect jump through the prefetch engine output register transfers the information from the data path to the instruction path; this jump is excited by the CPU.

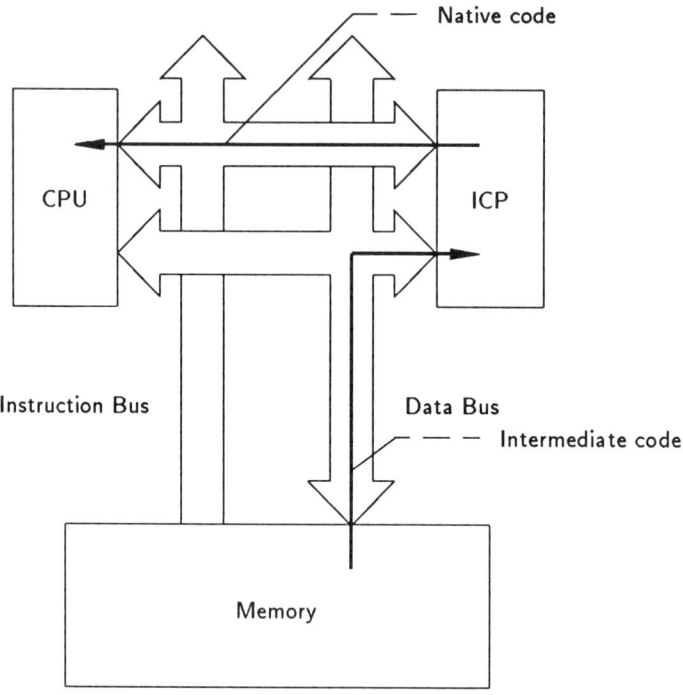

Figure 4.3
The instruction flow in a true instruction path coprocessor

4.2.2 A true instruction path coprocessor

In a next step we try to eliminate also the memory indirect jumps, and to truly locate the coprocessor in the CPU instruction path. The resulting instruction path coprocessor performs the same operations as the prefetch engine. In addition, it also generates the *actual semantic instruction sequences*, rather than just their starting addresses. Such an instruction-path coprocessor simultaneously behaves like a DMA device, fetching intermediate instructions, and like an *instruction* memory, generating machine instructions in response to the CPU's instruction fetch cycles. It is clear that such a coprocessor differs from conventional datapath coprocessors, in that it is located in the instruction path, between the actual (intermediate) instruction memory and the CPU. The communication between the CPU and the coprocessor is done implicitly, by means of instruction fetches, and the synchronization is based on the basic CPU/memory synchronization.

4.2. Instruction Path Coprocessors: the Concept

Figure 4.3 illustrates such a CPU/coprocessor configuration. One could say that the CPU behaves like a slave of the coprocessor: it simply executes the instructions handed over to it by the coprocessor. Alternatively one could say that the coprocessor is the slave, in fact performing a kind of on-demand dynamic native code generation based on intermediate instructions.

The instruction path coprocessor has some interesting properties which, at first sight, suggest a great potential:

- The dynamically generated code can be largely free of jump instructions, provided that the coprocessor can execute the jumps at the intermediate level.

- In addition to pasting together the semantic routines into a jump-free instruction stream, the instruction path coprocessor could embed literals appearing in the intermediate instruction stream into the generated native instruction stream. The instruction path coprocessor is in a position to perform these operations: it has access to the intermediate instruction stream, and it composes the native code stream. Therefore, it can merge intermediate literals with native machine code. The generated code is no longer generic in nature. To some extent, it is tailored towards the needs of the moment.

Hence, both the fetch/decode and literal passing overheads have been reduced to a minimal amount. A further reduction of the interpretation time is possible, for instance by using the top of stack optimization technique presented in the previous chapter. Further speedup would require a complex run-time optimization of the interpreter routines or more hardware support for semantic operations. The internal structure of a true instruction path coprocessor operating according to the above ideas is more complex than the simple prefetch engine, but it has much more potential. In addition to the resources already present in a prefetch engine, an instruction path coprocessor must contain:

- the actual code of the semantic routines, instead of just their starting addresses;

- a means to merge literals from the intermediate level into the native instruction stream;

- a native code queue to accumulate a sufficient number of generated native code bytes, instead of just one output register containing the starting address.

We shall now present two instruction path coprocessor prototypes that have actually been built and tested [VanC85,Deba86,Deba87,Deba88,VanC87]. In Section 4.4 we shall analyze some related issues more deeply.

4.3 Two Concrete Instruction Path Coprocessors

The instruction path coprocessor architectures we are about to present both operate in a standard i8086 microprocessor environment; in fact, they should fit in the standard Intel coprocessor environment. While it is true that this choice has some influence on the architectures of the coprocessors, we think that the principles illustrated by the examples are valid in a more general context. The prototypes of the instruction path coprocessors were realized using off the shelf standard TTL and MOS components, and were intended to explore the feasibility of instruction path coprocessing. Ease of implementation was deemed more important than obtaining an optimal result. One should therefore not consider either of the designs optimal or final.

4.3.1 An instruction path coprocessor for M-code

Structure. The M-code coprocessor consists of two main parts: the bus interface unit BIU, and the instruction synthesizing unit ISU (Fig. 4.4). Both units are connected by means of asynchronous queues: the intermediate code queue ICQ, and the native code queue NCQ.

The BIU contains the standard i8086 bus interfacing circuitry, enabling it to perform bus cycles autonomously. It contains the intermediate program counter AVPC, pointing to the next M-code to be fetched; and VPC, pointing past the M-code currently being executed. The AVPC register is used as a DMA address register. The structure of the ISU is very similar to a traditional microcoded architecture. The ISU consists of the following parts:

- a mapping memory, transforming the incoming M-code byte, concatenated with some internal status bits, into an internal starting address of the corresponding semantic routine;

- an instruction store IS, containing the code of the semantic routines, and a control store CS, containing internal control information. The control store bits can be looked upon as an extension of the corresponding instruction store byte;

- an instruction pointer IP, which simultaneously points into the internal instruction and control stores;

- a status register SR, holding status information obtained from the CPU;

- a byte-serial ALU, capable of performing simple unary operations such as ×2, ×4, padding, sign extension, etc.

- a control unit, which translates bit patterns from the control store into control signals for the other parts.

4.3. Two Concrete Instruction Path Coprocessors

Address	Operation	Effect
axxxxH	Fetch	obtain next native code instruction
axxx0H	Read	read contents of VPC
axxx0H	Write	Write contents of VPC and AVPC
axxx2H	Write	Write contents of SR
axxx4H	Write	Downloading operations
axxx6H	Write	Reset

Table 4.1
The M-code ICP viewed as a memory device. Note : a0000H is base address where coprocessor segment is located

External appearance and behavior. The M-code coprocessor presents itself in two ways to the i8086 CPU. The first way is as a memory device, consisting of one 64k byte segment of instruction memory, and a few registers which are memory-mapped in the i8086 address space. A memory map is shown in Table 4.1.

The second way in which the M-code coprocessor presents itself is as a DMA device, which can request the ownership of the system bus using the standard Request/Grant/Release protocol.

Operation. Both subunits of the M-code coprocessor work largely in parallel, although there are some points in time when a much closer interaction is necessary.

The BIU simultaneously observes the status of the intermediate code queue ICQ and the bus cycles issued by the i8086 CPU. When the CPU issues a fetch operation in the code segment axxxxH where the M-code coprocessor is mapped, a word from the native code queue NCQ is output to the bus. The BIU also intercepts accesses to the local registers of the coprocessor: the AVPC, VPC, and SR registers. Some of these accesses have complicated side effects which will be discussed later. When the BIU observes at least two empty byte locations in the ICQ, it will execute a DMA cycle so as to obtain the M-code byte pair pointed to by the AVPC register, which is then incremented by two. The bytes are put in the ICQ one by one. Fig. 4.5 shows a timing diagram of the fetch of an intermediate instruction byte pair.

The ISU observes the native code queue NCQ. As soon as a byte location is available, it will generate the next native instruction byte. This is done as follows. At the start of a new intermediate instruction, the M-code byte is obtained from the ICQ. This byte is appended to a number of bits which represent the internal state of the coprocessor. For example, these bits can encode the stack state when using top of stack optimization.

The output of the mapping memory is loaded into the instruction pointer IP. The instruction and control stores are accessed at the location pointed to by IP. If no special actions are coded in the control bits, the byte read from the instruction store

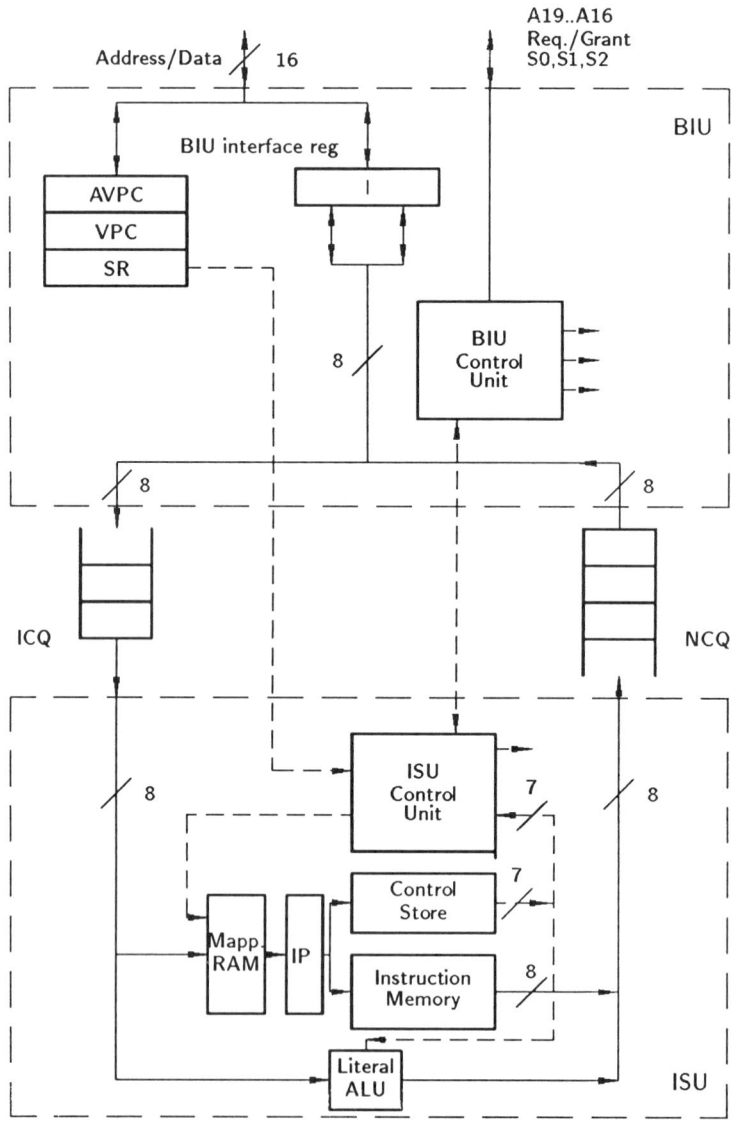

Figure 4.4
The architecture of an M-code instruction path coprocessor

4.3. Two Concrete Instruction Path Coprocessors

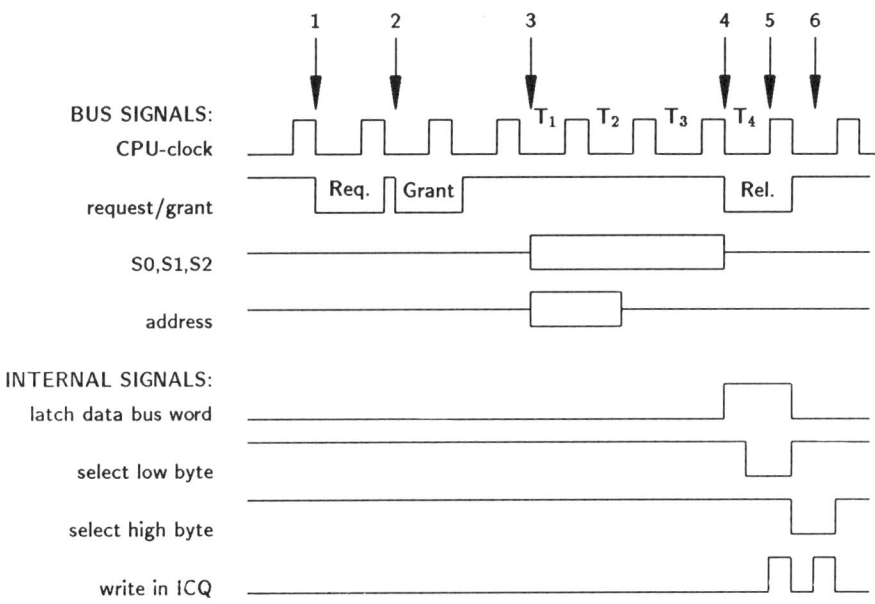

Figure 4.5
A timing trace of the DMA activity of an i8086 interpretive coprocessor: (1) the coprocessor requests the bus; (2) bus is granted; (3) DMA address is output; (4) data is read and bus released; (5) and (6) bytes are clocked internally

is output to the NCQ, and IP is incremented. Otherwise, special actions are carried out, such as the discarding of the (dummy) byte obtained from the instruction store, and replacing it by a byte computed by the ALU. In this way, literals can be extracted from the M-code stream, and can be embedded in the generated native code output stream. The dummy bytes in the instruction store are used as place holders, to allow the coding of the proper control bits in the corresponding control word. The place holder bytes also allow us to use a standard assembler to generate the contents of the instruction store. Note that, since the place holder bytes are discarded, they can be used as additional control bit patterns, e.g., as the operands for microcoded instructions from the control store. The control field has a width of seven bits; Table 4.2 provides a brief overview of the functions accomplished by these bits.

Group	Control Bits 6543210	Mnemonic	Operation
Main Control	0000xxx	GEN	generate code
	0001xxx	LIT	merge literal byte
	0010xxx	CPU	await register write by CPU
	0011xxx	EOS	end of sequence; reload IP
Literal ALU operations	000x000	Bx0	out=<abcdefgh>
(during LIT or GEN)	000x001	Bx2	out=<bcdefgh0>
ALU input =	000x010	Bx4	out=<cdefgh00>
<abcdefgh>	000x011	Cx0	out=<00000000>
Previous ALU input =	000x100	Cx2	out=<0000000A>
<ABCDEFGH>	000x101	Cx4	out=<000000AB>
	000x110	Wx2	out=<bcdefghA>
	000x111	Wx4	out=<cdefghAB>
Conditional jumps	0000000	JC	Local ICP jumps, similar
(only following CPU)	0010000	JP	to 8086 jumps.
	0100000	JA	Conditions are in SR register,
	0110000	JZ	target is in instruction store.
	0111000	JS	
	1000000	JNC	
	1010000	JNP	
	1100000	JNA	
	1110000	JNZ	
	1111000	JNS	
Next decoding state	0000xxx	Tmm	AX and NDP empty
(first CS byte in	0001xxx	T6m	TOS in AX
the sequence)	0010xxx	Tm7	AX empty, f.p. operand in NDP
	0011xxx	T67	TOS in AX, f.p. operand in NDP

Table 4.2
The microcode control bits in the M-code coprocessor

A few examples of the operation. From what has been explained above, the operation of the M-code coprocessor when executing non-jump intermediate instructions should be fairly obvious. Let us look at the execution of the following simple M-code example:

```
24          LLW4        ;load local word #4
12 00 01    LIW 100     ;load immediate value 100H
B8          UADD        ;unsigned addition
50 10       SGW 10      ;store result in global word #10H
```

4.3. Two Concrete Instruction Path Coprocessors

The contents of the coprocessor instruction and control stores IS and CS, relevant to the execution of these intermediate instructions are shown below. In this example, the AX register is used as the single top of stack optimization register. The expression stack of the M-machine extends into the native i8086 stack, all data is located in the DS segment, and the coprocessor registers are located in the CS segment. Local variables are indexed by SI (the L pointer), and global variables by BX (the G pointer).

```
M-code    CS      IS  8086 Instruction    Comments
------    --      --  ----------------    --------

LLW4mm:   T6m     8B  MOV AX,[SI+8]       ; T6m since AX will be full
          GEN     44
          GEN     08
          GEN     90  NOP                 ; padd to even length
          EOS     00                      ; next instruction

LIW6m:    T6m     50  PUSH AX             ; T6m since AX will be full
          GEN     B8  MOV AX,_WRD         ; _WRD is dummy operand
          GEN     90  NOP                 ; to prevent deadlock
          GEN     90  NOP                 ; with 8086
      LIT+Bx0     FF                      ; pass word literal
      LIT+Bx0     FF                      ; unchanged
          EOS     00                      ; next instruction

UADD6m:   T6m     5A  POP DX              ; T6m since AX will be full
          GEN     01  ADD AX,DX
          GEN     D0
          GEN     90  NOP                 ; padd to even length
          EOS     00                      ; next instruction

SGW6m:    Tmm     89  MOV [BX+_BYTx2],AX  ; Tmm since AX will be empty
          GEN     87                      ; _BYTx2 is dummy operand
      LIT+Bx2     FF                      ; pass literal x 2
      GEN+Cx2     01                      ; pass upper bits
          EOS     00                      ; next instruction
```

The execution of the intermediate code sequences results in the timing diagram shown in Figure 4.6. The total execution time amounts to 90 clock cycles; the software interpretation of the same sequence on the non-optimized Modula Corp.

interpreter takes 385 cycles; the speedup is more than 4.26. With respect to the well-optimized LEM interpreter, the speedup for this instruction sequence is 3.32. With a two-level top of stack optimization, the execution time of the above sequence would be 74 clocks, representing an additional speedup of 21%.

The execution of intermediate transfers of control is less efficient. Indeed, in the M-code coprocessor prototype presented here, transfers of control are preformed by the i8086 CPU, through a write operation to the VPC register, e.g.,

```
MOV CS:VPC,<target address>
```

As a result, the ICQ must be flushed. Since the CPU is *not* executing a native JMP or CALL instruction, its prefetch queue will not be flushed. Therefore, after having generated the MOV CS:VPS,<target address> instruction, one must be very careful to fill the NCQ either with useful instructions or harmless NOPs until the proper code can be generated for the intermediate instruction at <target address>. The internal coding of the intermediate unconditional relative jump JPF 02 is the following:

```
M-code   CS   IS  8086 Instruction    Comments
------   --   --  ----------------    --------
JPFmm:   Tmm  26  ADD CS:VPC,_BYT     ; Tmm since stack state unchanged
         GEN  81
         GEN  06
         GEN  00                      ; address of VPC
         GEN  00
      LIT+Bx0  FF                     ; low part is literal
         GEN  00                      ; high part of offset
         CPU  90  NOP                 ; wait till VPC written
         EOS  00                      ; next instruction
```

Its execution results in the timing diagram shown in Fig. 4.7.

Another problem which arises when programming the M-code coprocessor is the generation of machine instructions conditionally upon the status of the CPU. In some circumstances, this must be done for instance to compute the intermediate M-machine state, which resides on the stack after the execution of a relational operator. A similar problem exists with the execution of conditional intermediate jumps, or in the termination of a FOR loop. In a software interpreter this is accomplished through the use of conditional branches *in the interpreter semantic routines.*

However, a peculiar property of the coprocessor under consideration is that it totally ignores the contents of the i8086 CPU program counter. There is no relationship between the CPU program counter and the internal coprocessor instruction

4.3. Two Concrete Instruction Path Coprocessors

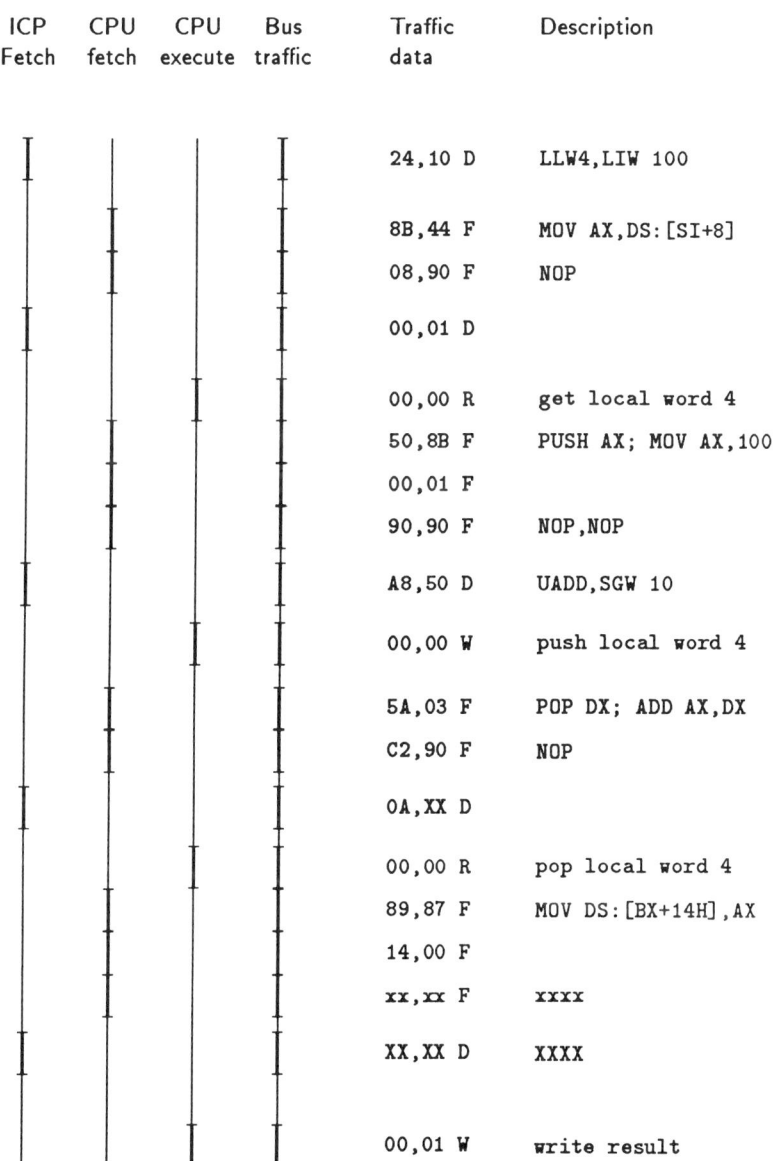

Figure 4.6
A timing trace of an instruction stream without transfers of control

144   Chapter 4. INTERPRETIVE COPROCESSORS

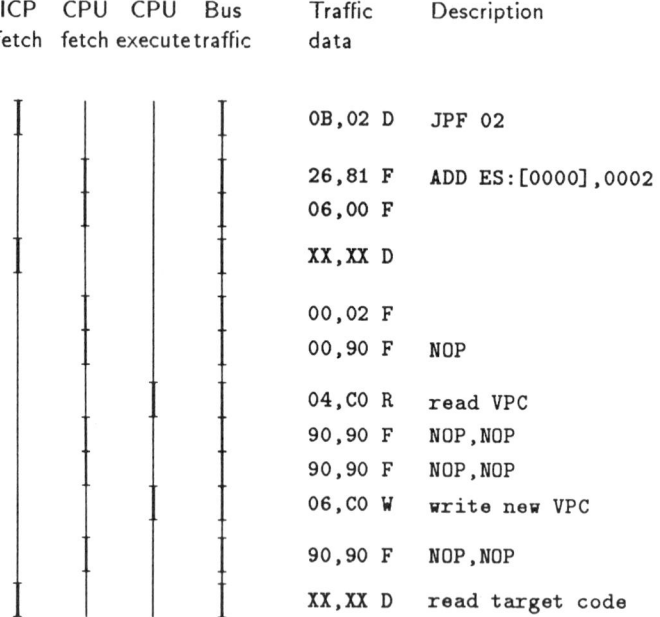

Figure 4.7
A timing trace of the execution of an intermediate unconditional transfer of control

pointer IP. As long as the i8086 code segment is mapped over the address range of the coprocessor, native code will be generated.

Generating a native jump to the CPU will only have as net effect that the instruction bytes generated immediately after the jump will *not* be executed, since the CPU flushes its prefetch queue. Thus in general, generating conditional jumps does not have the desired effect. When the generated code is free of jumps, the program counter increments and wraps around to 0 when reaching the offset 0FFFFH.

One way to solve this problem is to relegate the conditional generation of code entirely to the coprocessor. This is possible when the conditions involved are communicated to the coprocessor, which should now be equipped with a form of microcoded conditional jump. How this is done in the prototype is illustrated by the following example, which executes the intermediate code sequence

```
        C8      EQL             ; compare TOS elements & leave
                                ; result on stack
        1A 20   JPFC 020        ; take jump if condition false
```

4.3. Two Concrete Instruction Path Coprocessors   145

The internal coding of these instructions is as follows:

```
M-code   CS  IS  8086 Instruction    Comments
------   --  --  ---------------     --------
EQL6m:   T6m 5A  POP DX              ; AX will contain result
         GEN 39  CMP AX,DX           ; perform comparison
         GEN D0
         GEN 9F  LAHF                ; flags to AH
         GEN 26  MOV ES:SR,AH        ; send to ICP
         GEN 88
         GEN 26
         GEN 02                      ; address of SR
         CPU 00                      ; wait for SR written
         JNZ NE                      ; perform local jump
         GEN B8  MOV AX,1            ; TRUE=0001
         GEN 01
         GEN 00
         GEN 90  NOP                 ; padding
         EOS 00                      ; next instruction

NE:      GEN 31  XOR AX,AX           ; FALSE=0000
         GEN C0
         EOS 00                      ; next instruction

JPFC6m:
         Tmm 2E  MOV DX,CS:VPC       ; Tmm since AX will be empty
         GEN 8B                      ; read current value of VPC
         GEN 16                      ; (points at jump offset)
         GEN 00
         GEN 00
         GEN 03  ADD DX,AX           ; increment if jump not taken
         GEN D0
         GEN 48  DEC AX              ; jump taken if AX was 0000
         GEN 25  AND AX,_BYT         ; mask offset with AX
         LIT FF                      ; pass offset as literal
         GEN 00
         GEN 03  ADD AX,DX           ; compute new VPC
         GEN C2
         GEN 2E  MOV CS:VPC,AX       ; write new VPC
         GEN A3
         GEN 00                      ; address of VPC
```

```
            GEN 00
            CPU 90 NOP              ; pad & wait for VPC written
            EOS 00                  ; next instruction
```

As one can see, the code generated for **EQL** uses the status sent by the CPU, and performs a conditional local jump. The execution of these instructions results in the timing diagram shown in Fig. 4.8. It is clear that the speedup generated by the use of a coprocessor is significantly less than in the first example. Most of the delay is caused by the asynchronous nature of the coupling between the CPU and the coprocessor. There are some ways of reducing the negative impact of this coupling; a deeper analysis of the associated problems will be postponed till the next section.

4.3.2 An instruction path coprocessor for threaded code

The coprocessor for the execution of indirect threaded code programs was in fact designed as an extension to the M-code coprocessor. Consequently, both architectures are similar to some extent. In this section we shall only describe essential points of difference between the two approaches.

Architecture. A major point of difference between the architectures of the M-code coprocessor and the coprocessor for threaded code is that they must fetch different kinds of program representations. Indirect threaded code requires the access of two memory locations containing pointers before the first executable instruction of a semantic routine (primitive) is located. Furthermore, the indirect threaded code representation is *open*; intermediate **CALL**s use the same address representation as the primitives. Therefore, since the coprocessor is fully equipped to access the pointer structure, it is also capable of playing a more active role in executing intermediate **CALL**s than the M-code coprocessor.

We have therefore provided the threaded code coprocessor with more internal registers than the M-code coprocessor. The BIU now contains three registers **R1**, **R2**, and **R3**. These registers are intended to contain the intermediate instruction pointer **VPC**, the word address register **WA**, and the return stack pointer **RP**, respectively. The CPU holds the data stack pointer.

The ISU contains internal instruction and control stores, which are addressed using a 16-bit address. The instruction store contains the code for the primitives when the control store contains the **GEN** microinstruction at the corresponding location; otherwise the instruction store contains the parameters of the microinstruction. The intermediate program representation containing the definitions is stored in the CPU memory. The internal instruction pointer IP is loaded with the value of the direct primitive pointer loaded from memory at the address pointed to by **WA**. The structure of the threaded code coprocessor is shown in Fig. 4.9.

The control instruction repertoire of the threaded code coprocessor is somewhat richer than that of the M-code coprocessor. The control operations are listed in

4.3. Two Concrete Instruction Path Coprocessors

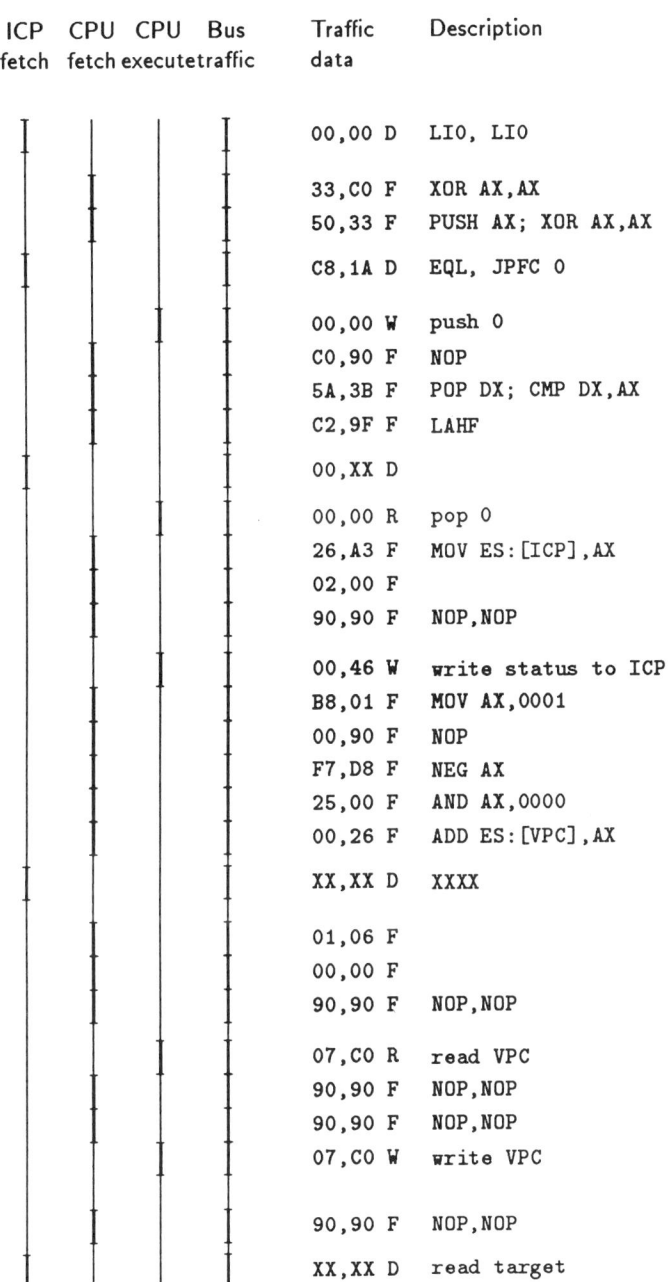

ICP fetch	CPU fetch	CPU execute	Bus traffic	Traffic data	Description
				00,00 D	LIO, LIO
				33,C0 F	XOR AX,AX
				50,33 F	PUSH AX; XOR AX,AX
				C8,1A D	EQL, JPFC 0
				00,00 W	push 0
				C0,90 F	NOP
				5A,3B F	POP DX; CMP DX,AX
				C2,9F F	LAHF
				00,XX D	
				00,00 R	pop 0
				26,A3 F	MOV ES:[ICP],AX
				02,00 F	
				90,90 F	NOP,NOP
				00,46 W	write status to ICP
				B8,01 F	MOV AX,0001
				00,90 F	NOP
				F7,D8 F	NEG AX
				25,00 F	AND AX,0000
				00,26 F	ADD ES:[VPC],AX
				XX,XX D	XXXX
				01,06 F	
				00,00 F	
				90,90 F	NOP,NOP
				07,C0 R	read VPC
				90,90 F	NOP,NOP
				90,90 F	NOP,NOP
				07,C0 W	write VPC
				90,90 F	NOP,NOP
				XX,XX D	read target

Figure 4.8
A timing trace of conditional code generation

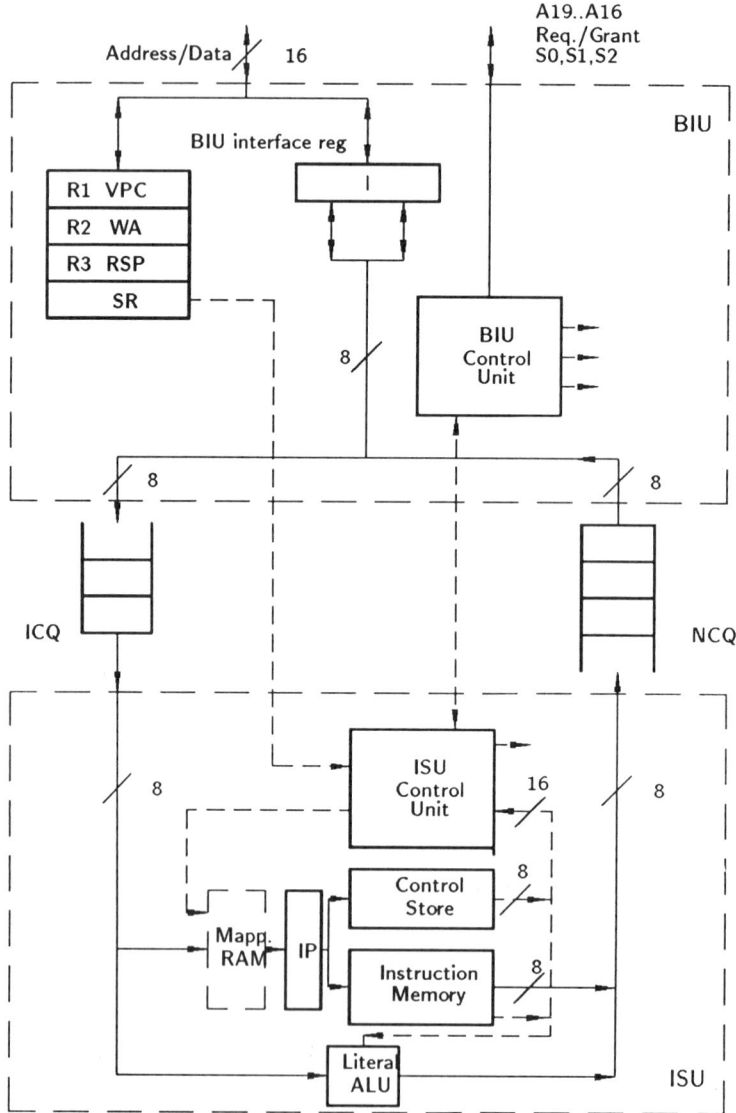

Figure 4.9
The architecture of an instruction path coprocessor for indirect threaded code

4.3. Two Concrete Instruction Path Coprocessors   149

Class	Mnemonic	Encoding	Comments
Generate	GEN	00H	Generate instruction byte for 8086
R-Inserts	INS1	11H	insert R1 in instruction stream
	INS2	09H	insert R2 in instruction stream
	INS3	19H	insert R3 in instruction stream
Operations	ADD	03H	perform addition
	MRM	0BH	move register to memory
	MRR	13H	move register to register
	MMR	1BH	move memory to register
	CFETCH	33H	fetch conditionally on room in ICQ
L-Inserts	LITx1	0DH	insert literal byte
	LITBx2	1DH	insert lower byte of doubled literal
	LITBx4	15H	insert lower byte of quadrupled literal
	LITWx2	35H	insert upper byte of doubled literal
	LITWx4	3DH	insert upper byte of quadrupled literal
	LITCx2	2DH	insert zero extension of doubled literal
	LITCx4	25H	insert zero extension of quadrupled literal
Jumps	JMP	07H	perform local jump
	JC	27H	perform conditional jump
	WAIT	17H	wait for CPU to write SR
Fetches	FBYTE	04H	decode byte from ICQ
	FWRD	24H	decode word from ICQ

Table 4.3
The microcode control operations in the threaded code coprocessor

Table 4.3. The operands of the control instruction are located in the instruction store IS. Table 4.4 lists their encodings.

Operation. The operation of the threaded code coprocessor is very similar to that of the M-code coprocessor. The problem of conditional code generation is also present. However, the problem associated with the execution of transfers of control are less severe with the current coprocessor, since CALL and RETURN operations can be largely executed autonomously by the coprocessor. We show the internal coding for two operations without transfers of control, and for the intermediate NEXT, CALL, and RETURN operations.

```
Primitive   CS  IS      8086 instructions and Comments
---------   --- ---     -------------------------------
ONE:        ADD R0,2                ; release bus to 8086
            GEN B8      MOV AX,1
            GEN 01
```

Class	Mnemonic	Encoding	Comments
Source registers	R0	00H	Register 0 controls bus release
	R1	40H	Register 1 (holds VPC)
	R2	80H	Register 2 (holds WA)
	R3	C0H	Register 3 (holds RP)
Destination registers	ICQ	00H	Intermediate code queue
	R1	10H	Register 1 (holds VPC)
	R2	20H	Register 2 (holds WA)
	R3	30H	Register 3 (holds RP)
Literals	-1	00H	
	+1	10H	
	-2	20H	
	+2	30H	
Status masks	SEL0	00H	select status bit 0 from SR
	SEL1	20H	select status bit 1 from SR
	SEL2	40H	select status bit 2 from SR
	SEL3	60H	select status bit 3 from SR
	SEL4	80H	select status bit 4 from SR
	SEL5	A0H	select status bit 5 from SR
	SEL6	C0H	select status bit 6 from SR
	SEL7	E0H	select status bit 7 from SR

Table 4.4
The encoding of operands of microcode control operations in the threaded code coprocessor

```
            GEN 00
            GEN 50      PUSH AX
            MMR R1,R2                ; [VPC] -> WA
            MMR R2,ICQ               ; [WA]  -> ICQ : fetch primitive
            ADD R1,2                 ; VPC+2 -> VPC
            FWRD --                  ; jump to next primitive &
                                     ; keep bus locked

ADD:        ADD R0,2                 ; release bus to 8086
            GEN 58      POP AX
            GEN 5B      POP BX
            GEN 01      ADD AX,BX
            GEN D8
            GEN 50      PUSH AX
NEXT:       MMR R1,R2                ; [VPC] -> WA
```

4.4. An Analysis of ICP Performance

Mnemonic	Dynamic Freq. (%)	LEM Interpreter (clocks)	Coprocessor (clocks)	Speedup Total	Semantic
JPFC	5.96	67	66(60)	1.02(1.12)	0.35
LLW4	5.20	73	20(17)	3.65(4.29)	1.59
RTN	4.23	115	95(92)	1.21(1.25)	0.75
UADD	3.53	76	9 (6)	8.44(12.67)	5.00
LLW7	2.89	73	20(17)	3.65(4.29)	1.59
LLW5	2.84	73	20(17)	3.65(4.29)	1.59
ENTR	2.81	118	42(36)	2.81(3.28)	2.00
EQL	2.78	84	35(32)	2.40(2.63)	1.19
LIW	2.68	69	20(11)	3.45(6.27)	2.09
LLW6	2.54	73	20(17)	3.65(4.29)	1.59

Table 4.5
Relative speedups of the ten most frequent M-machine instructions. Figures in parentheses do not count intermediate fetch DMA cycles

the improved code generated by the coprocessor.

Increased parallelism. The interpretive coprocessor works concurrently with the CPU as much as possible. In low-level intermediate languages such as M-code, the execution time of the mapping actions is of the same order as that of the semantic instructions. Not only can the ICP execute the mapping action *in parallel* with the operation of the CPU, it can also execute them *faster*, using direct hardware execution. Thus, for low-level intermediate languages, a large fraction of the coprocessor speedup can be attributed to this form of parallelism. Even when the mapping time exceeds the semantic time, total overlap of mapping and execution is possible, at least while executing a linear instruction stream.

Since the semantic execution times of intermediate instructions vary more markedly than their mapping times, a full exploitation of the parallelism requires the decoupling of the ICP and the CPU. The introduction of the native code queue NCQ allows this; its size is an important design parameter. Indeed, the ICP cannot generate more machine instruction bytes than can be held by the native code queue. When this queue is full or empty, either the ICP or the CPU must wait. So, its length should be larger than a certain minimum. On the other hand, making it too long is also bad, for reasons that will be explained below. In a similar way, the intermediate code queue ICQ allows the decoupling and parallel execution of the fetching of intermediate instructions, and their conversion into native code.

The presence of the intermediate and native code queues in the coprocessor, and the code expansion that takes place in the coprocessor, result in a virtual prefetch queue length which is significantly larger than in traditional CPUs. The virtual prefetch queuelength L_v seen by the CPU when driven by an ICP is given by

$$L_v = L_{CPU} + L_{NCQ} + \sum_{j=1}^{L_{ICQ}} NativeLength_j,$$

with

- L_{CPU} the length of the CPU prefetch queue;
- L_{NCQ} the length of the coprocessor native code queue;
- L_{ICQ} the length of the coprocessor intermediate code queue;
- $NativeLength_j$ the number of bytes into which the j-th byte in the ICQ will be expanded.

For example, the M-code coprocessor provides an average virtual queue length $L_v = 6+2+2.5\times 3 = 15.5$ bytes, where we have used 2.5 as an estimate of the intermediate code expansion factor. This virtual extension of the prefetch queue length allows a loose coupling of the ICP and the CPU, but it also makes the ICP/CPU pair more sensitive to pipeline break than traditional pipelined architectures.

Pipeline breaks limit the amount of parallelism that can effectively be achieved [Nico84,Rise72]; they are fundamentally caused by the feedback of information from the CPU to the coprocessor. Such feedback is used for two purposes:

- **Intermediate level jumps.** Intermediate level jumps are executed by writing a new value in the virtual program counter VPC. When new data is written into the VPC, the intermediate code queue ICQ must be flushed, and no new native code can be generated until ICQ again contains new intermediate instructions. The only native instructions that can be executed in the mean time are those still present in the native code queue NCQ at the time the VPC was written; often there are none.

  Several techniques can be used to increase the level of parallelism also in this case. At the level of the coprocessor architecture, techniques such as branch prediction and doubling the prefetch logic may improve the pipeline efficiency. The use of delayed jumps at the intermediate level could also provide great relief, but this requires the modification of the semantics of the intermediate program representation, as well as an optimizing compiler. Finally, the coprocessor hardware could be extended to execute at least the unconditional transfers of control autonomously, as was done in the threaded code coprocessor.

4.4. An Analysis of ICP Performance

- **Conditional code generation.** One of the ways in which the coprocessor can be made to generate condition-dependent code is to provide it with status information from the CPU. Communicating the status information to the coprocessor also limits the available parallelism. Indeed, when the status information is used *immediately* after the coprocessor has issued the write command to the CPU, code generation must be postponed until the CPU has actually transferred the status data. During this waiting time, no parallelism is possible, except perhaps for the fetching of subsequent intermediate instructions.

We shall come back to these problems in more detail in the next section, where we shall also provide some alternative solutions.

Improved code generation. While analyzing the causes of interpretive slowdown in Chapter 3, we have seen that the semantic routines of software interpreters do not make optimal use of the CPU resources for a variety of reasons. The presence of an instruction path coprocessor allows us to remedy this situation to some extent. Three notable points of difference are the following.

- **The number of jumps decreases.** No more decoding jumps are needed; the semantic code can thus better exploit the benefits of the CPU's prefetch pipeline. Conceptually it is even possible to generate native code totally free of jumps, although this may not be the most efficient solution.

- **The ICP frees CPU resources.** The coprocessor contains some frequently used registers which, in software interpretation, must be mapped onto CPU registers. Consequently, the semantic routines generated by the coprocessor can use the registers freed to additionally speed up their execution. For example, in the coprocessor version of the M-code interpreter, two-register top of stack optimization becomes possible, and also the M-machine G and S pointers can be kept in processor registers.

- **The code generated is less generic.** The merging and scaling of intermediate literals into the generated native code stream leads to a speedup of the semantic routines for two reasons: (1) fewer instructions are generated; and (2) no interface registers are needed to hold the literals. The use of these registers elsewhere can also speed up the execution.

The semantic speedup is shown in the rightmost column of Table 4.5. Note that intermediate instructions *not* using feedback communication to the coprocessor execute faster than in an optimized software interpreter. Those that do have a *slower* semantic execution. In particular, the semantic code generated for the conditional jump JPFC is significantly slower than the semantic instructions of a pure software interpreter. This has two causes. First, the old value of the VPC must be read from the coprocessor. The time elapsed between the issuing of the read instruction and its eventual execution is lost. Secondly, after writing the new value of the VPC, the entire prefetch system must be flushed, since no more useful code can be executed until the target M-instruction has been processed, and the corresponding native instructions have reached the execution unit of the CPU.

4.4.2 Weak points of instruction path coprocessors

Besides the above problems related to feedback, the simple examples of the previous chapter have revealed several weak points in the joint operation of an instruction path coprocessor and the CPU. A more comprehensive list of problem areas is the following:

- bus sharing and the deadlock problem;
- the ignorance of the CPU program counter;
- feedback conditional code generation;
- interrupts;
- the presence of instruction caches.

We shall now discuss these problems in somewhat greater depth, and present solutions where possible.

Bus sharing and the deadlock problem. In the instruction path coprocessor prototypes presented earlier, the data bus is shared between the coprocessor and the CPU. The coprocessor uses a DMA type protocol to acquire ownership of the bus to fetch intermediate instructions. From the timing traces of the M-code examples in Chapter 4, it follows that up to 20% of all bus cycles are coprocessor fetch cycles. Since these cycles are not present in native execution of compiled code, they limit the ultimate speedup attainable using a coprocessor. This is quite apparent from Table 4.5: the figures in parentheses show the speedup when the DMA fetch cycles and their bus arbitration overhead are not taken into account. This problem somewhat looses importance on 32-bit buses, for two reasons: first, the code expansion factor on 32-bit machines such as the MC68020 is slightly larger than on the i8086; and secondly, data transfer cycles are not necessarily reduced in number by using a wider bus. The intermediate code fetch cycles can be eliminated almost entirely by providing a small intermediate code cache on the coprocessor. From our analysis at the end of Chapter 3, it follows that caches of a few hundred bytes already provide excellent hit rates.

The common use of the bus by the coprocessor and the CPU also causes the frequent occurrence of the deadlock situations such as shown in Fig. 4.10. This

4.4. An Analysis of ICP Performance

program counter, and every now and then, it must generate a native jump to keep the program counter within the boundaries. Generally, the selection of the ICP address range depends on the most significant address bits. The ICP should generate a jump instruction when one of the most significant address bits changes, for instance, when the address offset exceeds half the length of the ICP address space. Thus only one address bit has to be traced and a jump is generated when this bit toggle from 0 to 1. Note that, similarly to NOP instructions, this jump instruction must be inserted at a boundary of machine instructions, and not within a machine instruction. A suitable place might be immediately after the expansion of an intermediate instruction.

In processors with a segmented address space having short, fixed-length segments such as the i8086, it suffices to allocate an entire segment for the ICP. Then the CPU program counter will wrap around, and no jumps are required. This technique obviously will not work when the segments can span the entire address range, or when segment boundary checks are performed by the segmentation unit (exceptions will be generated).

A additional problem arises when an interrupt arrives. Through the hardware generated call or jump, an interrupt changes the CPU's program counter to the address of the associated interrupt handler. If this handler is located *in* the ICP address space, the ICP continues sending instructions from the old intermediate instruction stream just as if nothing had happened; only some instructions already generated will be flushed. On the other hand, when the handler is *outside* the ICP address range, the same instructions will be flushed; they will not be regenerated on return from the interrupt handler. Therefore, interrupts require a special handling; we shall discuss this problem below.

Feedback and conditional code generation. We have already noted that the conditional generation of native code, which is needed at various places in an interpreter, can be realized provided the coprocessor contains the relevant status information; the example of the EQL M-code was used to illustrate the concept. The communication of status information from the CPU to the coprocessor is detrimental to performance. Therefore it is worthwhile to look somewhat deeper into this problem. It turns out that several ways exist to generate code with condition-dependent execution. Two classes of methods are available: those that use a form of *communication* from the CPU to the coprocessor; and those that use *computation* techniques, using fixed instruction sequences, of results that are usually computed using conditional execution.

- **Explicit communication.** The CPU explicitly writes its status to the ICP. This method was illustrated by the third M-code example in the previous section. It is imperative that the ICP wait for the CPU message to arrive before continuing the generation of the following (condition dependent) instructions.

When this waiting operation is started immediately after the generation of the write instruction, considerable dead time is introduced, since all previous instructions in the CPU prefetch queue must be executed first. During this dead time, a deadlock situation can be avoided by repeatedly generating NOP instructions.

Such a situation is very disadvantageous to the performance of the coprocessor. It is worse than the pipeline break caused by a native jump instruction. Indeed, whether or not the condition is true, it must be communicated, and the corresponding delay is incurred. This is not the case with direct execution of conditional jumps: the overhead is significantly lower when the jump is not taken. For example, on the i8086, the sequence

```
LAHF
MOV ES:SR,AH
```

always takes 21 clocks, while

```
JZ xxxx
```

takes 16 clocks when the jump is taken, but only 4 clocks when it is not.

Instead of generating NOPs, it might be possible to generate useful instructions. In the example of the EQL M-code of the previous chapter, the XOR AX,AX might always be generated after the MOV ES:SR,AH instruction. The effectively generated machine instruction stream then looks as follows:

```
            POP DX
            CMP AX,DX
            LAHF
            MOV ES:SR,AH
            XOR AX,AX       ; now replaces NOP,NOP pair
; only when equal :
            INC AX
```

This technique corresponds to a scoreboarding technique on the SR register. The scoreboarding bit should be set when the MOV ES:SR,AH is generated, and cleared when SR is written. The number of delay slots may be variable, as the time between the generation of the MOV ES:SR,AH instruction and its execution is not fixed; additional NOPs may be required. Therefore, it is useful not to code the NOPs in the code stream, but to equip the machine code queue with a facility that generates NOP instructions when it is empty, e.g., during

4.4. An Analysis of ICP Performance

the execution of the coprocessor CPU micro-instruction, which waits for the scoreboarding bit to be cleared. In this way only as many NOPs are inserted as are actually needed.

- **Implicit communication (snooping).** Another method to communicate status information is to indeed generate native conditional jumps, and to track the CPU's program counter. In jump-free instruction streams the program counter will be incremented by the word length after each fetch cycle. A taken conditional jump behaves differently, and can be detected on this basis. For example, the program counter may be kept the same, it may change by a different amount, or it may be reset to a fixed value. The detection of a taken jump requires additional hardware, which must be compared to the hardware needed to receive and test the CPU flags.

Let us look at an example. For the EQL M-code the generated machine instruction sequence looks as follows:

```
        POP DX
        CMP AX,DX
        JZ $+4         ; $+2 is same as not taken
        NOP            ; these NOPs will be executed
        NOP            ; when jump is not taken,
        NOP            ; otherwise they are merely fetched
        ...
; when not equal (jump not taken)
        XOR AX,AX

; when equal (jump taken)
        MOV AX,1
```

The NOPs generated after the generation of the conditional jump are necessary since the CPU performs prefetching cycles. Whether or not the jump has been taken can only be detected after several fetch cycles. If the jump was not taken, the instructions fetched in the mean time will be executed. As with scoreboarding, the generation of the conditional jump should set a flag which activates the program counter observation unit; eventually, it must be decided whether or not the jump was taken, e.g., after a sufficient number of fetch cycles. Thus, a fixed delay is incurred that only depends on the length of the prefetch queue of the CPU.

- **Direct computation of the intermediate status from the flags.** Sometimes conditional code generation can be transformed into unconditional code generation: the result is computed from the flags with a unique instruction sequence. Let us again look at the EQL M-code. This intermediate instruction must leave the intermediate status on the expression stack (the AX register), with 0 representing FALSE, and 1 TRUE. An unconditional and jump-free instruction sequence to compute this status might be:

```
POP DX
CMP AX,DX
LAHF
AND AX,Z_flag    ; mask away other bits
MOV CL,Z_pos     ; shift distance
ROR AX,CL        ; shift Z_flag to bit_0
```

This technique can be used for all conditions. An even faster technique for unsigned comparisons, e.g., UGTR (unsigned greater than or equal to) is the following:

```
POP DX
SUB DX,AX
CWD              ; extend sign bit of result into DX
MOV AX,DX        ; now AX=FFFF if AX > DX
NEG AX           ; convert to proper representation
```

- **Computation of intermediate conditional jump addresses.** The following example interprets a conditional intermediate-level jump, e.g., JPFC 008. The increment of the virtual program counter can be computed from the jump offset and the value of the intermediate status, using a fixed instruction sequence. The jump offset can be passed as a literal by the coprocessor.

```
MOV DX,CS:VPC    ; read current value of VPC (points
                 ;    past current M-code)
ADD DX,AX        ; increment if jump not taken
DEC AX           ; jump taken if AX was 0000
AND AX,008       ; compute jump offset with AX (0 or 8)

ADD AX,DX        ; compute new VPC
MOV CS:VPC,AX    ; (always) write new VPC
```

This technique was used in the third example of the previous section. Note that the VPC is *always* written, whether the jump is taken or not. This

4.4. An Analysis of ICP Performance

results in a uniformly slow execution. Some optimization is possible when the coprocessor hardware is capable of determining whether the VPC has actually been modified.

- **Computations exploiting the prefetch queue behavior.** A method to simulate conditional execution using a fixed instruction sequence is to have this sequence interpreted in a state-dependent way by the CPU. The idea is to make explicit use of the fact that the CPU does *not* execute instructions prefetched before a taken jump. For example, for the EQL M-code the synthesized instructions stream could be the following:

```
POP  DX
SUB  AX,DX        ; tests for equality
JZ   $+2          ; any target will do
MOV  AX,0FFFFH    ; unequal, result will become 0
NOP
...
NOP
INC  AX
```

If the operands are equal, after the subtraction AX will be 0, the conditional machine-level jump is taken, and the following machine instructions will be flushed. The INC AX instruction is executed, resulting in 1. If the operands differ, the jump is not taken, and AX is loaded with 0FFFFH. This will be incremented, and the result is 0. Care should be taken to ensure that the MOV AX,0FFFFH resides in the prefetch queue with certainty, and that the INC AX instruction can never reside in the prefetch queue at the moment it is flushed. Again, an appropriate number of NOPs is required. In the case of the i8086, observations have revealed that 4 instruction bytes are prefetched between the generation of the conditional jump and its execution.

Interrupts. In the case of external interrupts, problems similar to those of machine level jumps arise. During the servicing of an interrupt request, the address of the next instruction *to be executed* is saved; it is restored on return from the interrupt driver. The instruction bytes that were prefetched at the time of the interrupt are fetched again. The problem is that, even if the proper CPU program counter is saved and restored, the coprocessor is unaware of the fact that it has to regenerate the already generated but flushed machine instruction bytes. This problem is clearly related to the ignorance of the program counter. But there is more to it: once the machine code bytes have been generated by the ICP, it is hard to regenerate them, since some information may have been lost in their generation.

In other words, the operation of the finite state machine constituting the coprocessor is not invertible. The following strategy can be used to circumvent these problems[1]. Of the generated instruction bytes, the latest l are saved in a set-aside buffer (fifo queue), where l is the length of the CPU prefetch queue. In the event of a interrupt, all flushed bytes are in this queue. A snapshot of the current value of the (fetch) program counter is saved. On the return from interrupt, the reloaded value of the (execution) program counter is used to regenerate the proper number of flushed instructions from the set-aside buffer. Only a few program counter bits are needed for this purpose. Indeed, the difference between the prefetch program counter and the execution program counter cannot exceed l.

An easier solution to this problem might be to allow interrupts to be acknowledged only at intermediate instruction,boundaries. On receipt of an interrupt, the coprocessor might generate NOPs, which can be flushed in a harmless way. The problem is that the interrupt latency is increased. This is perhaps not a serious problem for low-level intermediate instructions, but it is for complex ones with large execution times, e.g., block move instructions.

Interrupts *at the intermediate level* can also be accommodated using an instruction path coprocessor. For example, in the M-code machine model, an intermediate level interrupt corresponds to the hardware insertion of a TRA intermediate instruction, performing a coroutine transfer from the current process to the associated interrupt driver process.

The last two solutions require that the coprocessor can observe the hardware processor interrupt line(s). Software generated interrupts or traps (overflow, divide by zero) caused by the execution process are more difficult to handle. In the case of traps, the CPU's program counter suddenly contains a new value. The ICP may detect this. Usually, the detection of the trap is more important than the correct recovery from it, and continuation of the trapped process (e.g., in the case of arithmetic overflow). This is different from software interrupts, which are used to implement system calls. A clean return from the system call is imperative. Luckily, in this case it is the coprocessor itself that has generated the interrupting instruction. Consequently, it may prepare the receipt of an interrupt in the same way as was done with machine-level jump instructions.

The presence of caches. As there is no fixed relation between the machine program counter and the generated machine code bytes, native instruction caches are useless and may even cause problems. In the ideal case, the code generated by the coprocessor is a linear instruction stream. Hence, it has very poor locality and a cache would not be effective. Futhermore it is possible, even probable, that eventually different machine instructions will be generated with identical values of

---

[1] This strategy is used in Knödler and Rosenstiel's Prolog Preprocessor, described in the next chapter.

the program counter. Then the cache contains the wrong code. To some extent, this is akin to the *cache coherence* problem in systems which allow memory mapped I/O, DMA, or multiprocessing. Consequently, on-chip instruction caches must not cache instructions fetched from the address range of the coprocessor. A more appropriate point of view is that the instruction path coprocessor actually *replaces* an instruction cache. Indeed, an ICP should be able to respond with machine code bytes without wait states, independently of the bandwidth of the main memory.

4.5 Conclusion

In this chapter we have investigated whether it is possible to adapt the well-known coprocessor concept to the support of interpretive execution on standard microprocessors, and in standard microprocessor environments. We have first looked briefly into the different varieties of traditional coprocessors. We have found that they are all datapath coprocessors, not intervening in the way in which the CPU obtains its own instructions from memory. The only exception to this situation is perhaps formed by memory management chips: they are located in the address path emerging from the CPU. Still, even memory management chips do not alter the instructions fetched by the CPU. Pure datapath coprocessors are not well suited to speed up the interpretation of low-level intermediate languages.

We have then analyzed how the time-consuming mapping actions of low-level intermediate languages could be accelerated by means of additional hardware. Simple prefetch engines provide some acceleration, but leave the ultimate decoding jump to the CPU. A true instruction path coprocessor provides a higher speedup. It behaves like a hardware run-time code generator for the CPU; this allows even the generation of less generic semantic code.

The general idea was illustrated by means of two concrete examples, one for M-code, and one for threaded code. The speedups obtained were significant, in that the interpretive slowdown can be strongly reduced. However, intermediate transfers of control and conditional code generation pose particular problems, which are aggravated by the asynchronous nature of the coupling of CPU and coprocessor. A deeper analysis has indicated that these weak points can be improved using techniques like delayed jumps, register scoreboarding, or by allowing the coprocessor to execute unconditional jumps autonomously.

5 CONCLUDING REMARKS

The feasibility of instruction path coprocessing as a means to speedup interpretive execution has become apparent from our exposure to the concept in Chapter 4. The two non-optimized coprocessors prototypes presented there accelerate software interpretation by factors of up to 5 w.r.t. commercially available software packages.

In this short and final chapter, we shall first look at some related published work. Indeed, it turns out that the concept of instruction path coprocessing has been used elsewhere, albeit in different contexts, and with different goals. Then we shall look at the applicability of the concept, as developed for the i8086 and intermediate languages like M-code or threaded code, in a broader context. In particular, we briefly investigate the applicability of the instruction path coprocessor concept in modern RISC architectures and in contemporary interpretive environments.

5.1 An Overview of Related Work

The concept of separate units for the execution, and for the fetching and decoding of instructions is not new [Lamp84,Thak86]. Such units have been used in dedicated machines, and are known as *instruction fetch units*. The separation between the fetch/decoding actions and the actual execution of instructions is natural, and is present in almost all contemporary microprocessors. As far as we know, the formulation of the fetch/decoding as a coprocessor task, and its introduction in general purpose and standard microprocessor environments in the way we have presented it, is new.

We now discuss some related approaches found in published case studies. Since the contexts of language, technology and design goals are specific to each case, we shall not attempt to compare the individual cases with respect to their performance and complexity. We shall limit our discussion to the following three cases:

- the instruction fetch unit of the Dorado;
- the instruction fetch unit of the G-machine;
- the Prolog preprocessor.

5.1.1 The instruction fetch unit of the Dorado

The Dorado [Lamp84] is a powerful microprogrammable personal computer built of ECL technology. To provide its processor with instructions at a maximum rate of one instruction every 60 ns, this computer contains a special instruction fetch unit.

Although, at first sight, there is a strong resemblance between the approach presented in this monograph and the instruction fetch unit of the Dorado, they are definitely not identical. Most dissimilarities arise from the fact that different types of execution engines are used. Our approach presumes a standard microprocessor as an execution unit, while the Dorado, being a dedicated computer, exploits all its degrees of freedom to speed up the interpretive process. The only task of the fetch/decode unit is to obtain the intermediate instructions from the program and to pass the information necessary to perform the corresponding semantic operations to the execution unit. Since the Dorado's execution unit contains the microcoded interpreter routines, a suitable form of communication is indeed the starting address of the proper interpreter routine (see the prefetch engine). In this sense, the Dorado is a good illustration of the concepts outlined in [Hoev74]. In our approach the communication between the two processors consists of the instruction sequences themselves, rather than their starting addresses. This is a consequence of the fact that the execution unit in our case is predefined and fixed. Generating the instructions rather than addresses is more efficient.

The method used for passing literal operands from the intermediate level to the machine level is also different in both designs. The Dorado has dedicated communication busses, while in our approach, the operands are embedded into the instructions to be generated. As a consequence of the strategies chosen the Dorado still needs instructions (and hardware) in the interpreter routines to pass these operands from the communication bus to the registers. In our approach the operands are fully part of the instruction stream.

5.1.2 The instruction fetch unit of the G-machine

The G-machine [Thak86,Peyt87] provides hardware support for functional languages based on the graph reduction technique. Its central processor is a dedicated RISC-like architecture and requires a high instruction bandwidth. An intermediate language (G-code) is used to represent the functional program and an instruction fetch unit fetches and translates the G-code into RISC-processor instructions.

The dedicated RISC-like processor resembles the Berkely RISC [Patt81], and is fed with instructions instead of starting or dispatch addresses as is the case in the Dorado. In order to be able to generate one instruction per cycle, the fetch unit contains a hardware decoding translation scheme, branch instruction support and different buffers to support the pipeline structure. The generated code is linearized: unconditional jumps are removed and executed at the fetch unit stage. The code enters the processor via a separate control bus. The literals are passed through a shared address/data bus to the processor. This strongly hardware supported processor achieves a considerable execution speed. However, the environment is strictly oriented towards G-code.

5.1.3 The Prolog Preprocessor

The Prolog Preprocessor [Knod86] speeds up the execution of Warren's WAM code, which is an intermediate representation of Prolog programs. The configuration consists of a standard MC68000 microprocessor and the dedicated preprocessor.

In contrast to both previous designs, it uses a standard commercial microprocessor as an executing unit, in which it resembles our approach. A point of distinction is that the preprocessor internally contains the **WAM** code representation of a Prolog program. In fact, this code acts as a high-level microcode which controls the operations of the preprocessor: synthesizing MC68000 instructions, spying on data references performed by the MC68000, controlling internal machine parts (sequencer, trail chip and comparator chip), etc. Our coprocessor acts as a fetch unit, which fetches intermediate instructions from the processor's memory space and translates it into an instruction sequence. The source of the intermediate sequences can be any of the sources available to the processor.

The Prolog Preprocessor expects its code to reside internally and hence achieves a higher performance (no bus cycles), at the cost of generality and limitations on the intermediate program size.

5.2 On the Applicability of Instruction Path Coprocessors

So far, we have focused mainly on the properties of the M-code instruction path coprocessor for the i8086. For this combination, the concept works fine, even without the use of delayed branching or scoreboarding. The introduction of these techniques can raise the efficiency of the instruction path coprocessor even more. Similar observations can be made concerning the coprocessor for threaded code: also there, a coprocessor can provide a cost-effective speedup of the interpretive process. But what about the usefulness of instruction path coprocessors in conjunction with other, more modern processors? What about its applicability to speedup other than low-level forms of interpretation? How general can a coprocessor for a given CPU be made while retaining its cost-effectiveness? A host of questions can be raised in this context. We shall not attempt to answer them all; rather, to end this chapter and this monograph, we shall focus on two aspects: the role of ICPs in RISC based systems, and the applicability of ICPs to support modern interpretive applications.

5.2.1 RISCs and the ICP concept

One of the aims of the RISC architecture is to provide single cycle execution of frequently used instructions. These instructions necessarily have 'simple' semantics, which allows current compiler technology to generate a more optimized machine code than for CISCs. The relative simplicity of these instructions, together with appropriate instruction encoding (few formats, fixed length) makes it possible to use hardwired decoding and hardwired control instead of microcoding. RISC instructions are often compared to the microinstructions used to implement CISC instruction sets. The performance levels that can be achieved using RISCs are (much) higher than these of CISCs with comparable hardware complexity. However, the effective exploitation of this computation power is not an easy matter.

- Pipelined RISC architectures achieve an execution rate of typically one instruction per cycle. Since cycle times can be as low as 30 ns, very fast instruction memories are required. Access times of less than 20 ns are needed [Mars88]. At this moment, large size memory devices of this performance are not available at low cost, and, therefore, the systems designer must resort to special memory techniques such as interleaving, high performance instruction caching, pipelining, burst mode accesses, etc., to circumvent the von Neumann bottleneck [Mars88]. While the raw processing power offered by modern RISCs is higher and cheaper as ever before, it is still a costly undertaking to harness it in a real environment.

- In contrast to CISC microprocessor families, which allow the use of existing compilers for their newer, upward compatible members, RISC code generators must be built from scratch. Moreover, so as to benefit from the speed offered by the hardware, RISC compilers must be sophisticated [Wirt87,Stal88, Henn83]. The lack of software portability and the stringent requirements on compiler quality may be a cause for the delayed acceptance of RISCs in industrial environments.

Software interpretation may offer a means to partially circumvent the software problem: interpreters are less complex than compilers, and are easier to port. Of course, the interpretive slowdown throws away a significant portion of the available computation power. As observed in Chapter 3, for low-cost systems, interpretation from a small fast memory may provide a sensible compromise between execution speed and cost. But for other applications, the use of interpretation is *imperative*; the interpretive technique will then allow significantly cheaper hardware without an additional speed penalty. In either case, an instruction path coprocessor may prove an interesting addition. Some aspects of instruction path coprocessors for RISCs are the following.

Speedup of semantic routines. The speedup of interpretation on a RISC by an instruction path coprocessor can be rather high, in particular for the support of complex addressing modes needed to implement the mapping actions and to access intermediate variables. In a software interpreter, these complex addressing modes must be implemented using several machine instructions. For example, on the Am29000, 6 instructions are needed for the M-code mapping actions; in contrast, only 2 are needed on the MC68020 CISC. The same situation also occurs in the semantic part of a software interpreter. Typical variable addressing modes in intermediate machines are the base+displacement and autoincrement/autodecrement

5.2. On the Applicability of Instruction Path Coprocessors

modes. Expression stacks and (indexed) allocation stacks are often used intermediate data structures. In software interpretation, the effective addresses needed to access these data structures are explicitly computed and used in a register-indirect way. The instruction sequence computing the effective address must be generic, and will generally consist of several RISC instructions. Provided that the coprocessor contains the base registers used, it can generate an instruction stream *literally using the effective address of the operand*. This is particularly useful in RISCs with large, directly addressed register files. For example, it is easy to map a stack structure onto a register file. Effective addresses are register numbers. Intermediate instructions referencing the stack (even indexing it) can be tailor-made, using the proper register number, when the coprocessor can dispose of the identity of the top of stack register. No explicit instructions incrementing or decrementing the stack pointer are necessary. This is an extension of the top of stack optimization method presented earlier. The method is not feasible with software interpreters, since too many stack states are needed.

Speed of instruction memory. The speed of the instruction memory used by an instruction path coprocessor can be lower than that of direct execution memory. Indeed, since the coprocessor generates code *without* using the CPU's program counter, it can address instruction memory *before* the new program counter is even known. The instruction memory should only have a sufficiently low cycle time; it does not have to meet additional stringent conditions regarding its access time.

Bandwidth reduction and instruction caches. A RISC requires nearly one instruction per cycle. Each RISC instruction, typically 32 bit wide, encodes a single primitive operation and, therefore, the information per bit is very low. CISC instructions carry more information per bit. In well designed intermediate languages, the information rate is even higher. Consequently, for a given execution speed, the required instruction bandwidth at the intermediate level is significantly lower than that for native RISC execution. The density of M-code compared to i8086 native code is between 3 and 4 [Wirt86]; and RISCs themselves are reported to have code densities one-half to two thirds of that of CISCs [Wirt87,Stal88], which suggests that the RISC instruction bandwidth is at least 6 to 8 times higher than that required by a RISC/ICP configuration running at the same speed.

Of course, traditional instruction caches too provide a strong reduction of the instruction bandwidth. However, because of the loose encoding of RISC instructions and their high execution rate, RISC caches are relatively complex and expensive. The Motorola MC88200 cache controller contains more transistors, and is more expensive than the MC88100 CPU. In [Flyn87], Flynn argues that RISC instruction caches must be twice as large compared to the CISC caches in order to achieve an equal hitrate. Similar figures are obtained in experiments described in [Davi87b]. A much smaller intermediate instruction cache would provide the same hit rate;

in addition, the resulting instruction bandwidth beyond the cache would be 6 to 8 times lower than for a native code cache. When the instruction and control stores are not taken into account, an instruction path coprocessor is significantly simpler than a cache controller.

On the architecture of ICPs for RISCs. The above considerations suggest that the instruction path coprocessor concept can also be deployed effectively in a RISC environment to speed up interpretation. However, it is clear that the architectures of the ICP prototypes presented in Chapter 4 cannot be used without modification in a RISC environment. The coprocessors for the i8086 use a clock which runs three times faster than the actual CPU clock. The internal control of the coprocessor is microcoded vertically, and the internal data paths are only 8 bits wide. This technique remains roughly applicable with other CISCs that use internal microcoding and multi-cycle instruction execution. In view of their much higher clock rates, and their essentially single-cycle execution, RISCs will no longer allow this technique, at least not if the same technology is to be used. Wide, 32-bit internal data paths, and horizontally microcoded control will be needed. On the other hand, some aspects of coprocessor design even become simpler: the Harvard architecture offered by most RISCs relaxes the deadlock problems; and word boundary problems vanish, since all RISC machine instruction lengths are words or multiples thereof.

5.2.2 ICPs and other interpretive applications

The rather high speedup of the interpretive execution of M-code results from the low semantic level of the intermediate instructions. It can still be improved by modifying the definition of the intermediate language, e.g., by including delayed jumps, and by using modern compiler optimization techniques to exploit these additions. When combining a high execution speed and a low instruction bandwidth is the goal, significant improvements could be obtained by designing intermediate languages that optimize the use of a coprocessor. It is not clear whether traditional instruction caches always present the optimal answer. Our interest in interpretation and instruction path coprocessors was not directed exclusively towards optimizing the speed/bandwidth product of a language implementation. The interactivity or the semantic definition of an application or language often require the use of interpretive techniques. Examples are spreadsheet programs; interactive data base query languages; and language environments such as Forth, APL, SMALLTALK, ASYST, and PostScript. Several AI languages provide only a subset of their full semantics when compiled into native code. In such cases, interpretation is needed to support interactivity and complete language semantics. Compilation, if any, is incremental and global compiler optimization techniques are ruled out. Hence we must raise the question whether or not the criteria that favor the use of an instruction path coprocessor in M-code are also present in the above applications and languages. This question is not void. On one hand, the speedup on languages such as Forth has been demonstrated. On the other hand, the average speedup of an instruction path coprocessor will be low when the semantic contents of intermediate instructions is high. For such intermediate instructions, the mapping overhead is relatively small, and the semantic instruction stream is likely to already be good. Indeed, when an intermediate instruction needs complex semantics, it pays to optimize the usage of CPU resources during its execution. Apart from their generic nature, a compiler or instruction path coprocessor could not significantly accelerate the execution of these semantic routines. Languages like APL, ASYST, or PostScript offer some very complex instructions. However, since these languages are still general purpose, they also provide very low level operations which can certainly benefit from the presence of an ICP.

5.3 Conclusion

In this monograph we have analyzed interpretive techniques. Interpretation was, and still is a preferred implementation method in many cases. It was found to have one major drawback, namely its low execution speed. In some interactive applications, the interpretive slowdown is not at all bothersome or harmful; in others, it is.

Software interpretation can be accelerated to some extent by using clever and appropriate programming techniques. A careful use of CPU resources, the omission of unnecessary jump instructions, and top of stack optimization techniques have allowed the authors to improve commercially available interpreters by a factor of two. Of course, this still is a long cry from the speed that can be obtained on modern processors, executing code produced by an optimizing compiler. Some of the remaining speed disparity is due to the residual interpretive slowdown; another part is induced by the nature of the intermediate machine and its architectural gap with the CPU.

The concept of interpretive coprocessors allows to further reduce the interpretive slowdown. Their effect is twofold. First, they execute the interpreter mapping actions faster, and concurrently with the CPU. Secondly, for the majority of the intermediate instructions, better code can be generated than a software interpreter can. The weak points of instruction path coprocessors are their poor performance in generating code conditionally on status information from the CPU, and in executing intermediate transfers of control. Both weaknesses can be improved by a combination of scoreboarding techniques and delayed branching, or even by having the coprocessor execute the intermediate jumps autonomously. Although the use of an instruction path coprocessor will never allow us to reach the performance level of a good optimizing compiler, accelerating interpretive execution by factors between 2 and 3 with respect to well-optimized software interpreters is achievable at low incremental hardware cost.

The concept of instruction-path coprocessing is not entirely new; several variations of the idea have been used elsewhere. Our processor/coprocessor approach was found to contain features of three existing applications. It has the generality of the Dorado's fetch unit, it generates instruction sequences, just like the fetch unit of the G-machine, and fits into a standard microprocessor environment, just like the Prolog Preprocessor.

The instruction path coprocessor concept remains interesting to speed up various modern interpretive applications; it also fits well in modern RISC environments, where it can be a very cost-effective replacement of expensive instruction caches whenever interpretation is used. The expected speedup of RISC-based interpretation is similar to the speedup observed in CISCs.

Bibliography

[AhoS86] Aho, A. V., Sethi, R., and Ullman, J. D. (1986), *Compilers: principles, techniques and tools*, Reading (Mass.): Addison-Wesley.

[Aike46] Aiken, H. H., and Hopper, G. (1946), "The automatic sequence controlled calculator, I, II, III," *Elec. Eng.* (Aus), vol. 65, pp. 384-528.

[Alle78] Allen, J. (1978), *Anatomy of Lisp*, New York (USA): McGraw-Hill.

[Alli86] Allison, A. (1986), "Riscs Challenge Mini, Micro Suppliers," *Mini-Micro Syst.* (USA), vol. (11), pp. 127-136.

[Arno86] Arnold, H. G. (1986), "Symbolic Processing Potential Of Forth-Based Microcomputers," *J. Forth Appl. & Res.* (USA), vol. 4(2), pp. 165-8.

[Atki87] Atkinson, R. R., and McCreight, E. M. (1987), "The Dragon processor," in: *Proc. of the 2nd Intern. Conf. on Architectural Support for Programming Lang. and Oper. Syst.*, Palo Alto, USA, 5-8 Oct. 1987, Washington, DC (USA): IEEE Comput. Soc. Press 1987, pp. 65-69.

[Back78] Backus, J. (1978), "Can programming be liberated from the von Neumann style? A functional style and its algebra of programs," *Commun. ACM* (USA), vol. 21(8), pp. 613-641.

[Ball84] Ballard, B. (1984), "Forth direct execution processors in the Hopkins Ultraviolet Telescope," *J. Forth Appl. & Res.* (USA), vol. 2(1), pp. 33-47.

[Bane82] Banerji, D. K., and Raymond, J. (1982), *Elements of microprogramming*, New Jersey (USA): Prentice Hall.

[Bark87] Barklund, J. (1987), "Efficient interpretation of Prolog programs," *SIGPLAN Not.* (USA), vol. 22(7), pp. 132-137.

[Bell73] Bell, J. R. (1973), "Threaded Code," *Commun. ACM* (USA), vol. 16(6), pp. 370-372.

[Bhuj83] Bhujade, M. R. (1983), "On The Design Of Always Compatible Instruction Set Architecture (Acisa)," *Comput. Archit. News* (USA), vol. 11(5), pp. 28-30.

[Blom87] Blomme, R., Brokken, D., and Van Campenhout, J. M. (1987), "Driemaandelijks aktiviteitsverslag, spilprogramma robotica, robotsturing IWONL conventie 4930," *Technical report*, Electronics Laboratory, State Univ. of Ghent, Ghent, Belgium.

[Boeh87] Boehm, H. (1987), "Constructive real interpretation of numerical programs," *SIGPLAN Not.* (USA), vol. 22(7), pp. 214-221.

[Bose83] Bose, P. (1983), "Instruction set design for support of high-level languages," *PhD dissertation*, UILU-ENG 83-2207, University of Illinois, pp. 1-175.

[Bose84] Bose, P., and Davidson, E. S. (1984), "Design of instruction set architectures for support of high-level languages," in A. Arbor (ed): *Proc. of the 11th ann. int. symp. on computer architecture*, IEEE Comp. Soc. Press, pp. 198-206.

[Brak82a] Brakefield, J. (1982), "Just What Is An Op-Code ? Or A Universal Computer Design," *Comput. Archit. News* (USA), vol. 10(4), pp. 31-34.

[Brak82b] Brakefield, J. C. (1982), "Talk On Interpreters," *Comput. Archit. News* (USA), vol. 10(6), pp. 21-28.

[Burs86] Bursky, D. (1986), "Optimized Processor Handles Forth, And More," *Electron. Des.* (USA), vol. 34(28).

[Carr86] Carr, H., and Kessler, R. R. (1986), "Forth For AI ?," *J. Forth Appl. & Res.* (USA), vol. 4(2), pp. 177-80.

[Cast88] Castan, M., Contessa, A., Cousin, E., Coustet, C., Durrieu, G., Lecussan, B., Lemaitre, M., and Ng, P. (1988), "MaRS: a parallel graph reduction multiprocessor," *ACM Comput. Archit. News* (USA), vol. 16(3), pp. 17-24.

[Chas87] Chase, B. B., and Hood, R. T. (1987), "Selective interpretation as a technique for debugging computationally intensive programs," *SIGPLAN Not.* (USA), vol. 22(7), pp. 113-24.

[Chow88] Chow, P., and Hennessy, J. (1988), "Reduced instruction set computer architectures," in V. M. Milutinovic (ed): *Computer architecture: concepts and systems*, New York: North-Holland, pp. 48-83.

[ChuA81] Chu, Y., and Abrams, M. (1981), "Programming languages and direct-execution computer architectures," *Computer* (USA), vol. 14(7), pp. 22-31.

[Chun78] Chung, K., and Yuen, H. (1978), "A 'Tiny' Pascal Compiler," *BYTE* (USA), vol. 3(9), pp. 58-155.

[Cive87a] Civera, P. L., Piccinini, G. L., and Zamboni, M. (1987), "Design considerations on a VLSI prolog interpreter," in: *Microprocess. & microprogram.* (Netherlands), Amsterdam: North-Holland, pp. 267-274.

[Clar87b] Clark, C. F. (1987), "The JADE interpreter: A RISC Interpreter for Syntax Directed Editing," *SIGPLAN Not.* (USA), vol. 22(7), pp. 222-228.

[Cohe85] Cohen, J. (1985), "Describing Prolog By Interpretation And Compilation," *Commun. ACM* (USA), vol. 28(12), pp. 1311-24.

[Coop88] Cooper, R. E. M., and Jones, G. (1988), "A microprogrammed Occam interpreter for the HLH Orion," *Software-Pract. & Exper.* (GB), vol. 18(1), pp. 63-71.

[Cord87] Cordy, J. R., and Graham, T. C. N. (1987), "Design of an interpretive environment for Turing," *SIGPLAN Not.* (USA), vol. 22(7), pp. 199-204.

[Crag83] Cragon, H. (1983), "Executable Instruction Set Specification," *ACM* (USA), vol. 11(1), pp. 25-43.

[Crag80] Cragon, H. G. (1980), "The elements of single-chip microcomputer architecture," *Computer* (USA), vol. 13(10), pp. 27-41.

[Davi87a] Davidson, J. W., and Gresh, J. V. (1987), "Cint: a RISC interpreter for the C programming language," *SIGPLAN Not.* (USA), vol. 22(7), pp. 189-98.

[Davi87b] Davidson, J. W., and Vaughan, R. A. (1987), "The effect of instruction complexity on program size and memory performance," in: *Proc. of the 2nd Intern. Conf. on Architectural Support for Programming Lang. and Oper. Syst.* Palo Alto, CA, USA, 5-8 Oct. 1987, Washington, DC (USA): IEEE Comput. Soc. Press 1987, pp. 60-4.

Bibliography

[DeBl86]   De Blasi, M., Gentile, A., and Pezzella, G. (1986), "Co-Processor Architecture for PROLOG," in M. De Blasi, and M. Luque (eds): *Microprocessor advanced architectures and design methodologies*, Fratelli Laterza Publisher, pp. 151-168.

[Deba86]   Debaere, E. H. (1986), "Language Coprocessor for Interpretive Execution of Modula-2 Programs," *IEE Electronics Letters*, (GB), vol. 22(24), pp. 1302-1304.

[Deba87]   Debaere, E. H. (1987), "A Language Coprocessor for the Interpretation of Threaded Code," in H. Schumny, and J. Molgaard (eds): *Microprocessing and Microprogramming*, Conference Proc. Portsmouth, United Kingdom, 14-17 sept. 1987, Amsterdam: North-Holland, pp. 593-602.

[Deba88]   Debaere, E. H. (1988), "The Extension of the Coprocessor-concept to the Instruction Path," in: *Proc. European Simulation Multiconference (1-3 June 1988)* Nice (France), pp. 294-299.

[Deba88]   Debaere, E. H. (1988), "Language coprocessor boosting the execution speed of threaded code programs," accepted for publication in *J. Forth Appl. & Res.* (USA).

[DeBo88]   De Bosschere, K. (1988), "Edulan, A tool for software education," in F. Lovis, and E. D. Tagg (eds): *IFIP conference, Computers in education*, Lausanne, Elsevier Science Publishers, pp. 99-105.

[DeMa89]   De Man, H. (1989), "Microelectronics and computer hardware," in: *Management van technologische complexiteit, 3e Vlaams technologisch wetenschappelijk congres (KVIV), 1 maart 1989*, Ghent, (Belgium), pp. 5.3.1-5.3.8.

[Denn70]   Denning, P. J. (1970), "Virtual memory," *Comput. Surv.* (USA), vol. 2(3), pp. 153-189.

[Dewa75]   Dewar, R. B. K. (1975), "Indirect Threaded Code," *Commun. ACM* (USA), vol. 18(6), pp. 330-331.

[Dewa77]   Dewar, R. B. K., and McCann, A. P. (1977), "Macro Spitbol - a Snobol4 compiler," *Software-Pract. & Exper.* (USA), vol. 7, pp. 95-113.

[Domm]   Dommergaard, O., "The Design Of A Virtual Machine For Ada," pp. 435-510.

[Dums83]   Dumse, R. (1983), "The R65F11 Chip," *Forth Dimensions* (USA), vol. 5(2), p. 25.

[Eccl19]   Eccles, W. H., and Jordan, F. W. (1919), "A trigger relay utilizing three-electrode thermionic tubes," *Radio Rev.*, vol. 1, pp. 143-146.

[Faus87]   Faustini, A. A., and Wadge, W. W. (1987), "An educative interpreter for the language Plucid," *SIGPLAN Not.* (USA), vol. 22(7), pp. 86-91.

[Feue]   Feuer, A. R., "SI – an interpreter for the C language," pp. 47-55.

[Flag78]   Flagging, F. (1978), "How VLSI impacts computer architecture," *IEEE Spectrum* (USA), vol. 15(5), pp. 8-31.

[Flyn66]   Flynn, M. J. (1966), "Very High-Speed Computing Systems," *Proc. IEEE* (USA), vol. 54(12), pp. 1901-1909.

[Flyn72]   Flynn, M. J. (1972), "Some Computer Organizations And Their Effectiveness," *IEEE Trans. Comput.* (USA), vol. C-21(9), pp. 948- 960.

[Flyn78]   Flynn, M. J. (1978), "A canonic interpretive program form for measuring 'Ideal' HLL architectures," *Comput. Archit. News* (USA), vol. 6(8), pp. 6-15.

[Flyn80]   Flynn, M. J. (1980), "Directions and issues in architecture and language," *Computer* (USA), vol. 13(10), pp. 5-22.

[Flyn83a]   Flynn, M. J., and Hoevel, L. W. (1983), "Execution Architecture: The Deltran Experiment," *IEEE Trans. Comput.* (USA), vol. C-32(2), pp. 156-175.

[Flyn83b]   Flynn, M. J. (1983), "Standford Emulation Laboratory," *SIGMICRO Newsl.* (USA), vol. 14(3), pp. 10-17.

[Flyn84]   Flynn, M. J., and Hoevel, L. W. (1984), "Measures Of Ideal Execution Architectures," *IBM J. Res. & Dev.* (USA), vol. 28(4), pp. 356- 369.

[Flyn85]   Flynn, M. J., Johnson, J. D., and Wakefield, S. P. (1985), "On Instruction Sets And Their Formats," *IEEE Trans. Comput.* (USA), vol. C-34(3), pp. 242-254.

[Flyn87]   Flynn, M. J., Mitchell, C. L., and Mulder, J. M. (1987), "And now a case for more complex instruction sets," *Computer* (USA), vol. (9), pp. 71-83.

[Fost71]   Foster, C. C., and Gonter, R. (1971), "Conditional interpretation of operation codes," *IEEE Trans. Comput.* (USA), vol. C-20, pp. 108-111.

[Fras84]   Fraser, C. W., Myers, E. W., and Wendt, A. L. (1984), "Analyzing And Compressing Assembly Code," *SIGPLAN Not.* (USA), vol. 19(6), pp. 117-121.

[Fura88]   Fura, D. A., and Milutinovic, V. M. (1988), "Computer design for Gallium Arsenide Technology," in V. M. Milutinovic (ed): *Computer architecture: concepts and systems*, New York: North-Holland, pp. 84-131.

[Furn87]   Furnari, M. (1987), "Pascal implementation of a LISP interpreter," *SIGPLAN Not.* (USA), vol. 22(5), pp. 42-46.

[Gabr85]   Gabriel, R. P. (1985), *Performance and Evaluation of Lisp Systems*, Massachusetts: The MIT Press.

[Gilb83]   Gilbreath, J., and Gilbreath, J. (1983), "Eratosthenes Revisited," *BYTE* (USA), January 1983.

[Glas85]   Glass, H. (1985), "Threaded Interpretive Systems and Functional Programming Environments," *SIGPLAN Not.* (USA), vol. 20(4), pp. 24-32.

[Gold83]   Goldberg, A., and Robson, D. (1983), *Smalltalk-80: the language and its implementation*, Reading (Mass.) (USA): Addison Wesley.

[Gold85]   Golden, J., Moore, C. H., and Brodie, L. (1985), "Fast processor chip takes its instructions directly from Forth," *Electron. Des.* (USA), vol. Mar 21, pp. 127-138.

[Gree86]   Green, R. (1986), "Abundance – a database language that can run backward in time," *BYTE* (USA), Oct., pp. 193-196.

[Gum86]   Gum, P. H. (1986), "The XA Interpretive Execution (Sie) Architecture," in: *Proc. Of The Seas Spring Meeting 1986* Expert Systems, Heidelberg, Germany, 6-11 April 1986, Nijmegen, Netherl.: SEAS, pp. 531-41.

Bibliography

[Gupt83]   Gupta, A., and Toong, HOO-MIND (1983), "Microprocessors – The First Twelve Years," *Proc. IEEE*, vol. 71(11), pp. 1236-1256.

[Harl86]   Harland, D. M., and Beloff, B. (1986), "Microcoding An Object-Oriented Instruction Set," *Comput. Archit. News* (USA), vol. 14(5), pp. 3-12.

[Harr87]   Harr, H., Evens, M., and Sprowl, J. (1987), "Interpreting ABF – A language for document construction," *SIGPLAN Not.* (USA), vol. 22(7), pp. 205-213.

[Harr80]   Harris, K. (1980), "Forth Extensibility Or How To Write A Compiler In 25 Words Or Less," *BYTE* (USA), vol. 5, pp. 164-184.

[Hart88]   Hartel, P. H., and Veen, A. H. (1988), "Statistics on Graph Reduction of SASL Programs," *Software-Pract. & Exper.* (USA), vol. 18(3), pp. 239-253.

[Haye87]   Hayes, J. R., Fraeman, M. E., Williams, R. L., and Zaremba, T. (1987), "An architecture for the direct execution of the FORTH programming language," in: *Proc. of the 2nd Intern. Conf. on Architectural Support for Programming Lang. and Oper. Syst.* Palo Alto, CA, USA, 5-8 Oct. 1987, Washington, DC (USA): IEEE Comput. Soc. Press 1987, pp. 42-49.

[Hell83]   Helliwell, A. M. (1983), "Implementation of highly portable Pascal interpreter using indirect threaded code techniques," *IUCC Bulletin*, vol. 5, pp. 124-127.

[Hehn76]   Hehner, E. C. R. (1976), "Computer design to minimize memory requirements," *Computer* (USA), vol. 9(8), pp. 65-70.

[Hend80]   Henderson, P. (1980), *Functional Programming: Application and Implementation*, London (UK): Prentice-Hall International.

[Henn83]   Hennessy, J., and Gross, T. (1983), "Postpass code optimization of pipeline constraints," *ACM Trans. on Programming Languages and Systems* (USA), vol. 5(3), pp. 422-448.

[Henn84]   Hennesy, J. L. (1984), "VLSI Processor architecture," *IEEE Trans. Comput.* (USA), vol. C-33(12), pp. 1221-1246.

[Hoev74]   Hoevel, L. W. (1974), "'Ideal' Directly Executed Languages: An Analytical Argument For Emulation," *IEEE Trans. Comput.* (USA), vol. C-23(8), pp. 759-767.

[Hoff83]   Hoffmann, R. (1983), "A classification of interpreter systems," *Microprocess. & Microprogram.*, (Netherlands), vol. 12, pp. 3-8.

[Horo84]   Horowitz, E. (1984), *Fundamentals of programming languages*, New York (USA): Springer Verlag.

[Husk76]   Huskey, H. D., and Huskey, V. R. (1976), "Chronology of computing devices," *IEEE Trans. Comput.* (USA), vol. C-25(12), pp. 1190-1199.

[Huss70]   Husson, S. S. (1970), *Microprogramming: principles and practices*, Englewood Cliffs (N.J.): Prentice-Hall, Inc.

[John71]   Johnson, J. D. (1971), "The contour model of block structured processes," *SIGPLAN Not.* (USA), vol. 6 (Feb), pp. 55-82.

[John82]   Johnsson, R. K., and Wick, J. D. (1982), "An Overview Of The Mesa Processor Architecture," *SIGPLAN Not.* (USA), vol. 17(4), pp. 20-29.

[Jona86] Jonak, J. E. (1986), "Experience with a FORTH-like language," *SIGPLAN Not.* (USA), vol. 21(2), pp. 27-36.

[Kari87] Karinthi, R. R., and Weiser, M. (1987), "Incremental re-execution of programs," *SIGPLAN Not.* (USA), vol. 22(7), pp. 38-44.

[Kavi82] Kavi, K., Belkhouche, B., and Bullard, E. (1982), "HLL Architectures: Pitfalls And Predilections," *Comput. Archit. News* (USA), vol. 10(3).

[Kell81] Keller, R. M., and Sleep, M. R. (1981), "Applicative caching," in: *Proc. Conference on Functional Programming Languages and Computer Architecture*, pp. 131-140.

[Kels]   Kelsh, J. P., and Hansen, J. C., "A simple virtual machine," *SIGSMALL/PC Notes* (USA), vol. 13(1), pp. 11-15.

[Kers81] Kershaw, J. (1981), "Two implementations of the 'Flex' machine," *SIGMICRO Newsl.* (USA), vol. 12(4), pp. 25-37.

[Keye81] Keyes, R. (1981), "Fundamental limits in digital information processing," *Proc. IEEE* (USA), vol. 69(2), pp. 267-278.

[Kirr84] Kirrmann, H. D., and Kaufmann, F. (1984), "Poolpo–A Pool Of Processors For Process Control Applications," *IEEE Trans. Comput.* (USA), vol. C-33(10), pp. 869-878.

[Klin81] Klint, P. (1981), "Interpretation techniques," *Software-Pract. & Exper.* (USA), vol. 11, pp. 963-973.

[Knod86] Knödler, B., and Rosenstiel, W. (1986), "A Prolog Preprocessor For Warren's Abstract Instruction Set," *Microprocess. & Microprogram.* (Netherlands), vol. 18, pp. 71-80.

[Kogg82] Kogge, P. M. (1982), "An Architectural Trail To Threaded-Code Systems," *Computer* (USA), vol. 15(3), pp. 22-32.

[Koko88] Kokol, P. (1988), "Spreadsheet language level: how high is it ?," *SIGPLAN Not.* (USA), vol. 23(6), pp. 121-134.

[Koop86] Koopman, P., and Haydon, G. (1986), "MVP Microcoded CPU/16 Architecture," *J. Forth App. & Res.* (USA), vol. 4(2), pp. 277-80.

[Koop87] Koopman, P. (1987), "The WISC concept," *BYTE* (USA), vol. 12(4), pp. 187-94.

[Kosk87] Koskimies, K., and Paakki, J. (1987), "TOOLS: a unifying approach to object-oriented language interpretation," *SIGPLAN Not.* (USA), vol. 22(7), pp. 153-64.

[Kral87] Krall, A. (1987), "Implementation of a high-speed Prolog interpreter," *SIGPLAN Not.* (USA), vol. 22(7), pp. 125-31.

[Kras83] Krasner, G. (1983), *Smalltalk-80, Bits of history, words of advice*, Reading (Mass.): Addison-Wesley.

[Kuck78] Kuck, J. D. (1978), *The structure of computers and computations*, New York (USA): John Wiley & Sons.

Bibliography

[Lamp84] Lampson, B. W., McDaniel, G., and Ornstein, S. M. (1984), "An instruction fetch unit for a high-performance personal computer," *IEEE Trans. Comput.* (USA), vol. C-33(8), pp. 712-730.

[Land63] Landin, P. J. (1963), "The mechanical evaluation of expressions," *Comput. J.* (GB), vol. 6(4), pp. 308-320.

[Laws71] Lawson, H. W., and Smith, B. K. (1971), "Functional characteristics of the multilingual processor," *IEEE Trans. Comput.* (USA), vol. 20(7).

[Lepp86] Leppala, K. (1986), "Interpretive Execution Of Program Code Increases Software Robustness In Embedded Computer Systems," *Microprocess. & Microprogram.* (Netherlands), vol. 18, pp. 63-68.

[Luqu88] Luque, E., Sorribes, J., and Ripoll, A. (1988), "Tuning architecture at run-time," *SIGMICRO Newsl.* (USA), vol. 19(1-2), pp. 15-22.

[Mall75] Mallach, E. G. (1975), "Emulator Architecture," *Computer* (USA), vol. 8(8), pp. 24-31.

[Marc86] Marcotty, M., and Ledgard, H. (1986), *The world of programming languages*, Berlin: Springer-Verlag.

[Mark80] Marks, B. (1980), "Compilation To Compact Code," *IBM Res. & Dev.* (USA), vol. 24(6), pp. 684-691.

[Mars88] Marshall, T. (1988), "Real-world RISCs," *BYTE* (USA), vol. 13(5), pp. 263-268.

[McCa60] McCarthy, J. (1960), "Recursive functions of symbolic expressions and their computation by machine," *Commun. ACM* (USA), vol. 3(4), pp. 184-195.

[McMi87] McMillan, T. C. (1987), "A small LISP interpreter as a project in programming languages course," *SIGCSE Bull.* (USA), vol. 19(3), pp. 10-14.

[Mira87] Miranda, E. (1987), "BrouHaHa – a portable Smalltalk interpreter," *SIGPLAN Not.* (USA), vol. 22(12), pp. 354-65.

[Modu84] Modula Corporation (1984), *Modula-2 Development system for IBM-PC*, Utah: Modula Corporation.

[Moor74] Moore, C. H. (1974), "Forth: a new way to program a mini-computer," *Astron. & Astrophys. Suppl.* (USA), vol. 15, pp. 497- 511.

[Moor80] Moore, C. H. (1980), "The Evolution Of Forth, An Unusual Language," *BYTE* (USA), vol. 5(8), pp. 76-92.

[Myer82] Myers, G. L. (1982), *Advances in computer architecture, 2nd ed.*, New York (USA): John Wiley & Sons, Inc.

[Myer86] Myers, G. J., Yu, A. Y. C., and House, D. L. (1986), "Microprocessor Technology Trends," *Proc. IEEE* (USA), vol. 74(12), pp. 1605-1622.

[Nico84] Nicolau, A., and Fisher, J. A. (1984), "Measuring The Parallelism Available For Very Long Instruction Word Architectures," *IEEE Trans. Comput.* (USA), vol. C-33(11), pp. 968-976.

[Noji86]   Nojiri, T., Kawasaki, S., and Sakoda, K. (1986), "Microprogrammable Processor For Object-Oriented Architecture," in: *13-th Annual International Symposium On Computer Architecture*, Tokyo, Japan, 2-5 June 1986, Washington, Dc (USA): IEEE Comput. Soc. Press, pp. 74-81.

[Nort83]   Norton, R. L., and Abraham, J. A. (1983), "Adaptive Interpretation As A Means Of Exploiting Complex Instruction Sets," *Comput. Archit. News* (USA), vol. 11(3), pp. 277-282.

[Notk87]   Notkin, D., and Griswold, W. G. (1987), "Enhancement through extension: the Extension Interpreter," *SIGPLAN Not.* (USA), vol. 22(7), pp. 45-55.

[Nowa87]   Nowak, L. (1987), "SAMP: A general purpose processor based on a self-timed VLIW structure," *Comput. Archit. News* (USA), vol. 15(4), pp. 32-39.

[O'ba87]   O'Bagy, J., and Griswold, R. E. (1987), "A recursive interpreter for the Icon programming language," *SIGPLAN Not.* (USA), vol. 22(7), pp. 138-49.

[Offu87]   Offutt VI, A. J., and King, K. N. (1987), "A Fortran 77 Interpreter for mutation analysis," *SIGPLAN Not.* (USA), vol. 22(7), pp. 177-188.

[Park83]   Parker, Y. (1983), *Multi-microprocessor systems*, Suffolk (USA): Academic Press Inc.

[Patt80]   Patterson, D. A., and Ditzel, D. R. (1980), "The case for the reduced instruction set computer," *Comput. Archit. News* (USA), vol. 8(6), pp. 25-33.

[Patt81]   Patterson, D. A., and Sequin, C. H. (1981), "RISC I: A Reduced Instruction Set VLSI Computer," in *Proc. of the 8-th annual symposium on Computer Architecture*, Minnesota: IEEE Press, pp. 443-450.

[Patt84]   Patton, C. (1984), "Data-Flow Architecture Unclogs The Bottleneck of von Neumann Systems," *Electron. Des.* (USA), pp. 60-62.

[Pemb82]   Pemberton, S., and Daniels, M. C. (1982), *Pascal implementation: the P4 compiler*, Chichester (UK): Ellis Horwood Ltd.

[Peyt87]   Peyton Jones, S. L. (1987), *The implementation of functional programming languages*, London: Prentice-Hall.

[Phil78]   Philips, J. B., Burke, M. F., and Wilson, G. S. (1978), "Threaded code for laboratory computers," *Software-Pract. & Exper.* (GB), vol. 8, pp. 257-263.

[Pier83]   Pier, K. A. (1983), "A Retrospective On The Dorado, A High-Performance Personal Computer," *Comput. Archit. News* (USA), vol. 11(3), pp. 252-269.

[Pitt87]   Pittman, T. (1987), "Two-level hybrid interpreter/native code execution for combined space-time program efficiency," *SIGPLAN Not.* (USA), vol. 22(7), pp. 150-2.

[Posa79]   Posa, J. G. (1979), "Programming Microcomputer Systems With High-Level Languages," *Electronics* (USA), vol. 52(2), pp. 105-112.

[Raus78]   Rauscher, T. G., and Agrawala, A. K. (1978), "Dynamic problem-oriented redefinition of computer architecture via microprogramming," *IEEE Trans. Comput.* (USA), vol. C-27(11), pp. 1006-1014.

Bibliography

[Raus80]   Rauscher, T. G., and Adams, P. M. (1980), "Microprogramming: a tutorial and survey of recent developments," *IEEE Trans. Comput.* (USA), vol. C-29, pp. 2-20.

[Rich71]   Richards, M. (1971), "The portability of the BCPL Compiler," *Software-Pract. & Exper.* (GB), vol. 1.

[Rise72]   Riseman, E. M., and Foster, C. C. (1972), "The inhibition of potential parallelism by conditional jumps," *IEEE Trans. Comput.* (USA), vol. C-21(12), pp. 1405-1411.

[Ritt80]   Ritter, T., and Walker, G. (1980), "Varieties Of Threaded Code For Language Implementation," *BYTE* (USA), vol. 5(4), pp. 206-227.

[Robi87]   Robinson, A. D. (1987), "The Illinois Functional Programming interpreter," *SIGPLAN Not.* (USA), vol. 22(7), pp. 64-73.

[Robi87]   Robison, A. D. (1987), "Illinois functional programming: a tutorial," *BYTE* (USA), vol. 12(2), pp. 115-125.

[Rosi69]   Rosin, R. F. (1969), "Contemporary concepts of microprogramming and emulation," *Comput. Surv.* (USA), vol. 1(4), pp. 197-212.

[Sach83]   Sachs, J. M., and Burns, S. K. (1983), "STOIC, an interactive programming system for dedicated computing," *Software-Pract. & Exper.* (USA), vol. 13, pp. 1-16.

[Samm82]   Sammer, W., and Schwärtzel, H. (1982), *CHILL eine moderne Programmiersprache für die Systemtechnik*, Berlin: Springer-Verlag.

[Schi88]   Schindler, M. (1988), "To assure software success choose a suitable language," *Electron. Des.* (USA), March, pp. 113-125.

[Schu82]   Schulthess, P., and Vonaesch, F. (1982), "OPA–A New Architecture For Pascal-Like Languages," *Comput. Archit. News* (USA), vol. 10(6), pp. 9-20.

[Siew85]   Siewiorek, D. P., Bell, C. G., and Newell, A. (1985), *Computer structures: principles and examples International Student Edition*, Singapore: McGraw-Hill.

[Silb86]   Silbey, A., Milutinovic, V., and Mendoza-Grado, V. (1986), "A Survey Of Advanced Microprocessors And Hll Computer Architectures," *Computer* (USA), vol. 19(8), pp. 72-85.

[Sked87]   Skedzielewski, S. K., Yates, R. K., and Oldehoeft, R. R. (1987), "DI: an interactive debugging interpreter for applicative languages," *SIGPLAN Not.* (USA), vol. 22(7), pp. 102-12.

[Smit82]   Smith, A. J. (1982), "Cache Memories," *Comput. Surv.* (USA), vol. 14(3), pp. 473-530.

[Smit85]   Smith, A. J. (1985), "Cache evaluation and the impact of workload choice," *Comput. Archit. News* (USA), vol. 13(3), pp. 64-73.

[Smit82]   Smith, J. E. (1982), "Decoupled Access/Execute Computer Architectures," *Comput. Archit. News* (USA), vol. 10(3), pp. 112-119.

[Smit84]   Smith, J. E. (1984), "Decoupled Access/Execute Computer Architectures," *ACM Trans. Comput. Syst.* (USA), vol. 2(4), pp. 289-308.

[Somm85]   Sommerville, I. (1985), *Software engineering, 2nd ed.*, Reading (Mass.): Addison-Wesley.

[Srid86]   Sridhar, R., and Manwaring, M. L. (1986), "An automatic microcode generator for high level language machines," *Microprocess. & Microprogram.* (Netherlands), vol. 18, pp. 263-268.

[Stal88]   Stallings, W. (1988), "Reduced instruction set computer architecture," *Proc. IEEE* (USA), vol. 76(1), pp. 38-55.

[Stan81]   Stankovic, J. A. (1981), "The types and interactions of vertical migrations of functions in a multilevel interpretive system," *IEEE Trans. Comput.* (USA), vol. C-30(7), pp. 505-513.

[Stev79]   Stevenson, J. W., and Tanenbaum, A. S. (1979), "Efficient encoding of machine instructions," *Comput. Archit. News* (USA), vol. 7(8), pp. 10-17.

[Suss81]   Sussman, G. J., Holloway, J., Steel, G. L., and Bell, A. (1981), "Scheme-79 Lisp on a chip," *Computer* (USA), vol. 14(7), pp. 10-21.

[Swee82]   Sweet, R. E., and Sandman, J. G. (1982), "Empirical Analysis Of The Mesa Instruction Set," *SIGPLAN Not.* (USA), vol. 17(4), pp. 158-166.

[Tane82]   Tanenbaum, A. S., Van Staveren, H., and Stevenson, J. W. (1982), "Using Peephole Optimization On Intermediate Code," *ACM Trans. Program. Lang. & Syst.* (USA), vol. 4(1), pp. 21-36.

[Tayl84]   Taylor, D. (1984), "A Portable Pseudo-Code For Pascal- Like Languages," *SIGPLAN Not.* (USA), vol. 19(1), pp. 68-77.

[Thak86]   Thakkar, S. S., and Hostmann, W. E. (1986), "An instruction fetch unit for a graph reduction machine," in: *Proc. of the 13th ann. int. symp. on computer architecture*, Tokyo: IEEE, Comput. Soc. Press, pp. 82-91.

[TheT82]   The Thanh, N., and Raschner, E. W. (1982), "Indirect Threaded Code Used To Emulate A Virtual Machine," *SIGPLAN Not.* (USA), vol. 17(5), pp. 80-89.

[Tred88]   Tredennick, N. (1988), "Experiences in commercial VLSI microprocessor design," *Microprocess. & Microsyst.* (GB), vol. 12(8), pp. 419-432.

[Turi36]   Turing, A. M. (1936), "On computable numbers, with an application to the Entscheidungsproblem," *Proc. London Math. Soc.*, vol. 42, pp. 230-265.

[Unga87]   Ungar, J. (1987), "Four C language interpreters," *BYTE* (USA), vol. 12(6), pp. 245-250.

[VanC84]   Van Campenhout, J. M., Stoop, R. G., and Decuypere, H. J. (1984), "The implementation of CHILL on a multi-interpreter architecture," in: *Proc. Third CHILL Conference*, Cambridge (Sept. 23-28), ITT, pp. 49-54.

[VanC85]   Van Campenhout, J. M. (1985), "Language coprocessors in a multi-interpreter environment," *Technical report, State University of Ghent, Ghent, Belgium*, pp. 1-18.

[VanC86]   Van Campenhout, J. M. (1986), "The Combination of Interpretation And Multiprocessing: A Marriage Of Reason?," *Proc. Intern. Conf. Parallel Computing 85*, pp. 389-393.

Bibliography

[VanC87] Van Campenhout, J. M., and Debaere, E. H. (1987), "Language Coprocessor to support the Interpretation of Modula-2 Programs," *Microprocess. & Microsyst.* (GB), vol. 11(6), pp. 301-307.

[VanC88] Van Campenhout, J. M., and Debaere, E. H. (1988), "A concurrent high-level language based real-time controller," *Journal of the IERE (UK)*, vol. 58(2), pp. 57-62.

[Vegd88] Vegdahl, S. R. (1988), "Architectures that support functional programming languages," in V. M. Milutinovic (ed): *Computer architecture: concepts and systems*, New York (USA): North- Holland, pp. 405-453.

[vonN45] von Neumann, J. (1945), "First draft of a report on the Edvac," *Technical Report Univ. Pennsylvania*, Philadelphia (USA).

[VonP83] Von Puttkamer, E. (1983), "A microprogrammed Lisp machine," *Microprocess. & Microprogram.* (USA), vol. 12, pp. 9-14.

[Vose87] Vose, G. M. (1987), "QuickBasic 4.0," *BYTE* (USA), vol. 12(13), pp. 111-114.

[Wada82] Wada, K., Kaneda, Y., and Maekawa, S. (1982), "System design and hardware structure of a FORTH machine system," *Syst.- Comput.-Controls* (USA), vol. 13(2), pp. 11-18.

[Wake87] Wakefield, S. P., and Flynn, M. J. (1987), "Reducing execution parameters through correspondence in computer architecture," *IBM J. Res. & Dev.* (USA), vol. 31(4), pp. 420-434.

[Wall87] Wall, D. W., and Powell, M. L. (1987), "The Mahler experience: using an intermediate language as the machine description," in: *Proc. of the 2nd Intern. Conf. on Architectural Support for Programming Lang. and Oper. Syst.* Palo Alto, CA, USA, 5-8 Oct. 1987, Washington, DC (USA): IEEE Comput. Soc. Press 1987, pp. 100-104.

[Wall83] Waller, L. (1983), "Forth Interpreter On Microcomputer Eases Programming," *Electronics* (USA), vol. 56, pp. 47-48.

[Warr83] Warren, D. H. D. (1983), "An Abstract Prolog Instruction Set", Technical Note 300, SRI International pp. 1-30.

[Wass82] Wasserman, A. I., and Gutz, S. (1982), "The Future Of Programming," *Commun. ACM* (USA), vol. 25(3), pp. 196-206.

[Week86] Weeks, J., and Berghel, H. (1986), "A comparative feature-analysis of microcomputer Prolog implementations," *SIGPLAN Not.* (USA), vol. 21(2), pp. 46-61.

[Wegn76] Wegner, P. (1976), "Programming languages – the first 25 years," *IEEE Trans. Comput.* (USA), vol. C-25(12), pp. 1207-1225.

[Wijn89] Wijnands, H. E. R., and Bruijn, P. M. (1989), "A Forth based software tool for real-time multiprocessing," in J. Zalewski, and W. Ehrenberger (eds): *Hardware and software for real-time process control*, Amsterdam: North-holland, pp. 109-119.

[Wilk84] Wilkes, J. L. (1984), "Architecture of a VLSI multiple ISA emulator," *SIGMICRO Newsl.* (USA), vol. 15(4), pp. 31-36.

[Wilk51] Wilkes, M. V. (1951), "The best way to design an automatic calculating machine," *Technical report, Manchester University Computer Inaugural Conference*, London, UK, pp. 16-21.

[Wiln72] Wilner, W. T. (1972), "Design Of The Burroughs B1700," *The Fall Joint Conference*, pp. 489-497.

[Wirt81] Wirth, N. (1981), "The Personal Computer Lilith,": *Technical report ETH Zürich*.

[Wirt82] Wirth, N. (1982), *Programming in Modula-2*, Berlin (Germany): Springer-Verlag.

[Wirt86] Wirth, N. (1986), "Microprocessor Architectures: A Comparison Based On Code Generation By Compiler," *Commun. ACM* (USA), vol. 29(10), pp. 978-90.

[Wirt87] Wirth, N. (1987), "Hardware architectures for programming languages and programming languages for hardware architectures," in: *Proc. of the 2nd Intern. Conf. on Architectural Support for Programming Lang. and Oper. Syst.*, Palo Alto, CA, USA, 5-8 Oct. 1987, Washington, DC (USA): IEEE Comput. Soc. Press 1987, pp. 2-8.

[Wulf81] Wulf, W. A. (1981), "Compilers and computer architecture," *Computer* (USA), vol. 14(7), pp. 72-85.

[Yama81] Yamamoto, M. (1981), "A survey of high-level language machines in Japan," *Computer* (USA), vol. 14(7), pp. 68-78.

Index

A

accuracy, 95
address, **7**
  logical, 7
  physical, 7
  translation, 7
address expressions, **8**
  index registers, 8
  indirect addressing, 8
  segmented memory, 8
addressing modes, **8**
AI, *see* artificial intelligence
algorithm, 1, 21
ALU, *see* arithmetic/logic unit
analytical engine, 2
APL, 100
architectural gap, 106
architecture, 1
  decoupled access/execute, 20
  decoupled execute/access, 11
  dedicated, 42
  direct execution, 42
  Harvard, 19
  indirect execution, 44
  instruction set, 36
  language corresponding, 45
  language directed, 44
  pipelined, 39
  very long instruction word, 19
arithmetic/logic unit, 4
artificial intelligence, 22
associative table lookup, 7
ASYST, 100

B

backtracking, 96
bandwidth, 58
block transfer, 8
branch prediction, 154
bus, **18**
  arbitration overhead, 18, 128, 151, 156
  bandwidth, 18, 47
  interfacing circuit, 18
  protocol, 18
  signal travel time, 18
bus interface unit, 136
C, 92

C

cache, 40, 47, 59, 122
  coherence, 165
  for interpreters, 123
  instruction, 40
  training, 123
calculating machines, 2
CISC, *see* complex instruction set computer
code compactness, 37, 54, 93
  M-code, 171
  RISCs vs. CISCs, 171
code expansion factor, 158
compiler, 35
  code generator, 41, 94
  incremental, 35
complex instruction set computer, 10, 38
computer science, 94
conditional code generation, 155, 157, 159
  using direct computation, 161
  using prefetch queue behavior, 163
  with communication, 159
  with snooping, 161
conditional intermediate-level jump, 162
context-dependent decoding, 131
contour model, **59**
control store, 136, 146
control unit, 4, **9**, 136
  hardwired, 39
  microcoded, 9, 38
coprocessor, 17, 42, 125
  communications, 125
  data transfer, 125
  floating point, 17
  graphics, 17, 125
  I/O, 11, 17, 125
  numeric, 125
  speedup, 125
coroutine transfer, 164

D

data path, 4, 129
data path coprocessors, **125**
  activation schemes, **126**
    independent, 128
    peripheral, 127
    spying, 127
  complexity, 126
  interfaces, 126
  speedup, 126
  synchronization, **128**
    dedicated signal, 129
    polling, 128
    using interrupts, 129
data representation, 107
  big-endian, 107
  little-endian, 107
data stack pointer, 146
DCA, *see* direct correspondence architecture

DEA, *see* architecture, direct execution
deadlock, 156, 160
debugging, 33–34, 92
decoding jump, 165
definitions, 56, 146
DEL, *see* directly executable language
delay slots, 160
delayed branch, **120**
  at the intermediate level, 154
delayed effect of internal registers, **120**
DIL, *see* directly interpretive language
direct correspondence architecture, 58
direct execution, 99
direct memory access, 11, **125**
  address register, 136
  bus protocol, 137
  coprocessor, 127
  fetch cycles, 156
directly executable language, **58**
directly interpretive language, **60**
  evaluation metric, 61
  set of transformations, 60
dispatching table, 52
DMA, *see* direct memory access
do interpretive loop, 49
DTC, *see* threaded code, direct
dynamic instruction count, 58, 152
dynamic load sharing, 64
dynamic size, 40

E

education, 94
emulation, 31, 97
Eratosthenes' Sieve benchmark, 102, 152
evaluation mechanisms, 96
  applicative, 96
  data-flow, 96
  demand driven, 97
  reduction, 96
execution actions, 49
execution phase, 49
execution speed, 34, **38**
extensibility, 33, 35, 90

F

feedback of information, 154
fetch/decode phase, 49
finite state machine, 54, 131
Flynn bottleneck, 19
formal languages, 22
Forth, **72**, 90
  compiling words, 74
  control stack, 75
  data stack, 74

defining words, 74
definition, 73
dictionary, 75
FORGET, 74
primitive, 73
primitives area, 75
threaded code, 74
word, 73
frame addressing, 55
functional languages, 168

G

G-code, 168
garbage collection, 86
general purpose microprocessor, 125
  mass production of, 125
generic code, 101, 155
graph reduction, 168
graph rewriting, 58

H

Harvard architecture, 19, 157, 172
HLL, *see* programming language
Huffman coding, 131

I

I/O controller, 11
I/O systems, 4, 10
ICP, *see* instruction path coprocessor
ignorance of the program counter, 163
indexing, 7
indirect threaded code, 146
infix notation, 55
information content, 8
information hiding, 22
instruction, 19
  functional, 19
  movement, 19
  procedural, 19
instruction bandwidth, 171
instruction caches, 164, 171
instruction fetch unit, 167
  of the Dorado, 167
  of the G-machine, 168
instruction path, **125**
instruction path coprocessor, 125, **129**, **134**
  architecture for RISCs, 172
  differences with datapath coprocessor, 134
  general configuration, 134
  internal structure, 135
  performance analysis, **152**
  prototypes, **135**
  related work, **167**

Index

speedup, 152
  thru improved code generation, 155
  thru parallelism, 153
  weak points, **156**
  feedback, 159
  ignorance of the CPU program counter, 158
  interrupts, 163
  the presence of caches, 164
applicability, 169
  for other applications, 172
  on RISCs, 169
instruction set, **9**
  addressing modes, 38
  compactness, 8
  completeness, 36
  complex instruction set computer, 10
  encoding, 38
    frequency based, 37
    operand addressing, 37
  reduced instruction set computer, 10
  regularity, 36
  semantics, 38
instruction set architecture, 36
instruction store, 136, 146
instruction synthesizing unit, 136
interactive applications, **30**
interactivity, 33, 35, 47, 92
intermediate architecture, 107
  confluent machine, 107
  overlapped host, 107
  partially mapped, 107
  well-mapped, 107
intermediate code, 31, 48, 65
  execution mechanism, 48
  interpretation, 31
intermediate code cache, 156
intermediate code queue, 136–137, 154
  flushing, 154
intermediate instruction, 50
  boundaries, 164
  decoding, 130
  encoding, 50
    pointer based, 51
    subroutine, 50
    tokenized, 52
  fetch, 130
  mix, 101
Intermediate level jumps, 154
intermediate M-machine state, 142
intermediate program counter, 51, 136
intermediate program representation, 50, 53, 100
  context-free, 54

linked, 57
openness, 54
regular, 54
semantic level, 100
sequential allocation, 55
syntactical structure, 54
threaded, 55
  direct, 57
  indirect, 57
compactness and caching, 123
interpretation, **31**, 34, 59, 99
resource usage, 106
  adaptive, 95
  bibliographical notes, 90
  conditional, 93
  hardware support, 97
  interpretive environment, 35
  principles, 96
  resource usage, 105
    addressing modes, 106
    jump instructions, 105
    move operations, 106
interpreter, **31**, 70
  inner-interpreter, 36
  M-code, 70
  microprogrammed, 33
  multi-interpreter, 64
  outer-interpreter, 36
  program dependent, 94
  two-level, 32
interpreter optimization, **108**
  optimal use of host resources, 110
  bridging the architectural gap, 111
    delayed coprocessor operand fetching, 116
    top of stack optimization, 112
  choice of intermediate language primitives, 108
  code reorganization, 111
    alignment, 111
    in-line jumps, 111
  escape instructions, 108
  global speedup, 123
interpretive coprocessor, **125**
interpretive loop, 48
interpretive overhead, **100**
interpretive process, 125
interpretive slowdown, 99
interrupt, 11, 159, 163
  at the intermediate level, 164
  driver, 164
  handler, 159
  latency, 164

ITC, *see* threaded code, indirect

J

jump-free instruction stream, 135

L

language, **21**
  algorithmic, 21
  assembly, 21
  binary machine, 21
  declarative, 23
  high level, 21
lazy operand fetching, **116**
LCA, *see* architecture, language corresponding
LDA, *see* architecture, language directed
Lilith, 65
linked representations, 130
Lisp, 84, 90
  atom, 84
  dotted-pair, 84
  function, 84
    higher-order, 84
    recursive, 84
  Lispkit, **84**
  list, 84
  SECD-machine, **84**
  symbolic expression, 84
literal value, **68**
  as operands, 101
  embedding, 135
  little-endian representation, 68
  passing of, 168
locality, **7**, 164
loosely coupled tasks, 128

M

M-code, 55, **65**, 100, 130, 171
M-code instruction path coprocessor, **136**
  examples, 139
    conditional code generation, 142
    intermediate jumps, 142
    non-jump sequence, 140
  external appearance and behavior, 137
  microcontrol, 139
  operation, 137
  structure, 136
M-machine, 65
  code frame, 65
  data frame, 65
  data frame table, 66
  module, 65
  stack frame, 66

mapping actions, 49, 100, 129
mapping memory, 136
memory, 4
  bandwidth, 58
  shared, 64
  speed disparity, 63
memory bandwidth, 40
memory device, 137
memory hierarchy, 4–5, 7–8
  caches, 6
  dynamic optimization technique, 7
  hardware stack support, 7
  programmed overlays, 7
  read only storage, 10
  register optimization, 7
  registers, 5
  replacement algorithms, 7
  static optimization technique, 7
  transfer rate, 18
  virtual memory, 7
  writable control store, 10
microcode, 94, 168
microcoded architecture, 136
microinstruction, 10
microprocessor, 13
  architecture, **15**
  bit-slice, 17
  complex instruction set computer, 18
  complexity, 13
  general purpose microprocessor, 15
  instruction set, 36
  microcomputer, 15
  microcontroller, 15
  microprogrammable, 97
  reduced instruction set computer, 18
  transistor count, 14
microprogramming, **9**, 61
  control store, 10, 61
Modula-2, **64**
  coroutine, 66
  process descriptor, 66
modularity, 22
multiprocessor, 12
  distributed, 12
  shared memory, 12
mutation analysis, 92

N

native code, 31
  direct execution, 31
  execution speed, 33
native code queue, 136–137
NDP, *see* coprocessor, numeric

NOP filling, 142, **158**, 160

O

operation sequencing, 2
optimization scope, 120
optimizing compiler, 7, 34, 41, 120, 154
  code motion, 34
  elimination of common subexpression, 34
  peephole optimization, 34
overlapped memory references, **120**

P

P-code, 55, 100, 130
parallelism, 4–5, 11, 18, 153
  coprocessing, 23
  macroscopic, 11
  microscopic, 11
  MIMD, 12
  multiprocessing, 23
  SIMD, 12
  SISD, 12
  speeding up interpretation, 117
    coprocessor parallelism, 117
    RISC parallelism, 119
peripheral device, 11
piggy-back, 158
pipeline break, 154, 160
pipelining, 11
pointers, 130
portability, 33–34, 94
postfix notation, 73
prefetch engine, **131**
  communication and synchronization, 132
  features, 132
  operation, 132
  structure, 132
prefetch queue, 142, 144, 158
  flushing, 142, 144, 158, 163
primitives, 55, 146
processor, 12
  array, 12
  associative, 12
  pipelined, 12
program analysis, 95
program counter, 164
  execution, 164
  fetch, 164
program structures, 151
  deep, 151
  shallow, 151
programming language, **21**
  applicative, **26**
    referential transparency, 26
  classification, **24**
  dedicated, 29
  functional, **26**
  history, 21
  imperative, **24**
  implementation techniques, **31**
  logic, 28
    fact, 28
    Horn clause, 28
    rule, 28
    rule-based, 29
  object oriented, **27**
    class, 27
    inheritance, 27
    method, 27
    object, 27
    polymorphism, 28
  compilers, 22
PROLOG, 100
Prolog Preprocessor, 168

R

random access memories, 3
  ultrasonic mercury delay lines, 3
  electrostatic Williams tube, 3
  magnetic core memory, 4
  registers, 4
reduced instruction set computer, 10, **18**, 38, 157, 167
  code generators, 170
  delayed branch, 41
  memory access time, 170
    reduced by ICP, 171
register architecture, 107
register files, 171
representation size, 33, 35, 59
result caching, 95
return stack pointer, 146
reverse polish, 55
RISC, *see* reduced instruction set computer
robustness, 94
run-time code generator, 165

S

scaled index, 110
scoreboarding, 41, 160
SECD-machine, 84
  car, 85
  cdr, 85
  control list, 85
  dotted-pair cell, 85
  dump, 85
  environment, 85
  number cell, 85
  stack, 85

secondaries, 56
segmented address space, 159
semantic gap, **31**, 41
semantic routines, 101
semantic speedup, 152
sequential representations, 130
shared-memory multiprocessing, 128
simulation tools, 95
Smalltalk, 90
software engineering, 22
  formal specification, 23
  rapid prototyping, 23
  requirement capturing, 23
  verification, 23
software interrupts, 164
software tools, 40
space/time trade-off, **58**, 93
speedup, 142, 152
stack, 54
  control, 55
  data, 73
  environment, 55
  evaluation, 54
stack architecture, 37, 99, 131
  data locality, 100
stack marking, 55
stack state, **113**, 131, 137
state memory function, 2
static size, 58
status register, 136
stored program computer, 3, 6
system calls, 164

T

technology, **12**
  evolution, 61
  integrated circuit, 12
    LSI, 12
    MSI, 12
    SSI, 12
    VLSI, 12
  transistor, 12
testing, 92
threaded code, **55**
  direct, 79
  direct token, 81
  Forth, 74
  indirect, 75
  indirect token, 81
threaded code instruction path coprocessor, **146**
  architecture, 146
  microcoding, 146
  operation, 149

  speedup, 151
threaded representations, 130
tokenized encoding, 52
tokens, 130
top of stack optimization, 135, 137, 142, 151
total speedup, 152
transformationally complete format set, 59
transformations, 2
translator, 45
  hardware, 45
  software, 45
traps, 164

V

virtual memory, 7
  address translation, 7
  management chips, 125
  paging table, 7
  translation look aside buffer, 7
virtual migration, 96
virtual prefetch queuelength, 153
virtual program counter, 67
VLIW, *see* architecture, very long instruction word
von Neumann, 1, 3–4, 9
  bottleneck, 6, 18–19

W

Warren's abstract machine, 100, 168
WCS, *see* memory hierarchy, writable control store
  bus sharing, 156
  deadlock, 156
word address register, 146
word addressability, 67
working set, 7, 40

The MIT Press, with Peter Denning, general consulting editor, and Brian Randall, European consulting editor, publishes computer science books in the following series:

ACM Doctoral Dissertation Award and Distinguished Dissertation Series

Artificial Intelligence, Patrick Henry Winston and J. Michael Brady founding editors; J. Michael Brady, Daniel G. Bobrow, and Randall Davis, current editors

Charles Babbage Institute Reprint Series for the History of Computing, Martin Campbell-Kelly, editor

Computer Systems, Herb Schwetman, editor

Exploring with Logo, E. Paul Goldenberg, editor

Foundations of Computing, Michael Garey and Albert Meyer, editors

History of Computing, I. Bernard Cohen and William Aspray, editors

Information Systems, Michael Lesk, editor

Logic Programming, Ehud Shapiro, editor; Fernando Pereira, Koichi Furukawa, and D. H. D. Warren, associate editors

The MIT Electrical Engineering and Computer Science Series

Research Monographs in Parallel and Distributed Processing, Christopher Jesshope and David Klappholz, editors

Scientific Computation, Dennis Gannon, editor

Technical Communication, Edward Barrett, editor

JUN 2 1 1990